*A Childhood
for Every
Child*

A Childhood
for Every
Child

THE POLITICS OF PARENTHOOD

Mark Gerzon

*"Arise, and take the young
child and his mother ... for
Herod will seek the young
child to destroy him."*
Matthew 2:13

A Sunrise Book E. P. Dutton & Co., Inc. New York

Grateful acknowledgement is made for permission to reprint lyrics from
Cat Stevens' "Where do the Children Play," Copyright 1970, Freshwater
Music, Ltd. (England) Controlled in Western Hemisphere by Irving Music
Inc. (BMI) All Rights Reserved.

Standard Book Number: 0-87690-088-0
Library of Congress Catalog Number: 72-97986
Copyright © 1973 by Mark Gerzon
First published in the United States of America in 1973
Printed in the United States of America
All rights reserved including the right of reproduction
in whole or in part in any form.

Design: Anne Hallowell Obuck

Second Printing June 1973

Outerbridge & Lazard, a subsidiary of
E. P. Dutton & Co., Inc.

To all the parents of my children

PREFACE
AND ACKNOWLEDGEMENTS

What is the relationship between political and parental responsibility? What is the political meaning of being a "good parent?" And what does "good politics" mean in terms of raising children?

These are the kinds of questions which this book faces. It focuses on children who are *not* disadvantaged, who have parents with money and time to read and write books like this one. It calls for action, not on behalf of starving Vietnamese children or hungry ghetto children, but on behalf of our own children. If we will not save them, we will save no one, not even ourselves.

When one faces the prospect of becoming a parent, one can no longer be an activist alone. The political and the parental must coalesce. Because I plan to be a father, I am reaching out to those who are seeking to create a community which will organize itself to be responsible for, and to, its children. By learning to feel more like brothers and sisters to each other, we will find it easier to be fathers and mothers for our kids. Our liberation depends on our children's; and theirs depends on the larger struggles for liberation occuring all around us.

In these pages, then, I describe where politics and parenthood meet. Politically, I am writing an analysis of how the American technocracy treats children. Personally, I am laying the cornerstone of my children's home.

I want to acknowledge several people who have shared their insight with me. The work and teaching of Erik Erikson have influenced me greatly, compelling me to examine both the history which surrounds me and the life history within.

During the past few years, Kenneth Keniston has encouraged me with care and criticism that have helped me to integrate the political and the psychological without, I hope, over-simplifying either. In clarifying the focus of this broad-ranging essay, Alan Williams made essential suggestions, and showed a continued interest in this project which has meant much to me. In the final stages, Paul De Angelis's editorial advice and personal friendship helped me to bring the work to completion. I also received helpful advice from Morton Gorden, Robert Haggerty, Laura Nader, Niles Newton, Lon von Renner, and James Shuman.

I am especially grateful, of course, to the friends with whom I lived while I wrote who gave me time, space, and care to think things through: Michio Araki and Eiki Hoshino on Chicago's South Side; Sam Lipman, Ellen Lindgren, Bart Casey, and especially Barbara Hancock in Maine; and Kathy Messenger, Shelley Kessler Cohen, and Bill Roth in New Haven.

I should end with whom I began: my parents, my two brothers, and my sister. The warmth and loyalty we have shared have enabled me to envision a family of my own. To those, known or unknown, who have breathed life into this vision, I dedicate this book.

Mark Gerzon
January, 1973

CONTENTS

Introduction

not any thing will do

Do your own thing.
             Counter culture proverb.

*If you're not part of the solution,
then you're part of the problem.*
   Black Panther, New Left slogan

*Do one's own thing, yes, but the
time has come to learn that not any
thing will do.*
             Herbert Marcuse

Like so many other young people in the late 1960s, I rebelled against the "conservative" attitudes ingrained in me during my schooling and became deeply involved in "radical" causes. I marched in anti-war demonstrations, turned in my draft card, obstructed the movement of high government officials, joined university strikes, and sat in at the Pentagon. Surrounded by tear gas and blood, I once yelled obscenities at the National Guard. I supported the black movement in America, and liberation movements in the Third World. I favored drastically altered corporate structures, wages scales, and national priorities. I opposed American economic and military interventions in the internal affairs of other countries. I had been to the Soviet Union and planned to go to Cuba and China. And I rolled joints, swam nude, grew organic vegetables, lived on a commune, and made love without a license.

Although these were adequate credentials, I found that I was unable to call myself a "radical." Nor could I claim to want a "revolution" in America. These terms no longer seemed to bear any relation to social and political reality. Radicals and revolutionaries were split among themselves and increasingly isolated from others even within the same generation. Even supporters must acknowledge that they failed to develop any consensus about how to bring about revolutionary social change.

The "Movement"—that mixture of political dissent and cultural experimentation which came to be called the "counter culture"—involved only a few of us. It attracted the support of others, and the hostility of many more. In 1968 the young gave a higher percentage of votes to Eugene McCarthy than did any other age group, but they also gave a higher percentage to George Wallace! The polarization of our generation manifested itself within the Movement also. It disintegrated into warring political organizations, establishment activists, Zippie-Yippie-and-Hippie factions, apolitical communes, and drug-rock freaks.

A One-Generation Movement

We pointed with pride at old activists, gray-haired matrons, or mothers pushing strollers, who joined us for our marches. But they were few, too few. Throughout the Sixties and early Seventies "the Movement" was almost entirely comprised of students, young professionals, minority youth, and recent college graduates. As a result, the Movement had all the enthusiasm, energy, and fervor characteristic of youth. We felt we had found the place for which Archimedes had been searching, a fulcrum with sufficient leverage so that—despite our small numbers and our inexperience—we could change the world.

This fulcrum was a time of life called youth: a time beyond our childhood but before our children. With no parents or children to stop us, we were free to sit in in Washington, work for weeks in McCarthy's New Hampshire campaign, throw ourselves behind local anti-war congressmen, disappear to ashrams or rock festivals or SDS conventions. Throughout our protest we gained strength in the knowledge that we knew more than our parents, or cared more, or maybe both. We could not make their mistakes, nor embody their hypocrisies. While we branded others "fascists," or at best "sell-outs," we formed a political congregation. Lined up with our radical brothers and sisters like parishioners in their pews, we reaffirmed our political righteousness and ethical superiority.

This is not to say that we did not effect some changes. After all, we helped remove Johnson from office; make corporations accept some social responsibilities; prompt universities to restructure; and perhaps even infuse a "new consciousness" into American culture. But even at the height of our victories, our demise was already in sight. Reflects Rennie Davis, a veteran of every March on Washington, and a co-defendant in the Chicago 7 conspiracy trial:

> We have seen that national mobilizations that build no permanent organizations are inadequate, if not self-defeating. Our rhetoric and "revolutionary" style have created obstacles to communicating with people. We see that a movement unable to relate to tens of millions of Americans who are angry and frustrated is a movement that is out of touch with its own country and times . . .[1]

By the early Seventies the first members of the Movement reached their middle or late twenties. Some of them, of course, took jobs and settled down. Just as the decline of Haight–Ashbury brought a deluge of reports about the death of hippiedom, so did the first signs that our generation was geting older trigger a spate of epitaphs for the Movement. The campuses were quiet, the marches small. Jobs were scarce and students were hitting the books. SDS was divided; the Panthers were in jail; the Weathermen had disappeared; and Abbie, Jerry, and the other Yippies were passing out McGovern buttons to no avail.

In restrospect, it seems natural that the counter culture which grew out of the anti-war movement expressed more a youthful revolt against parental authority than a mature commitment to social change. The absence of any deep alliance with older established traditions of dissent left our movement uniformly young. Harold Cruse described us as "the victims of historical discontinuity . . . this new generation is called upon to make up for lost time—about forty-five years of it." Paul Goodman agreed: "The young are honorable and see the problems, but they don't know anything because we have not taught them anything."[2]

But we not only lacked the radical training and tradition which could have given depth to our opposition; we also lacked time. Our movement was born in crisis—opposing a war which decimated civilian populations and which was documented, filmed, and debated as no other war has ever been. The immediate, essential goal of stopping the war necessarily made us less willing to think about fundamental, long-range strategies for dissent. We would have been morally callous to make scholarly analyses of our society and cautious strategies for reform. Our ethical outrage required militant action to stop the killing.

So we have historical and political excuses for why our movement exhausted its own ideas and demonstrated the mindlessness of its tactics. Nevertheless, they are excuses. For several years all we offered the American public was what Christopher Lasch has called "warmed-over Marxism."[3] Daniel Yankelovich, who made the most extensive study of youth attitudes during the years 1967–1972, concurs: ". . . the version of Marxism, as held by the mass of students and applied by them to our contemporary American society, is steeped in invincible ignorance and will neither yield productive insights nor produce effective programs for social change."[4]

Our failure to generate meaningful contemporary social criticisms has led, as it had to, to our failure to generate effective political dissent. Since we ourselves were "incapable of formulating the future" (as one SDS president admitted)[5] and failed to articulate "a vision of what we are working towards" (as radical professor Howard Zinn has charged),[6] we can hardly blame middle America for not taking us seriously.

Both hostile critics anxious to write epitaphs and those hoping for a renewal of the Movement's energy recognize its critical weakness. From Andrew M. Greeley's "The End of the Movement":

> . . . the movement was simplistic, self-righteous, naive, romantic, and inept. It preached relevance and commitment and yet when the going got tough, it abandoned politics. . . . It wanted to remake the world, but it never had time to formulate clearly its own vision of what the world ought to be, much less to articulately communicate this vision to others. It claimed political sophistication, but demonstrated incredible naiveté about how you convert other human beings to your cause. . . .[7]

Even a friend of the Movement has harsh words for us. From Staughton Lynd's "The Movement: A New Beginning":

> I sense a hardness and bitterness growing in the movement which not only turns me off, but which I think will prove politically self-defeating. [The movement needs] a style which seeks to empathize with those who do not yet stand with it, but who may stand with us, especially if we make some effort compassionately to grasp their situation.[8]

Both criticisms pose the same problem: what happens now as the passionate, committed cultural and political "revolutionaries" of the 1960s become "adults?" As we take jobs, make homes, and start families, what will become of our "radical" vision of a more democratic politics and a more fulfilling life style?

Do we refuse to grow up at all because our utopian dreams are not taking form before our eyes? Or do we reject our revolutionary vision outright as useless fantasy and hire ourselves out to the highest bidder? Or do we seek a comfortable bourgeois compromise by devising on the one hand a sensual, open life style, but on the other hand giving up ever trying to change society?

Clearly no alternative will be acceptable which transcends generations unless somehow the youthful protest movement becomes a movement of all generations which will last not a week or two, but a lifetime; which will take place not in the streets, but in offices, homes, and communities; and which will be judged not by journalists, administrators, or congressmen, but by our children and their friends.

Hip Bigotry and Violence

To achieve such a movement will require several qualities we have sorely lacked in the Movement. The first is endurance. In our surge of ethical concern we used to visualize ourselves sparking a democratic overthrow of existing policies: in one night, we could close the Pentagon; in one week, transform politics; in one month, end the war. We thought perseverance meant staying up all night, or missing dinner at the dorm, or not going to Chemistry during the strike. We really thought we would change history if we spent a few weeks campaigning or organizing protests, and we thought older people, who found our timetable naive, were simply conservative. Few if any of us would yet think in terms of a life-long struggle rather than a one-year stand.

It is not surprising that we could be deluded by our own rhetoric. The mass media had blown up the word "radical" until it was bound to burst. Suddenly, Weathermen and Jesus shared the same label. So did Jerry Rubin and Ralph Nader; living in communes and working on Capital Hill; organic foods and speed; free schools and dropping out; *Das Kapital* and *The Greening of America;* meditation and carrying guns; Che Guevara and Buckminster Fuller; being poor and gaining power; and so on. "Radical" seemed to apply to *any* new social movement, even those moving in opposite directions; almost anything new or faddish could be called "radical."

We let ourselves be deceived by the attention we received. For a while it seemed our revolutionary theatrics—our instant demonstrations, mimeographed analyses, media-magnified marches, occupied buildings, and finger-pointing logic—had actually won the battle. We hoped the curtain would fall and our performance be declared a success. Except that the show went on.

But if it was our lack of endurance that crippled the Movement, it was our arrogance that killed it. Our hip elitism drove potential supporters away from us and into "the silent majority." Even if we escaped the romantic appeal of believing in a greening-of-America Consciousness III, which was supposed to sweep across the American continent like a psychedelic prairie fire, too many of us still adopted the righteous superiority of a cultural vanguard. We wanted to believe that we were free of the political authoritarianism, racial bigotry, intellectual parochialism, and sexual repressions that characterized "middle America" and the politics it supported. We not only deluded ourselves with our all-too-flattering self-image, but more seriously, we also crippled our movement with our negative counter stereotype of the American public.

Too many of us held the remote, rigid view of the mass of Americans as people mired in "false consciousness," apathy, and hypocrisy. Our radical stereotype was in many ways just as prejudiced as the mass bigotry it opposed. Supposedly, the noble capacity to empathize with the down-trodden allowed student "radicals" to place themselves in the position of oppressed groups. But, as one Yale student wrote:

> This theoretically leads them to empathize with the ghetto blacks and therefore to distrust the "authorities" who oppress them. Unnoticed goes the fact that the "authorities" who get hated are the lower-middle-class police. . . .[9]

The "cop" is not the elite mentality's only stereotype. The military, "party hacks," hardhats, Southern whites, business executives, and countless other groups have been the object of "radical" students' contempt. The problem is that our empathy for blacks, for the Vietnamese, or for the "Third World," can be translated into concrete political changes only when it ceases to be an excuse for the most flagrant lack of empathy with our neighbors, with the rest of our generation who became mechanics, accountants, salesmen, or policemen.

Unfortunately, even those of us trying to change the schools have been as guilty of this elite bigotry as those engaged in political change. Angry at the apparent meaninglessness of much of our own education, we have all too often carried our own dissatisfactions into communities with needs and aspirations quite different from our own.

> There's not much that a poor, black 14-year-old can do in cities like New York and Boston if he cannot read or write enough to understand a street sign or read a phone book. It is too often the rich college graduate who speaks three languages with native fluency, at the price of 16 years of high-cost, rigorous, sequential education, who is most determined that poor kids should make clay vases, weave Indian headbands, play with Polaroid cameras, and climb over geodesic domes.[10]

We have feigned certainty to hide our inexperience, and thus created dogma in our attempt to fight it. Consequently, concludes Jonathan Kozol, we have tended to undermine "our passion and our intensity by sacrificing truth and candor for the sake of putting on a good show for the larger audience."

Nowhere was our failure more evident than when we turned to violence. It was terribly easy to blame "middle America" for its unwillingness to share radical goals. But it was far more difficult to construct a compelling image of the society we wished to create, a clear vision of a more liveable future which they could share. Because we failed to do the *real* work of revolution, we should not have been surprised that the American people not only boycotted our revolutionary performances, but defeated the "radical" candidate in 1972 by a landslide.

Even though they called and still call themselves a vanguard, those who were enraptured with violence were in fact a political anachronism. They conceived of revolution more simplistically than Lenin ever did, and ignored the changes that have taken place in the past half-century. Castro referred to this puerile militance when he spoke of "theoretical super-revolutionaries . . . capable of smashing imperialism with their tongues . . . without the slightest notion of reality and of the problems and difficulties of revolution."[11]

Yet rationales for violence were inevitably proposed. Even after our disastrous foreign policy in Southeast Asia, some "radicals" at anti-war rallies still shouted "fight for peace." That it was the identical phrase which first led us to Vietnam evidently escaped them. Although they portrayed themselves as "urban guerillas" fighting a "revolution in the streets," such demonstrations as the 1971 Mayday traffic-blocking in Washington were little more than childish games. An officer in the Washington police force acknowledged that, with even minimal skills of communication and organization, such a group *could have brought* the capital city to a standstill. As it turned out, the only skill we did not lack was the skill of offending the vast majority of the American populace.

Our problem was not that we were radicals, but that we were not good radicals. A close and self-critical reading of Karl Marx, that venerable radical, could have explained to us why we failed to inspire others to share our vision of a better society. As Marx put it: *"If you want to exercise influence over other people, you must be a person with a stimulating and encouraging effect on other people."*

> Every one of your relationships to man and to nature must be a *specific expression* . . . of your *real individual* life. If you love without evoking love in return—that is, if your loving as loving does not produce reciprocal love; if through a *living expression* of yourself as a loving person you do not make yourself a loved person, then your love is impotent . . . .[12]

The primary power of our movement rested in communication. And communication depended on mass media whose story line inevitably cast us as court jesters of the status quo. So we were forced to compete for the attention of an audience under circumstances that Marx could never have envisioned.

But let us not blame the media for our short-lived movement. We did not transform the culture because, in Erik Erikson's words, we "reversed rather than transcended the original culture."[13] We set up new stereotypes as we discarded old ones—and so arrived not at a "higher consciousness," but simply at a more fashionable one.

"Negation is not itself a form of liberation," writes one radical economist:

> The son/daughter who acts on the negation of parental and societal values is not free—he/she is merely the constrained negative image of that which he/she rejects . . . .[14]

Whenever an action is merely a reaction, it can only be reactionary.[15] We may do the opposite of what we have been told; we may become "the people our parents warned us about;" we may choose to become, in Erikson's phrase, our "negative identity." But if we stop there, we have not created new values, but simply become the mirror image of the selves we destroyed.

Simply put: we lacked *creativity*. We lacked the imagination to formulate creative criticism to deal with the historically unprecedented obstacles and opportunities presented by our technological society. We either borrowed models of revolution from other societies with fundamentally different structures, or did with no models at all. We were sure we knew what was wrong with our technological society, but were incapable of finding a way to set it right which was not either anachronistic or adolescent. All too often we thought we could be radical simply by proclaiming it, thus avoiding the more difficult task of *creating* an authentic radicalism.

The Politics of Parenthood

Some might say this analysis of the Movement is harsh, subjective, or even reactionary. On the contrary, what is truly reactionary is the absence of such an analysis. It is true the technological society placed barriers between the Movement and its audience. But, more important, this technological society deeply influenced the childhood and psychological development of those who later joined the Movement. Our own radical critique of society therefore requires us to examine not only the society itself, but also what that society has done to our own abilities to oppose it.

By its very nature, youth is a time of life preoccupied with its own unfolding. The search for identity, the questioning of values, the rebellion against authority, the raising of consciousness—these are all admirable, but self-centered, quests. Unless the insights we gained during youth are practiced during parenthood, these insights will be lost with the birth of our children. If our generation as parents does not free its children to redesign the fatal technological trajectory on which "spaceship earth" has been launched, children throughout the world will face bleak prospects of surviving as human beings. Only if the values of radical youth are sustained and expressed in parenthood will the human strengths which gave birth to our generation's creativity survive. Our reactions *against* technology must grow into actions *for* our children. Otherwise our revolt will die as soon as our adulthood begins.

The oppression of children by adults has continued after every previous revolution which adults have engineered. Our youthful revolution will fail in the same way unless the values of youth culture come to embrace the virtues of parenthood.

The members of our generation have often been simplistically divided into a vocal radical minority who seek revolution, and a patriotic conservative majority who simply want to work and raise their children. Perhaps as young people we were so divided, but as parents we can no longer afford to be. Neither part of our generation will succeed in their aims unless they embrace the concerns of the other.

The pages ahead seem to point to one lesson: that good radicals must think more like parents, and good parents must think more like radicals.

I.

And she brought forth her firstborn son,
and wrapped him in swaddling clothes,
and laid him in a manger; because
there was no room in the inn.

Luke 2:7.

1.
Radicalism

the cradle of the child

A man has come into the world; his early years are spent without notice in the pleasures and activities of childhood. As he grows up, the world receives him when his manhood begins, and he enters into contact with his fellows. He is then studied for the first time, and it is imagined that the germ of the vices and virtues of his maturer years is then formed.

This, if I am not mistaken, is a great error. We must begin higher up; we must watch the infant in his mother's arms; we must see the first images which the external world casts upon the dark mirror of his mind . . . we must hear the first words which awaken the sleeping powers of thought . . . if we would understand the prejudices, the habits, and the passions which will rule his life. The entire man is, so to speak, to be seen in the cradle of the child.

Alexis de Tocqueville

Since 1965, we have been repeatedly told, a generation has been "radicalized." This is the belief of adults whose hope for the peaceful transformation of America rests with the young, and the belief of many of the young themselves. What does this process of "radicalization" mean? Is it simply a leftward migration on the political spectrum? Or is it a new "consciousness," an evolutionary adaptation? If young Americans can claim to have been radicalized by everything from a drug raid to a year at the Harvard Business School to the 1968 Democratic Convention in Chicago, then we are left with a word so amorphous as to appear useless.

During the period in which I was gaining political awareness, it seemed there were basically two ways of reacting to those who called themselves "radicals:" one saw them either as a blessing, or as a curse. America seemed polarized between the profound hatred or devotion the young "radicals" inspired.

My feelings about the word "radical" were very clear then. My adolescence had coincided with the decade when "radicals" compelled America to diagnose the failure of our Vietnam policy; triggered national awareness of our threatened environment; focused attention on repression of minority groups; and exposed corporations who exploited the consumer. For me, as for so many members of the postwar generation, to call an idea or person "radical" was virtually a benediction. It meant the idea was truthful and just; the person, courageous and humane. Quite reasonably, I adopted "radical" views on social and political issues, and experimented with a "radical" life style.

Born into the world a decade earlier, perhaps I would have accepted the inflammatory, derisive definition of "radical" common to other generations of Americans. Perhaps I too would have willingly accepted that a "radical" idea was destructive and alien, that a "radical" person was dogmatic, violent, and subversive.

But "radicalism" was not an either–or question. When I left America in the autumn of 1968 to travel for a year in Asia, the Middle East, and Europe, I learned that there were not just two sides to the words "radical" and "revolution." There were dozens, each a mirror reflecting the character of its adherents. I witnessed "radical" movements, particularly in the USSR, which had become conservative. They resisted change, opposed new ideological or artistic movements, and severely limited freedom of expression. These erstwhile "revolutionary" movements were called "reactionary" by other "radical" governments, such as that of China. A third country would then brand the former two as repressive (Yugoslavia). Neutral nations, pursuing their own revolutionary paths, could criticize all three (India). Finally, "radical" student movements throughout the world did not hesitate to call all these governments "authoritarian" or "bourgeois" or "elitist." Traveling through this verbal gauntlet, I could barely remember what the word had previously meant to me.

On my guard, I returned home to find that the word "radical" had grown beyond recognition. The mass media had popularized the positive definition, and the negative definition had rapidly lost its meaning. "Radical" could no longer mean paid agents of Moscow, underground cells, or spies. The youth movement had grown so rapidly that those bewildered Sherlock Holmeses who were always trying to find "card-carrying communists" at every anti-war demonstration or ghetto riot simply had to give up. They came to realize that it was not foreign infiltrators sitting in at the Pentagon, but their own kids. Perhaps the Soviets could continue to blame "Western influences." And the Chinese, with two foreign bogey men, could blame American "imperialists" or Soviet "revisionists." But in America that game was up. The younger generation had called the convenient cold war bluff. At last people had to listen to their own children again.

But the sudden popularity of "radicals" also blurred and distorted the definition of the term. With hip capitalists, organic farmers, and grim-faced SDSers all sharing the same label, one could no longer distinguish what was radical from what was not.

I resented losing the word "radical." I was still critical of "conservative" American politics and culture as well as of its "liberal" opposition; a word like "radical" defined issues and goals that both wings of the normal political spectrum seemed to ignore. Without this word, I had no name to call myself, no vision of what I was working for.

It became important for me to find a meaningful and durable definition of radicalism.

Words as Weapons

According to *Webster's Dictionary*, any big change was radical. The adjective "radical" was defined as "marked by a considerable departure from the usual or traditional: extreme; tending or disposed to make extreme changes in existing views, habits, conditions or institutions; of, relating to, or constituting a political group associated with views, practices, and policies of extreme change."[1]

Such a general definition of change was not very helpful in a country which was *already* changing at an incredible rate. The heart of the American tradition was innovation, particularly when it promised more profits. Henry Ford's automobiles and the Wright brothers' airplane, for example, certainly resulted in "a considerable departure from the usual or traditional." Yet the Ford Motor Company and Pan American can hardly be called radical institutions. The conquest of space will certainly lead to "extreme changes in existing views, habits, conditions," etc. Yet by the standard criteria of the late 1960s, radicals were against, not for, the use of federal funds for the space race.

The dictionary search left me back where I started. The definition of "radical" was so general as to be meaningless. As long as "radical" was applied to *any* drastic change, it was perfectly natural that books, articles, and advertisements felt they could legitimately refer to the "information revolution," the "revolution in hair-styling," the "sexual revolution," or even to the "miniskirt revolution." Someone could argue convincingly that perhaps the only truly "radical" thing in our age would be something that did not change at all.

After the international conflicts, domestic divisions, and linguistic evasions, my question still remained: *which* among all the extreme changes with which I was surrounded could be called "radical?" And *who* among their proponents and detractors could rightly be called "radicals?" I almost decided to delete the word from my vocabulary altogether.

This semantic search may seem like an over-complication of an essentially simple issue. It is not. Rather it is a necessary house-cleaning of words that obfuscate rather than clarify. George Orwell's premonition was that through mass communications our language would close in on itself. In his novel *1984*, a straight-jacket prose became the official language, and no one was permitted to deviate from its vocabulary. This can still happen if we permit a word such as "radical" to be destroyed. The linguistic means for expressing our individuality would then be eliminated and we would be left with words which can only mechanically endorse orthodox views. First our tongues are trained; our minds follow.

The Root Is Man

Continuing my search for a definition, I returned to the word "radical" itself, and to its Latin origin, *radix,* which means "root." As an adjective: "of or relating to, the origin: *fundamental.*" Seeking the human meaning of this abstract clue, I found myself, to my surprise, turning to Karl Marx. "*To be radical,*" the young Marx wrote boldly, "*is to go to the root, and the root is man himself.*"[2]

Radicalism for Marx did not primarily mean either philosophic ideas or political actions. It meant human growth. "Communism as such," he wrote in 1844, "is not the aim of human development."[3] Communism was then only the means to reach what Marx considered the real goal: a society in which "*the free development of each is the condition for the free development of all,*" and in which "*the full and free development of each individual becomes the ruling principle.*"[4] Marx's ultimate aim was a human society where every man was provided with the social conditions necessary to ensure his full development as a human being.

Following Marx's approach, it becomes clear that any extreme change in society is not necessarily radical. Radical or revolutionary changes are only those changes which *promote growth in those who are affected by the new conditions.*

This important criterion of radicalism has immediate value, since it justifies the exclusion from our language of such phrases as "Ku Klux Klan radicals" or "the Nazi revolution." However, the criterion is so abstract that it leaves most problems unsolved. In fact, this definition of radicalism sounds little different from what politicians from Kennedy to Johnson to Nixon have said in their official speeches for over a decade. The 1960 report of President Eisenhower's Commission on National Goals beautifully echoed Karl Marx:

> All of our institutions—political, social and economic—must . . . promote the maximum development of [each individual's] capabilities. The first national goal to be pursued . . . should be the development of each individual to his fullest potential . . . .

Similar rhetoric pervaded Johnson's "Great Society" speeches as well as Nixon's orations on "the reach of the human spirit."

To avoid the pitfalls of such rhetoric, we must make our ideal of human development more concrete. Political factions pay lip-service to the concept of "full human development," but they do not take into account the physiological and psychological factors necessary to insure this development.

As early as embryonic and infant development, the human potentials which underlie capable social and political participation are being formed in the individual. While still in the womb, a fetus may be permanently damaged if the mother herself is malnourished. The most common cause of impaired mental ability is, in fact, malnutrition: a lack of protein inhibits the development of brain cells during the first four years of life when virtually all such cell growth occurs. Beyond physical nourishment, the infant also requires the stimulation and care of adults. As studies of infants in institutional care have shown,[5] too little care may result in decreased intellectual and emotional development, or even in disease and death.*

Child Development: The Psychological Ideal

Psychological factors become crucial for development as an individual grows out of infancy into childhood and adolescence. Certain fundamental cognitive stages of growth must be achieved in childhood in order that the emotional, intellectual, and ethical traits we associate with maturity may develop. The man who has perhaps best outlined these stages of development is Jean Piaget.

Piaget described the emergence of increasingly complex

---

* Bruno Bettelheim tells the story of an experiment carried out long ago in Prussia in order to determine the "true" human language. The king took a dozen babies, isolated them in a room, and instructed the caretakers not to speak to them, and not to touch them in any way not required by mere feeding and cleaning. The purpose was to discover what language would emerge among these "culture-free" children.

They never found out, concludes Bettelheim, because every one of the children died. They had no reason to live.

processes of reasoning during the years of childhood without which creative ideas and independent action would be impossible during adulthood. He observed in five- to eleven-year-old children a level of reasoning which he called *concrete operations*. The child at this age is capable of organizing, ordering, and classifying what is immediately present. He is rooted to the given rather than the potential. He can take existing structures of reasoning—for example, simple mathematical formulas—and apply them to new content. But he is not yet able to approach new material by constructing and testing a new hypothesis.

Piaget observed in later childhood and adolescence an important advance beyond this level of reasoning, an advance which alters the child's perception of *the relation between the real and the possible*. Piaget calls this more complex level of reasoning *formal operations,* a logical process based on hypothetical reasoning.

> Reasoning is thus conceived as a special subset within the totality of things which the data would admit as hypotheses; it is seen as the "is" portion of a "might be" totality . . . the empirically given comes to be inserted as a particular sector of the total set of possible combinations.[6]

The achievement of formal operations is symbolized, according to Piaget, by the ability to formulate "but what if . . ." thoughts. It extends the child's world to include the "hypothetical, the future, and the spatially remote."[7] It enables him to envision alternatives to the here-and-now, the given. Clearly, this basic cognitive growth is a precondition for creative social action.

When we later examine a generation's development in the modern technological state, these cognitive changes will be quite important. However, the influence of society on individual development is also critical in late adolescence and youth, *after* these basic stages of cognitive growth have been achieved. During youth, growth is more social and interpersonal than cognitive. To outline briefly these "psychosocial" aspects of development we must turn to Erik Erikson.

According to Erikson, the central conflict in later child-hood concerns the desire to learn and to make. Hoping to become skilful, the older child fears that he will fail to meet the expectations of the adults who are responsible for his training. During this period, he or she is primarily occupied with achieving *competence* and displaying *workmanship*— with finding out "what works."

> All cultures . . . meet this stage with the offer of instruction in perfectible skills leading to practicable uses and durable achievements . . . . This child at this stage, then, is ready for a variety of specializations and will learn most eagerly techniques in line with that ethos of production which has already entered his anticipations by way of ideal examples . . . .[8]

It is usually the family and the school which provide these ideal examples, and indicate to the child what social and technical skills must be acquired in order to later cope with the world as an adult.

Typical of this age is dualistic thinking—conceptualizing in polarized terms of "we-right-good vs. they-wrong-bad," and investing authority unquestioningly with knowledge of truth and purpose.[9] It is also characterized by what another psychologist has called conventional morality, the automatic acceptance of community values and standards of behavior.[10] The conventionally moral person is not necessarily confident that he can live according to the moral code endorsed by his community, but he does not question that the code is right. It seems objective, immutable, and authoritative.

Dualistic thinking and conventional morality are both an integral part of the stage of growth which Erikson calls the stage of *industry*. During this stage the adolescent is preoccupied with demonstrating his ability to perform assigned tasks and his worthiness to "graduate" to more difficult assignments. He must postpone direct and critical appraisal of the ethical and intellectual assumptions which determined what those assignments were to be.

According to Erikson, if growth is unhindered, this preoccupation with skills evolves into a concern about values.

This he has called the stage of *identity*. A young person becomes less concerned about his ability to work, and more concerned about its purpose. A qualitatively new ability is now required, "the ability to sustain loyalties freely pledged despite the inevitable contradictions of value systems." He searches now not for greater skill proficiency alone, but for "an inner coherence and durable set of values."[11]

Young people often being to wrestle with the issues of identity by the time they leave for college. There dualism gives way to a new relativism of values, and conventional morality is often superseded by a morality based upon independently chosen, personal principles. In the stage of identity, previous dualistic structures can no longer deal with the multiple and conflicting versions of right and wrong which friends and adults represent. Authorities become fallible; past "givens" become present questions; rules become hypotheses. Faced with interdependent occupational, interpersonal, and political choices, a young person realizes that he alone can determine what his loyalties and values are to be. He can no longer passively accept inherited values, but must actively commit himself through his adult work.

By searching for their identities, the members of a young generation enter history. Looking for "men and ideas in whose services it would seem worthwhile to prove oneself trustworthy," a generation's growth can no longer be adequately described in terms of "acquisition" of knowledge, "incorporation" of values, or "identification" with persons. At last, a generation ceases to be simply molded by their society, but begins to change it.

> [I]n youth the tables of childhood dependence begin to turn:
> it is no longer for the old to teach the young the meaning of life.
> . . . . It is the young who, by their responses and their actions,
> tell the old whether life as represented by their elders and as
> presented to the young has meaning.[12]

To transpose psychological terms into political ones, this generational process can be termed dialectical. The cycle of generations is the most concrete representation of a thesis which creates its own potential antithesis. *By encouraging the "full development" of their children, a generation of parents enables them to reject or affirm freely what their parents have created.*

Every psychological theory of human growth emphasizes the need for an individual to develop a vision of what he is moving *toward*. Freud viewed man as struggling to overcome oral and anal fixations by molding them into a more mature, ego-based *genital* orientation. Fromm speaks of relatedness and *individuality* as opposed to narcissism and conformity. Similarly, Riesman suggests *autonomy* as the goal of development. Others have written of the *open* versus the closed mind (Rokeach); of the anti-authoritarian or *tolerant* personality (Adorno); or, quite simply, of the process of "becoming a *person*" (Rogers).

In all these "humanist" psychologies, as in those of Jung, Sullivan, and many other contemporary theorists, some concept of *health* is essential—a vision of the person discovering within himself, and bringing to his species, a greater humanity. All of these theories recognize that the process by which children become parents of children of their own is the flesh and blood of history, the human measure of all progress.

The biological mechanism by which a new generation differentiates itself from its forebears is integral to all evolution. For *Homo sapiens* this is a cultural process, a generational safeguard against the unforeseen consequences of our species' extraordinary inventiveness. No matter how locked into a technocratic plan, new generations will ideally react to their parents' handiwork and reassess it. Deeply rooted in the successive stages of human growth, this ceaseless redirection of human culture ensures mankind's flexibility and creativity. This above all is our insurance against overspecialization and, ultimately, extinction.

Child Development:
The Social Reality

Until now we have defined radicalism in psychological terms, examining those aspects of an individual's growth during childhood and adolescence which enable him to develop a creative radicalism. We must now broaden our scope to include the external factors which may have an influence on an individual's development. Only by taking into account the society as a whole can we ascertain whether its social conditions favor or discourage the widespread development of creative radicalism. Unless this radicalism becomes more the rule than the exception, we cannot entertain any hopes of significant "revolutionary" change.

Erikson argues that, in principle, societies are constituted to encourage "the proper rate and the proper sequence of the unfolding human potentials." He is fully aware, however, that societies in fact are often constituted quite differently. Full development is less likely in some societies than in others, and under certain social conditions is nearly impossible. Even Piaget, whose cognitive research is less directly related to social conditions than Erikson's work, recognizes that his description of growth is based upon observations of a specific group of privileged youngsters.

> A particular environment remains indispensable for the realization of these possibilities. It follows that their realization can be accelerated or retarded *as a function of cultural and educational conditions.* This is why the growth of formal thinking . . . remains dependent on social conditions as much as and more than on neurological factors.[13]

The ideal development of the child described by Piaget and Erikson occurs only *if* growth continues unimpaired. How often this potential development is actually realized depends upon biological, economic, political, and technological conditions which psychologists rarely study in depth. Our task is to examine whether these conditions in a modern technological society enhance or impair a generation's progress toward the goal of full development. Only then may we move beyond *psychological ideals* of human development to discover the *social reality* of an actual generation.

Unfortunately political theories, even "radical" political theories, tend to stress economic and social factors and end up ignoring this critical psychological process. Although the potential contribution of psychology to radical theory has been apparent ever since Freud, the two strands of thought have long been antagonistic toward each other and each has tended to exclude the other's insights.

Once the bridge between Marxism and Freudianism had been clear: Freud warmly praised Marx for his "sagacious indication of the decisive influence which the economic circumstances of men have upon their intellectual, ethical, and artistic attitudes," and modestly claimed that the psychological factors he studied were involved in the formation of the economic conditions which Marx studied.[14] Like Marx's later position however, Freud's final stance became so rigid that he narrowed all causality to one set of forces. Shortly before his death, Freud maintained that "the events of human history are *no more than*" (italics mine) individual psychology "repeated on a wider stage."[15]

Freud thus became guilty of the psychological reductivism for which Marxists would criticize him. The level of technology or the structure of the economy was relegated to a secondary, peripheral position. As Anna Freud explained concisely, her father's commitment to psychoanalysis led him to assume that "the patient suffers from a conflict, not with the environment but within the structure of his own personality."[16] Personality, Freud took pains to point out, was formed early in childhood, before an individual entered the economic marketplace.

Marx's commitment to socialism led him to precisely the opposite conclusion. He ignored the development of man before he assumed an active role in the economy. Although as a young man he had wrestled with the contradictions of personal development, particularly as expressed through religion, he obfuscated this early interest in alienation which began before labor, and claimed that all conflict originated in the economic structure. Because the old Marx seemed to be entirely preoccupied with the alienation *of* labor, the final form of Marxism had little if any thing to say about childhood and youth, only about adulthood. Just as Freud did not analyze his work from the perspective that was then already called Marxist, Marx never analyzed his work from the perspective that would later be called psychoanalytic. Both have suffered from this mutual isolation.

The ideological barrier between social development and individual growth should never have been constructed. Because there was no adulthood in Freudianism, and no childhood or youth in Marxism, we must draw from both the Marxists and the Freudians in order that the whole life cycle of man may be present in our definition of radicalism. We cannot pursue Marx's and Freud's shared aim of liberating man unless we focus on the crucial interconnections between personal growth, on the one hand, and political, economic, and technical development, on the other.

Distinctions between the inner and outer world are not always easy to maintain: the morning headlines *are* our dreams, and our dreams the morning headlines. Personal growth and a free social order hang together in a delicate balance, each dependent upon the other. John Lukacs poses the problem for our age in his book *Historical Consciousness*:

> From now on "know thyself" should mean, know your historical circumstances, in order to be aware of yourself and of your tendencies as fully as possible; in order to be able to transcend them.[17]

To understand how a social order controls the individual's development is necessary in any historical period. It is more important than ever in a technological era which has witnessed the massive interference of technical organization in every stage of human life: from conception to maturity to old age and death.

It is not by choice, therefore, but by necessity that we include childhood and youth within our concept of radicalism. For in the modern technological state, the ultimate repression is not the opposition of a society to certain radical *ideas,* as with the Soviet censorship of newspapers. Nor is it punishment by a society of certain radical *actions,* as with the harassment and prosecution of the radical opposition in

America. The ultimate repression, greatly facilitated by technology, is the *undermining of the human process which produces these ideas and actions.* By the systematic intrusion of a technical, political, and economic system into the years of childhood and youth, it is possible to alienate a generation from the human capacity to create radical ideas or perform radical actions long before its members have become working adults.

2.
The Technological Revolution

tell me, where do the children play

Well, I think it's fine building Jumbo planes
I'm taking a ride on a cosmic train,
switch on summer from a slot machine,
just get you want to, if you want,
cause you can get anything.
I know we've come a long way,
we're changing day to day,
but tell me, where do the children play?

Cat Stevens

"Revolution" and "revolutionary" are tricky words. They have been applied to such diverse historical phenomena as the mere replacement of one ruler by another without any accompanying social change, or even to the attempted restoration of an earlier form of government.

Of the many historical definitions, one pair has survived into this century. According to *Webster's,* they apply to political movements which use violence to "overthrow a government, form of government, or social system, with another taking its place." *Webster's* provides as examples: "the English Revolution (1688), the American Revolution (1775), the French Revolution (1789), the Chinese Revolution (1911), and the Russian Revolution (1917)." This usage suggests that more profound change is required than simply a change of rulers. But it does not specify any criteria by which change might be judged "revolutionary;" nor does it explain what the overthrows mentioned here had in common; nor does it explain why some overthrows (e.g., the "Nazi revolution") are not included.

Modern dictionaries, however, have introduced a new definition for "revolution" and also made a verb out of it. According to *Webster's*:

revolution: any movement which brings about drastic change in society. (Examples: The Industrial Revolution; a revolution in modern physics).

revolutionize: alter drastically or radically; as "the automobile has revolutionized American life."

No wonder Movement people had trouble defining the "revolution" they wanted. As *Webster's* examples indicate, they were trying to design a "revolutionary" strategy in a society which was *already* in the process of continuous revolution: technological revolution.

The ascendance of the technological society has in fact totally transformed the nature of the political and social dialectic. Because their technology was so primitive, previous revolutionaries always had technological expansion as one of their basic goals. Marx had complete faith in science (he even wanted to dedicate *Das Kapital* to Charles Darwin). Lenin was so enraptured with the wonders of technology that he once defined communism as "soviets plus electrification." And Maoist China has agonized over an unceasing dispute about the relative importance of being "red" (ideologically dependable) or of being "expert" (technically trained).

With this shared desire for technological development, previous revolutionaries considered the production of capable, specialized technicians to be one of their most pressing tasks. To accomplish this they needed more capital, more schools, more raw materials, and more jobs. It appeared to them that they did not need freedoms of speech, of assembly, or of the press, since technical competence could be acquired without these liberties.

Unlike Marx, Lenin, or Mao, we live in a society that *already* has the most advanced technology in the history of man. In America, as in Northern Europe, Japan, and the USSR, technical knowledge has been developed and applied to every industry and to virtually every sphere of social and personal life. No major social function—whether building roads, selling produce, teaching children, or communicating news—has been left untouched. Enormous numbers of trained

workers perform the specialized tasks on which these economies depend. Rapidly growing educational and research
institutions have been created to ensure the continued
expansion of technical knowledge. In such drastically altered
social circumstances, concepts of revolution valid in other
cultures or in other eras do not apply.

No matter how flamboyantly the Movement invoked
the Bolshevik, Chinese, or Cuban scenarios for revolution,
these scenarios obviously did not fit in modern America.
From the perspective of most Americans, we activists were
trying to tear down society without having anything to put
in its place.

Again, our problem was not that we were radicals, but
that we were not creative ones. Had we only studied Lenin
more closely, we would have seen that, even during the Bolshevik revolution, technology was a force to be reckoned
with.

The Bolsheviks:
Little Science

Although the role of technology in prerevolutionary Russia
was far more limited than it is today, Lenin had to confront
some of the troublesome issues it raised. Socialist theoreti-
cians—"whether Bolshevik or Menshevik,"[1] lamented Lenin
—had left unexamined many concrete policy questions. One
of these questions was the role of technical knowledge.

Lenin had to defend himself on this point against the
charges of so-called "left Communists" who supported the
idea of "total revolution," of overthrowing the "past" and
establishing the "new." They wanted to rid themselves of
the entire bourgeois intelligentsia who had been technicians,
administrators, and intellectuals under the Czar. These "bourgeois specialists" were part of the old society, they argued,
and therefore should have no power in the new society.
Lenin's policy, however, had been to assign many of these
specialists to important positions in the economy, the army,
and the government. Consequently, the left Communists

charged Lenin with revisionism and challenged his leadership.

Lenin's reply to them was brief and to the point. Calling
their view "Left-Wing Childishness," Lenin wrote:

> Ninety-nine percent of the organizers and the first-class tech-
> nicians of really large-scale and giant enterprises, trusts, and
> other establishments belong to the capitalist class. But it is pre-
> cisely these people who we . . . must appoint to "manage" the
> labor process and the organization of production, for *there are
> no other people who have practical experience in this matter*.[2]

Even at this relatively low level of technology, Lenin found
that the "organizers and first-class *technicians*" could not be
dismissed by the revolution. Lenin inherited an economy
sufficiently complex so that dialectical change could not be
"mere negation," but "negation as a factor of connection,
as a factor of development, retaining the positive."[3]

Because the number of "knowledge" workers is astronom-
ically greater in contemporary society than in Lenin's time,
the strategy of a tightly organized vanguard of violent revolutionaries taking over a nation has become even weaker.
Today such a vanguard would have to turn to its opponents
in order to keep society functioning. Thorstein Veblen
understood this a half-century ago when he wrote in *The
Engineer and the Price System*:

> No movement for the dispossession of the Vested Interests in
> America can hope for even a temporary success unless it is
> undertaken by an organization which is competent to take over
> the country's productive industry as a whole, and to administer
> it from the start on a more efficient plan than that now pursued
> by the Vested Interests.[4]

In countries which rely on knowledge workers for food,
housing, clothing, fuel, medical care, transportation, communication—indeed for virtually everything—a definition
of revolution which presumes only a small number of specialized, technical workers is fatally anachronistic.

Unlike previous forms of wealth, such as land, money, or

property, all of which could be confiscated by chopping off their owner's head, knowledge cannot be so easily appropriated. Technical knowledge, the new "mental capital," is firmly embedded in those heads. They cannot be severed from their respective bodies without losing the value of what they contain.

Technology has completely invalidated the mechanistic interpretation of revolutionary change, which fails to recognize the continuity which must be sustained even through the revolution. As Stalin's Yugoslav critics have persistently argued, to define revolution as the negation of the "old" and the establishment of the "new" is deceptive. The new is part of the old and, especially in a technological society, the old must be part of the new.

> Negation of the "existing" is not something external to the "existing" but something within it, a part of the "existing" . . . . Continuity in social progress cannot be assured by removing the "existing" but rather by the emergence of the "new" within it. In life's continuity, therefore, the "old" cannot be discarded as long as the "new" depends on it.[5]

To argue that the new society must inevitably be built on the ashes of the old is to argue that "the conception of every human being would simultaneously mean the death of the mother."[5] Both the child and the revolution could be born, perhaps, but neither would have much chance to grow.

The old definition of revolution accepted the illusion of "The Revolution," the illusion that only one generation of radicals was needed to achieve significant change. Born in a pretechnical era, this definition was based on the assumption that society is basically unchanging. Revolutionary violence would therefore result in a new order which, though different from its predecessor, would be equally unchanging. Although Marx and Engels said plainly: "We have no intention to dictate to mankind laws valid forever," revolutions in their name have bound their children tightly to immutable laws.

The epitaph of such revolutions was written by Czech

students on the walls of Prague during the Soviet invasion. "Socialism, yes; occupation, no," they wrote. *"Fathers, liberators; sons oppressors."*

The Technicians:
Big Science

Technology has altered the lines of conflict in modern society. Historical methods of social analysis are no longer adequate today. "Clearly the concepts used to analyze 19th and 20th century capitalism," argues Herbert Marcuse, "cannot simply be applied to its present form."[6]

In industrial society, the *organization of labor* was of paramount importance in political debate. Relations between those who managed labor, and those who labored; between those who paid, and those who were paid; between those who had too much, and those who had too little; were the central questions of the time. These contradictions still remain, but to them have been added new ones.

In the classical scenario of industrial capitalism, workers struck against the management for higher wages. In the classical scenario of technological capitalism, management and labor together defend their factory against anti-pollution or anti-war groups who are seen as threats to the growth of the enterprise. (In Japan, victims of pollution poisoning have actually been barred entrance from the guilty factory by angry workers who did not want them to register complaints with the management out of fear for their jobs.) "This does not, of course, mean that the old contradictions have disappeared," writes Roger Garaudy, "but rather that they have been profoundly transformed by fresh contradictions."[7]

Technology, broadly defined, is the *"organization of knowledge* for the achievement of practical purposes."[8] This shifting emphasis from physical labor to knowledge work rests at the very heart of American society.[9]

The economy now requires vast numbers of trained workers whose expertise is not so much with things, nor with money, nor with people, but with technical knowledge which may be applied to all of them. From 1947 to 1965, white-collar workers—those who primarily worked with knowledge —increased by 9.6 million, while blue-collar workers decreased by 4 million. These knowledge workers who staff Galbraith's "technostructure" are displacing blue-collar workers.[10] White-collar jobs have become so central in the technological society that only one-quarter of the present generation will have to enter the agricultural and productive occupations which are subsumed under "labor."[11] The remainder are emerging as a vast work force the members of which we will call quite simply, *technicians.*

One major reason for the overall increase in knowledge-based jobs is the growth of the "knowledge industries." Although its central component industries—education, research and development, communications, information machines, and information services—are difficult to measure economically,[12] the growth of this field is reliably estimated at *twice* the rate of the rest of the economy.[13] Half of every dollar spent in the American economy in 1975 will be in the production and distribution of knowledge.[14] The growth of the knowledge sector of the economy has been discussed not only by experts on management and economics, but by everyone from the president of IBM to socialist critics like Michael Harrington. Relying on US Department of Labor manpower projections for the year 1980, Harrington identifies a "knowledge revolution" which is creating "new industries:"

> The occupation with the greatest growth during the seventies is that of "professional and technical workers," which will increase by fifty percent, while operatives (assemblers, truck drivers, bus drivers) will grow by only ten percent. As a result, in 1980 it is estimated that there will be slightly more professionals than operatives . . . .[15]

We would be foolish not to realize the enormous benefits that this technological revolution has brought us. It is true that technology has increased the yield from our farmlands and reduced the incidence of epidemic disease. Technology has freed many of us from jobs of drudgery and physical strain and given us the freedom to move to new places and to learn of new worlds. Technology has made the home, the office, and the factory more efficient environments, and spread wealth to an unprecedented percentage of our population. Perhaps most important, the technological revolution's demand for highly-skilled workers has created a burgeoning educational industry that has brought a college education to millions of young Americans and virtually created a new, highly educated middle class.

Men and women who have played a role in this historic technological revolution—whether skilled metal workers and telephone repairmen, or nuclear physicists and physicians— feel insulted to be called "conservative" or "traditional." Together they have created a new world far different from anything their parents could have built, or even imagined. The technicians surmounted many of the challenging problems that had faced their parents' generation. They are, naturally, quite proud.

Armed with unsurpassed technical knowledge, they feel that their revolution is based upon the only means by which men can truly progress: scientific knowledge. Instead of social classes fighting over who gets how much of the existing wealth, they have created *new* wealth. Social groups no longer need to oppose each other for a larger share of the economic pie, they explain, because an amazing method now exists for making the pie continually bigger. Their technological revolution has provided food, clothing, and shelter to virtually all Americans; medical science is the most advanced in the world; more children than ever before receive free public education; and unprecedented levels of per capita income enable the vast majority of the citizenry to acquire the consumer goods they want. Perhaps the best symbol of the technicians' extraordinary success is the chart in virtually every economics textbook which demonstrates that the number of hours the average American must work to purchase a given commodity is but a fraction of the hours an average Russian must work.

Their faith in technology seemingly justified, *the techni-cians are confident that whatever problems remain to be solved are all subject to technical solutions.* We may rely, said President Nixon in his 1970 State Of The Union Mess-age, on the "same reservoirs of inventive genius" that have brought us this far. The technicians are so impressed with their achievements that they assume that if a problem does not have a technical answer, either the problem has not been properly formulated, or it is simply not a *real* problem.

By their bold and innovative "technological radicalism" they feel comfortable with "social conservatism."[16] In essence, they tell their children: because we have engineers we no longer need radicals.

Supported by their economic charts and technical experi-ments, the technicians are quite justified in claiming to have made a revolution. As their definition requires, they can certainly prove that they have "brought about a drastic change in society." Even their determined critics such as Herbert Marcuse must admit that their argument is impres-sive. "What is really so terrible about this system," Marcuse asks, "which continually expands social wealth so that strata of the population that previously lived in the greatest poverty and misery today have automobiles, television sets, and one-family houses?"[17] The technicians—the white-collar archi-tects of our technetronic wonderworld—can logically con-clude that technology has in fact "liberated" their children, and that their children should be duly grateful.

Children of the Technocracy

Why then do so many of the technicians' offspring reserve their greatest animosity for the highly-developed technology of which their parents are so proud? Young people all across America have turned to everything from oriental religion to psychedelic drugs to communal farming in an effort to escape from the technological system and its strait-jacket rational-ism. The assembly of young people gathered at the White House Conference on Youth in 1971, hardly a band of wild-eyed hippies, focused on "uncontrolled technology" as the primary danger to mankind, and felt obliged to call for "a recognition of Life as the Supreme Value which will not bear manipulation for other ends."[18]

This generation's opposition to the influence of technology is particularly striking because its members are, literally, the first "children of technocracy," the first generation to be raised after the gigantic application of scientific knowledge to the problems of everyday life. The revolution which heralded the triumph of technology can be accurately tied to the moment in history when abstract science became applied science, that is, when general scientific knowledge was used to affect human life and social organization.[19]

In this transition from basic science to applied technology, argues Barry Commoner, "World War II is a decisive turning point..."

> The twenty-five years preceding the war is the main period of the sweeping modern revolution in basic science, especially in physics and chemistry, upon which so much of the new productive technology is based. In the approximate period of the war itself, under the pressure of military demands, much of the new scientific knowledge was rapidly converted into new technologies and productive enterprises. Since the war, the technologies have rapidly transformed the nature of industrial and agricultural production. The period of World War II is, therefore, a great divide between the scientific revolution that preceded it and the technological revolution that followed it.[20]

Therefore, the first postwar generation may also be called the first post-technological generation. (Generations born in the late fifties and sixties, of course, felt the impact of the technological revolution even more intensely than the first, but those born in the first decade following the war are the only ones who have had time so far to react as young men and women to the technological colossus that has surrounded them since birth.) This first post-technological generation has felt the heavy influence of technology at all stages of their development from child to adolescent to young adult. This influence can be broken down into three concrete areas: economic planning, educational control, and ecological exploitation.

1. Economic Planning. Of the changes in economic life in the twentieth century, writes John Kenneth Galbraith, "the most visible has been the application of increasingly intricate and sophisticated technology to the production of things."[21] Although "socialists" like Michael Harrington and "conservatives" like Milton Friedman interpret the impact of this transformation somewhat differently, the thrust of Galbraith's point is sound.

Increasingly elaborate technology, first of all, has required a heavier investment of capital. Second, it has required a greatly increased lapse of time between the decision to produce a given product and its emergence on the market. Third, after making such an enormous commitment of time and money, it has required that the market demand for the product be conditioned and controlled to a certain extent by the producer. In other words, one of the imperatives of technology is *economic planning*.

Today these are economic truisms. Even independent socialist economists are in accord with this view of technological economy. Roger Garaudy, the leading French Marxist theoretician, has written of this "new scientific and technological revolution." He maintains that the use of highly developed technology in production is the crucial determinant of the structure of advanced societies. Like Galbraith, he argues that this technological revolution *"demands long-term planning* . . . an increasing time-lag between production plans (prepared at research and development level), the commencement of production and the product's appearance on the market."[22]

Because of this extensive coordination of capital, research, development, materials, manpower, promotion, and markets, it is economically unfeasible to alter the original plans in any fundamental way during the many years between the initiation and completion of the project. This is the essence of economic planning.

The material advantages of this highly complex, long-term regulation of economic life are clear. To be doubly sure that we would recognize them, the technicians have inundated our world—from the roadside landscape to the flickering living room—with ingenious reminders. From their point of view, of course, economic planning has raised the standard of living, saved us from scarcity and unpredictability, and facilitated efficient organization of resources without which technical progress would be impossible.

From the perspective of the planners' children, however, there is a serious flaw in this apparently rational scheme. *Long-term economic planning, as it reaches its most highly developed form, binds one generation to the production priorities of its predecessors.* So tightly interlocking are the functioning parts of the technological economy—finance, research, manpower, production, and marketing—that its designers can rationally argue that any attempt to restructure the whole apparatus is inconceivable.

Like the cyclist who cannot change gears because he refuses to stop pedaling, the technological revolutionaries have so deeply committed themselves to achieving present goals of production that they cannot change speed or direction. Their children have no choice but to accept the overall plan, and to satisfy themselves with making minor adjustments whenever possible. To paraphrase Emerson: technology is in the saddle and is riding mankind.

"Our present method of underwriting advanced technology is exceedingly dangerous," writes Galbraith. "It could cost us our existence."[23] Similarly, Erich Fromm asks: "Are *we* really planning, or are we *planned to plan* according to certain principles which we do not question and for which we have no responsibility?"[24] For all that the architects of advanced economies have provided for their children, they have taken one crucial thing away: the freedom to change directions.

2. *Educational Control.* Of what value would be even the most refined economic blueprints if properly trained personnel were not available in adequate numbers? Only a cursory reading of trade journals and newspapers is necessary to realize that an integral part of economic planning is

the accurate estimation of the aggregate demand for workers with various kinds of specialized training. Somehow it can be authoritatively announced by an omniscient administrator that by 1985 America will need 40,000 more data processors or 27.5% more engineers. To guarantee that a proper distribution of manpower will be available when industry requires it, the technicians have felt more than justified in adopting a policy of compulsory education with highly specified curriculum. This second imperative of technology, then, is *educational control*.

The expansion of the technological enterprise requires that ever greater numbers of children be exposed to ever more intensive specialized instruction. So important is technical knowledge to the modern corporation that some economists maintain it has become more important than capital or property. This transition from a dependence on physical labor to a dependence on trained minds has tremendously increased the economic importance of childhood. If the struggle of the industrial society revolved around the adult's willingness to work in privately owned factories at subsistence wages, then the struggle of the technological society today revolves around the child's willingness to study in highly structured schools about officially designated subjects. Naturally, the technicians feel this protracted training is a privilege for their children, since it enables them to compete for the most remunerative positions. This training also assures the continued expansion of the economy.

The technicians' children, however, once again feel that their lives had been unduly predirected: not only in terms of the jobs they are required to hold as adults, but also in terms of the activities they are required to pursue as children. The absorption of childhood into the economic process is particularly offensive because it begins to mold the individual's needs and goals long before he has achieved the ability to recognize and defend his self-interest.

This educational control is by no means limited to the public schools (over which, in theory, the individual parent exerts some control). It is still more evident in the use of the media of mass communication, which, once again, are based on new technology.

3. Ecological Exploitation.   Technology is based upon a twofold assumption: that man can devise processes and manufacture products superior to nature's; and that man can devise inventions which can perform necessary services at ever lower cost. These have become the axioms, the basic commandments, that have fueled the technological revolution. In many areas of life, these assumptions have been repeatedly validated. The technicians' error was to assume that what was true in many areas was true in all. It would be naive to denounce technology itself as destructively and inevitably opposed to nature. After all, nature itself embodies a constant interplay of destruction and creation, or growth and decay. Long before the development of complex technology, man was intervening in nature. Each time a field was cleared and planted, or animals were bred, or a river adapted for iririgation or power, or a tree felled, or a stone shaped, man was entering into a natural process and altering it to serve his welfare. Pre-technological man was not a pure creature whose activities never altered natural events, but rather the first evolutionary being to employ the resources of nature systematically to enrich his own existence.

A fundamental difference exists, however, between mild intervention and wild exploitation. For some time man has used technology to exploit nature at the expense of other species. And, of course, men have also used technology to exploit nature at the immediate expense of other men. But never before in human history has there been such a wholesale exploitation of the global environment at the expense of future generations.

The term "ecological exploitation" refers not only to the exploitation of man's external environment, but to the exploitation of man himself (perhaps in fact "bio-ecological exploitation" would more nearly convey my meaning). Between the emission of a pollutant into the environment and its impact on human health there is an extraordinarily long time lag. This delay includes both "the passage of the pollutant through air or rivers or soil and into the food chain, and also the time from human ingestion or absorption of the pollutant until clinical symptoms appear."[25] For example, several years may elapse between the use of DDT and its absorption into our food supply and our bodies. If the use of DDT were to be progressively diminished beginning this year, DDT concentration in fish we eat would continue to climb for eleven more years. Still more startling: it would persist in concentrations higher than its current level for at least 25 years, that is, *until the beginning of the 21st century.*[26]

Thus, if we were now to discover scientific proof that DDT (or some other chemical) contributed to the increased incidence of cancer (or some other disease), our children and even our children's children would continue to be damaged by it. Quite literally, we are exploiting nature at our children's expense.

This environmental time bomb particularly endangers our children. Published estimates of the toxic effect of a given chemical are generally established by averaging the results from a statistically reliable sample of *adults*. Unfortunately, as we shall later examine more thoroughly, many substances have disproportionately injurious effect on children, infants, and fetuses. This is not only true for many chemical pollutants, but also for radioactivity.

Dehumanization of Values

Through economic planning, educational control, and ecological exploitation, the new technological state demonstrated its pervasive grip upon postwar America. This state had grown up in a time of need and crisis—first the Depression, then World War II, then the Cold War provided the impetus for driving the technocratic machine onwards. But the technological state needed a rationale for perpetuating its ascendancy on the national scene, especially in the atmosphere of detente and humane idealism of the sixties. It found this

rationale in technology itself: the achievements of the technological system became not ways of satisfying essential
human needs, but ends in themselves. From the arms race to
the space race to the Vietnam War itself, goals were formulated as technical problems with technical solutions and
technical rewards. The USA may possess the capability of
destroying all of the Soviet Union fifty times over, instead
of just once, but what is the use of that if the USA would inevitably be destroyed in the process? The astronauts may
have brought back twenty pounds of moon rocks, but of
what use is that to the ghetto mother whose four kids are
strung out on heroin? The average household may own more
cars and more TV sets than ever before, but at the same time
more and more kids have become delinquents, more and
more parents are divorced, and more and more city streets
have become unsafe. The technological state presented the
world with the subtle and pervasive *dehumanization* of all
national priorities.

The technicians and their generation have undoubtedly
been sincere in their desire to provide a comfortable material
base for their children. But the methods they have used to
achieve that comfort have been so "successful" that they have
become ends in themselves. The technicians did not (and
do not) realize that while the undeniable need for a generation recovering from scarcity is to obtain material security,
material comfort is not an adequate goal for a generation
raised on abundance. The technicians' children have recognized that the economic, educational, and ecological exploitation which have met all their material needs have ignored
other needs, individual and social. They have been told that
they could not convert war-related industries into industries
for social peace because it would disrupt the balance of the
economic system; they have been told they must not question
the goals or relevance of the education they have received
because they would understand later; they have been told
that they could not stop the ecological poisoning of their
environment because pollution is the price of progress. But
these children have no stake in a war-related economic

system or an educational regimen that prepared them to take part in that system; nor have they been willing to pay the ecological price for that sort of "progress." They are alienated from these technicians' dehumanized goals because the technicians have not been able to explain them in human terms.

Vietnam gave the lie to the technicians' real priorities. So far removed had these men become from the needs of their children that, once their systems-analysis military solution failed to work, they not only refused to accept their own *human* failure, but they continued to use their children as sacrifices to their "adult" sense of honor.

Like most Americans, I once believed that childhood was unimportant. The child does not vote, does not earn wages, does not pay taxes, does not contribute to scientific or cultural wisdom. The child is merely an investment, one which will pay handsome dividends when it matures.

My own attitude toward childhood began to change when my childhood ended—when I realized that, although my friends and I knew virtually nothing about America and its international involvements (we were still in our teens), many of us were being ordered to kill and be killed. I noticed that all the newspaper pictures of American soldiers dead or missing in Vietnam had two things in common: the men wore uniforms, and they were young.

Before I knew it, I was a young man, and the pictures were of my friends. I couldn't help but wonder if someday someone would be looking at my picture. And I began to wonder: why is our age group first in line for military sacrifice?

My anger mounted with each death. What signified the end of my childhood was not the anger itself but rather my ability to identify its cause. I listened to the refrain of Phil Ochs's song "I Ain't Marchin' Anymore," and for the first time I understood. "It's always the old who lead us to war," he sang, but "always the young to fall." One pediatrician, sent to Japan to care for the children of American men and women in the Armed Forces, soon found himself treating wounded soldiers who had been airlifted from Vietnam.

After seeing teenagers without limbs and without purpose, the painful irony of a pediatrician who was treating "grown" soldiers struck him: "I soon realized that the troopers they were pulling off those med evac choppers were only children themselves."[27]

For me, too, the war changed the meaning of childhood. Childhood has become a political question.

3.
The Children's Revolution

organizing for children

---

*Adults should be organized, not for
themselves, but for their children.*
Maria Montessori

A revolution to achieve technology and a revolution to control it require different politics.

During the Depression, while the technicians were growing up, the goal was clear. "A chicken in every pot and a car in every garage." While this goal was remembered, and achieved, another was forgotten. "At the turn of the century," recalls Robert Coles in *Children of Crisis*, "the labor movement asked for 'a childhood for every child.' "[1] This goal has yet to be reached.

As Orwell's *1984* and Huxley's *Brave New World* have illustrated, the possibility exists of a society based on technical wizardry in which all citizens are fed, clothed, sheltered, educated, medicated, and employed; but who have simultaneously been so biologically, psychologically, and socially manipulated from birth onward that they have no vestige of individuality. We must realize that this is the perfect technique of totalitarianism: a liberal technocracy. Unlike crass communist control, the ultimate technicians would, on the one hand, defend individual freedoms but, on the other hand, ensure that no one had ever had the chance to develop the independence of mind to use those freedoms.[2] Is this not what Marcuse means when he writes: "psychological categories . . . have become political categories"?[3]

Although our technological society has not yet become a "brave new world," present intrusions into the years of childhood are having deep and disturbing effects on the growing personality which, if permitted to intensify, could fulfill those anti-utopian visions. Technological society has already altered childhood, particularly two phases of growth vital to the development of the healthy adolescent: industry and identity. To oversimplify: more industry has been required, but less identity.

Before the advent of technology, the job market did not require large pools of young people with the ability to innovate. As previously noted, blue-collar labor until recently absorbed the overwhelming majority of the rising generation. These jobs required hard work, but not innovation. With the ascendancy of technology, virtually all work was transformed. The new by-words of American industry were research, innovation, specialization, reorganization, automation, development, etc.

Quite suddenly, society wanted a generation capable of discovering new ways of doing things. The technicians valued change, not repetition. They could not simply socialize their children—that is, train them to do things in traditional ways. On the contrary, the entire system of production and administration required that the young learn new information and methods and apply them at an ever accelerating rate. As Kenneth Keniston wrote, technology required a "priority on cognition," an intensified emphasis on "men's capacities for achieving accurate, objective, practically useful" knowledge.[4]

In order that sufficient numbers of children would develop these cognitive potentials, they had to be raised differently soon after birth. The real pressure became most visible, however, during the phase of early adolescence which Erikson calls the stage of industry. Roughly corresponding to the years of high school, this is society's "last chance" to stimulate and control the human potentials without which technocracy cannot be maintained.

As Americans have quickly remarked about education in the Soviet Union, a generation can produce technical experts despite the absence of human freedoms. In fact, the absence of broader freedoms may have even made Soviet youth more loyal, diligent technical workers. Americans have been much slower to realize that their own capitalist version of training for technology also places very stringent limitations on the kind of creativity developed in the young. The sort of creativity fostered can be called *technical creativity*.

Creativity for Hire

Technique means the use of specialized knowledge for the achievement of predetermined ends.[5] The very nature of technology requires that it is almost always someone other than the knowledge worker himself who selects these ends. In technologically based systems, a process or problem is first broken down into manageable units. These component elements are then divided and subdivided so that highly specialized knowledge can be applied to each unit. As symbolized mechanically by the computer, someone (or something) else must decide what each fragmented unit should be required to do, when it should be done, and how the aggregate should be fit together. At its most rigorous, this problem-solving technique is called systems analysis.[6]

By following technology's lead, by letting it determine what knowledge is important and applicable, the technicians have created a "how-to-do-it society, not a what-to-do society."[7] While the technicians permissively encouraged their children to be as creative as they could, they also dictated the specific frame of reference within which that creativity could be expressed. Behind the revolutionary demand for creativity of skills lurked the reactionary demand for conformity of values.

Values—beliefs based upon ethics, not statistics—have no place in the creativity technicians want. After defining their problem (which may be anything from increasing electric power to making children learn), they seek a technical solution to be implemented as soon as they deem it efficient and economical. They define social problems so that the solutions seem to "require a change only in the techniques of the natural sciences, demanding little or nothing in the way of change in human values or ideas of morality."[8] Only later, when the remedy chosen on technical grounds has been implemented, does the truth become apparent: changes *are* demanded in "human values" and "morality" after all. *And such changes must correspond first to the prerequisites of the technical "solution," and only second—if at all—to the prerequisites of human growth.*

Technical creativity, then, is based on a *false frame* of analysis: a frame which rigorously examines technical feasibility, economic productivity, organizational efficiency, and other measurable components (the means) ; but which fails to reexamine the needs of individual growth and the ethical goals of society (the ends). After separating a problem from its social and human contexts, the technicians consider it to have been effectively solved until, days or years or decades later, the unanticipated economic, ecological, and emotional costs must be paid by those who were but children when the handsome profits were made.

Although popular American mythology views the technologist as "a kind of scientific sorcerer," scientist Barry Commoner concludes that "he is less a sorcerer than a sorcerer's apprentice." Commoner is referring to the technicians' "tubular vision," which leads them to define problems without grasping the whole systems of which those problems are integrated, functioning parts. He validates his point by a series of illustrations—detergents, automobiles, plastics, chemical manufacturing, fertilizers—and concludes:

> Ecological survival does not mean the abandonment of technology. Rather, it requires that technology be derived from a scientific analysis that is appropriate to the natural world on which it intrudes.[9]

To argue that technology itself is the enemy is as naive as to maintain that it is our savior. What will condemn or rescue mankind is the quality of our creativity. We must transform shallow technical creativity, which overemphasizes man's tools and tool-making abilities, into a deeper and more mature *radical creativity,* which recognizes man above all as part of a human community and as part of nature. The present youth generation may initiate this post-technological revolution, but it is their children, and their children's children who will complete it.

Subsequent chapters will concretely criticize technical creativity and the professional and political groups which rely on it. But the simplicity inherent in such categories should not lead us to self-serving smugness or holier-than-thou polemics. Technical creativity is not an alien ideology but an extreme form of our own alienation; and the technicians are not a ruthless enemy but a caste of experts on whom each of us has at some time depended. Each criticism we make of the technological order, then, is potential self-criticism as well.

Radical Creativity

Creativity is at the very heart of radicalism. It describes in a psychological way the philosophical assumption of dialectical theory: that synthesis must finally emerge out of contradictory forces. Beginning with the present state of society (thesis), dialectical theory posits a movement which negates society (antithesis). Out of the struggle between these conflicting forces finally emerges a radical reconceptualization which transcends both (synthesis).

It is only in the act of synthesis, of overcoming and transcending both the given *and* its opposite, that creativity is required. Without it, dialectical change remains locked into stereotyped rigidity and cannot move toward a new and higher level of social conflict. This is why genuine creativity, as Brewster Ghiselin's extraordinary book *The Creative Process* implies, is *radical.*

> [It] is not an elaboration of the established, but a movement beyond the established . . . . The first need is therefore to transcend the old order. Before any new order can be defined,

the absolute power of the established, the hold upon us of
what we know and are, must be broken.[10]

The very existence of "the Movement" or the "counter
culture" attests to the resilience of human creativity. Told to
sit still, we asked about our bodies. Told to fight, we asked
why. Told to work, we asked for whom. We reacted against
the technicians' mentality and tried desperately, often chaot-
ically, to grow beyond it.

Some members of the first post-technological generation
succeeded in extending their creative thought beyond the
narrow framework specified by the technicians. That this
group of creative young men and women grew out of the
technicians' revolution should not surprise us. For if a society
reaches that point of self-intensifying complexity at which it
can no longer sustain itself without developing new levels
of technical creativity, then, no matter how hard it may try,
that society cannot prevent some genuine creativity from
emerging. If creativity concerning practical skills is required,
then how can at least some creativity concerning critical
values be prevented? As Jim Kunen said with lovely brevity
in *The Strawberry Statement*: "When my parents sent me
to college, they took the chance that I might learn something."[11]

This is the built-in tension of a society which on the one
hand stands up for individual freedom and yet on the other
hand bows to the dictates of technology. When the technicians' children realized that they could act as well as react, lead
as well as be led, and have children as well as be children,
the well laid plans of the technological revolution began to
meet its first real challenge.

Children Come Last

During the civil rights and anti-war movements of the 1960s,
young people without established power found new political
leverage. Indeed, during the 1968 elections attitudes toward
the "youth rebellion" were among the most salient charac-

teristics which determined voting patterns. As a result, by 1972 the 18-to-21-year-olds had been enfranchised. Both Richard Nixon and George McGovern pursued the "youth vote" with the special age-oriented zeal which had previously been devoted to the "senior-citizen vote." Thus in the 1970s the political system officially conferred on youth the rights of citizenship, as it had done for blacks and women in previous decades.

Clearly only one age group as such remains disenfranchised: children. This is generally not of great interest in political discussions because it is assumed that other institutions— first the family, and now schools, hospitals, welfare and planning agencies, etc.—attend to the needs of children. Periodically, when political pressure groups vigorously complain that some children's needs are being outrageously neglected, a new program is established, such as the school lunch program, Headstart, the Office of Child Development, and so on. Most often, however, the assumption stands unchallenged that, despite the transformation of modern society by technological innovation, the growth of children is somehow still adequately defended by traditional institutions.

Unfortunately, the opposite is true. Subsequent chapters will demonstrate that various stages of growth during childhood and adolescence are not only left unprotected, but are actually exploited.

In their *Report to the President,* the White House Conference on Children in 1970 anxiously called for "a reordering of priorities at all levels of American society so that children and families come first." And Urie Bronfenbrenner, chairman of the conference's committee on the family, concluded starkly:

> The evidence indicates that American society, whether viewed in comparison to other nations or to itself over time, is according progressively less attention to its children.[12]

While some of the poor countries of the world which have yet to reap the benefits of technology devote a generous share of their scarce resources to their children's welfare, technological states like the US and the USSR are squandering their wealth.[13]

How little has changed, in fact, since the turn of the century when that brave educator Maria Montessori wrote: *"the greatest crime that society commits is that of wasting the money which it should use for children on things that will destroy them and society itself...."*

> Nature furnishes no examples of adults who devour everything for themselves and abandon their own offspring to misery. And yet nothing is done for the child. His body is kept alive and that is all. When, because of its wastefulness, society has urgent need of money, it takes this from the schools, and especially from the lower schools that shelter the seeds of life. It takes it from these schools because there are no voices to defend them.[14]

How true this still is today in this era of extravagant overseas wars and miserly school lunch programs.

The requirements of modern technology make this age-old adult wastefulness even more damaging to the quality of life. Highly developed weaponry, both nuclear and nonnuclear, requires an unprecedented commitment of national resources to military programs. This commitment includes not simply money, but manpower. These military enterprises in turn require broad-based scientific and industrial support from the "heavy industry" which receives defense contracts. In this way an incredible amount of valuable technical expertise is funneled into projects which cannot be applied to civilian needs, or which, at best, can be applied only indirectly and with great delay and further expense. America's previously unchallenged superiority in the world market has been undermined for precisely this reason: while the resources of our economic competitors have been almost totally devoted to *non*military research and development, as much as one-half of America's technical energy has been directed toward "defense" strategies only marginally related to genuine national growth.

The tight civilian budget which results from this waste fits precisely Montessori's description. Welfare, day care, child health delivery, schools, etc., receive decreased appropriations. As Charles Hampden-Turner observes,

> . . . modern America produces techniques of staggering sophistication, side by side with unmet needs of equally staggering yet tragic proportions, for which there are no available techniques or resources. This inexorable divergence between what is feasible technically and what is needed humanly is the result of decades of groveling before the God of Technique, of resolving what to do next by following meekly the direction in which the tool itself pointed, even though it pointed away from human needs and towards the "opportunity" of a circus in space and other distractions.[15]

In each of the case studies we pursue in this book, we will find this description—harsh as it may seem—frighteningly accurate.

From the engineer testing wing stress on a new military transport plane to the Army logistics expert to the Lockheed executive—thousands of trained, sometimes brilliant men could be devoting their time, energy, and knowledge to solving the host of problems which confront men, women, and children in their daily lives. Yet this pacification and humanization of technical work and industrial production seems further away than ever before. Few adults seem ready to boldly redirect the use of national resources because they are more committed to sophisticated adult games—called "space race," or "corporate profits," or "missile gap," or "world respect"—than to the growth of children. As the early communist William Morris once said: "children have as much need for a revolution as the proletariat have."[16]

Let no misunderstanding arise here. It is obviously still preferable to be a rich child rather than a poor one; to have parents with stock options rather than parents on welfare; and to have a lovely suburban home rather than a crumbling tenement. But technology has altered society so profoundly that radical analysis is incomplete if it relies on the simple principle: give the poor what the rich have got. Certainly the inadequate nutrition, unsafe homes, and inferior medical care which poor children live with bears no comparison with the relative affluence of middle-class America. Still, even the privileged children in society today are subjected to an environment which threatens their growth.

The technological scenario is rapidly displacing the industrial one. The old blue-collar labor force is diminishing in numbers as a new one of knowledge workers grows daily. We must lend our support to the resolution of these old economic contradictions and not ignore them. But we must also recognize the new forces which have arisen in the country, and respond to the challenges they present. Both the rich and the poor child still fit Maria Montessori's painful description written over fifty years ago:

> Much has been said in recent years of the rights of the workers, but it is now time to speak of the social rights of the child. A recognition of the rights of workers is a matter of fundamental importance for society since it is solely by human toil that humanity survives. But if workers produce what men consume and are the creators of countless objects, the child produces humanity itself and consequently his rights have still greater need of recognition.[17]

In their myriad forms—biological, chemical, mechanical, electronic, nuclear—the inventions of technology now affect *all* children's lives long before they encounter the conditions of labor or the institutions of government. Although the technicians could defend their inventions in terms of productivity, efficiency, power, precision, speed, or scale, their potential impact in children was rarely considered important enough to delay or to limit their production or application.

We must begin with the premise that no previous revolutions have faced: *that human childhood inevitably provides a potential basis for exploitation.*[18] Other revolutionaries could claim that they would end forever the social basis for exploitation, but they overlooked the human fact that there will always be children. And children will always be dependent on the society of adults, not only economically, but also psychologically and biologically. It is true that the activity of labor divided men into two major classes, one of which exploited the other. But it is also true that the activity of human development divided men into two generations, one of which is in position to control the other.

Erich Fromm writes:

> Children could defend themselves even less than women and slaves. Women have fought a guerilla war against the patriarchate in their own way; slaves have rebelled many times in one form or the other. But temper tantrums, refusal to eat, constipation, and bed-wetting are not the weapons by which one can overthrow a powerful system. The only result was that the child developed into a crippled, inhibited, and often evil adult, who took revenge on his own children for what had been done to him.[19]

Because we have begun with the premise that a revolution's children are the measure of its success, we must challenge the technological revolution not only in terms of political freedoms, such as the right to vote or to assemble; and not only in terms of economic freedoms, such as the right to work or to strike; but also in terms of the freedom of development during childhood and youth. Since none of the claims of the technological revolutionaries have assured us that this freedom of development has been guaranteed to their children, we must closely examine their revolution and judge for ourselves.

But where do we begin? At what point were the lives of the post-technological generation first affected by the technological revolution?

Certainly when they entered the labor force. The kinds of work required by industry had been profoundly altered by the impact of technology. And when they entered school, their experiences were molded by the strenuous, specialized, and prolonged training demanded of those who aimed to become technicians. At still younger ages, of course, new inventions (most prominently, the mass media) intimately entered their daily lives. And even before that, the child was affected by the way his parents and brothers and sisters reacted to the new circumstances wrought by technology.

In fact, the first post-technological generation had already been exposed to the benefits and hazards of technology well before they took their first breath of life. That is why their political biography must begin in the protected sea of their mothers' wombs.

II.

And whoso shall receive one
such little child in my name
receiveth me.

Matthew 18:5

4.

The Embryo

the sanctity of human life

Unrestricted abortion policies or abortion on demand I cannot square with my personal belief in the sanctity of human life—including the life of the yet unborn.

Richard Nixon
San Clemente, April 3, 1971

Our best hope for meeting the nation's growing demand for clean energy lies with the fast-breeder [nuclear] reactor.

Richard Nixon
Speech to Congress, 1971

In 1945 the first postwar babies were born. If our purpose was praise, we might say these babies were conceived beneath the victorious American flag at the moment when the Axis powers surrendered to the Allies. But rehearsing eulogies is not patriotism. It would be more fitting to place the act of conception under the first atomic mushroom cloud.

The year after the end of the war the Atomic Energy Commission was established. The AEC was given the authority to develop the military and civilian potential of atomic and nuclear energy.

By the time the first postwar children were five years old, the two major nuclear powers had exploded no less than twenty-nine bombs.[1] This was not war, simply testing for war. Though important to politicians, this distinction did not protect the natural chemistry of our bones. We became the first generation in history to grow up with strontium-90 built into our bones, and iodine-131 embedded in our thyroid glands.[2]

Who Is To Be Solomon?

All this time, the technicians claimed to have the situation well under control; the Federal Radiation Council assured the public that they were proceeding with all due caution.

> The establishment of radiation protection standards involves a balancing of the benefits derived from the controlled use of radiation and atomic energy against the risk of radiation exposure . . . any radiation exposure involves some risk, the magnitude of which increases with the exposure . . . the various benefits to be expected *as evaluated by the appropriate responsible group* must outweigh the potential hazard or risk.[3] [Italics mine.]

Of course, the "appropriate responsible group" was none other than the technicians themselves. The AEC was delegated the responsibility both to promote nuclear energy *and* to control its safety. Although democratic practice has always held that—as stated by James Madison in *The Federalist Papers*—

> No man is allowed to judge in his own cause; his interest will certainly bias his judgment, and, not improbably, corrupt his integrity. With equal, nay, with greater reason, a body of men are unfit to be both judges and parties at the same time . . .[4]

the AEC proceeded to judge its own cause, armed with the conviction that James Madison knew nothing about nuclear physics, and that nuclear physics was not subject to normal political or moral judgment. It was a technical question.

Fortunately, the spirit of democracy has not been completely buried by technique. A scientist and ecologist like Barry Commoner feels required to raise the issue:

> . . . who is to be the Solomon of modern technology and weigh in the balance all the good that comes of it against the ecological and social costs? Or, who will strike the balance between the concern of the prudent manager of a nuclear power plant for economy and the concern of a mother over the health of her child?[5]

The technicians appointed themselves Solomon in dealing with nuclear arms tests. Who else knew enough physics to judge?

Taken within the false frame of cost-efficiency analysis, nuclear weapons tests were deemed necessary on the grounds that, if not conducted, the Russians might win the "nuclear arms race" and jeopardize our national security. The technicians were not unaware that levels of radioactivity climbed during the 1950s; that the nature and rate of genetic mutation may well have been altered; and that the level of strontium-90 in cows' milk soared.[6] According to their decision-making abacus, the gain in "national security" was well worth these risks.

Technology did not rest with arms tests. By the time the first postwar babies were ten years old, nuclear power had expanded from military to civilian use. The technicians proudly told their critics that this awesome power of the atom had finally been adapted for a peaceful purpose: generating electrical energy. In 1957 came the first nuclear power plant; by 1965 there were eleven; by 1975 there will be 84. By 1980 over one-third, and by 2,000 over half, of America's electrical output will be derived from nuclear plants,[7] if present plans are carried out.

The AEC's jurisdiction over civilian nuclear power includes the setting of standards for "permissible radiation," and the siting of nuclear power plants.

The setting of standards determines in great measure how costly construction of the power plants will be. The more stringent the safety standards are, the higher construction and maintenance costs must be.[8] An efficiency-minded AEC somewhat lackadaisical about safety would therefore be a boon to industry. The power to pick the site of civilian nuclear plants further extends the AEC's economic clout. It represents a basketful of economic plums which the AEC can distribute, much as the military has for years doled out its installations. If one locality raises an ecological stink, the AEC may simply go on to a second site which promises to pose less environmentalist resistance in return for the new jobs and additional revenue. Siting also determines whether plants will be located close to urban centers or in more "remote" locations. The further away the plant is built, the greater the safety *and* the greater the cost.[9]

The AEC asures the public that their powers are not being

misused. In long technical papers, officials patiently explain laymen how nuclear energy will generate enormous electrical power while exerting only "a minimum of strain on energy sources and the environment." The AEC asks for increased funding and public support to ensure that their experts can solve the technical problems at hand. With this backing, everyone may be assured of adequate electrical energy at less cost, and so of more comfortable and more secure lives.[10]

The Weakest Link

Well, almost everyone. The children growing inside the womb but still unborn may never have the chance to enjoy this surplus electrical energy.

A growing group of scientists outside the AEC fiefdom has become concerned about the health risk of nuclear explosions and nuclear reactors, particularly to the unborn child. Startling studies in the mid-1950s showed that the children of mothers who received Xrays during pregnancy had a higher risk of cancer than those babies who mothers were not X-rayed. This was startling because it indicated that *an embryo might be far more vulnerable to low-level radiation than a full-grown person.*[11]

Dr. Ernest Sternglass, a professor of radiation physics, has advanced controversial evidence that a sharp increase in cancer and leukemia among school-age children in America and England occurred during the years immediately following World War II, precisely the years when nuclear testing began. Based on a county-by-county statistical analysis, he has tried to show how infant mortality rates are higher following nuclear explosions and higher in areas adjacent to nuclear reactors. He has concluded that hundreds and perhaps thousands of children died before birth because of these new sources of power.[12]

Beneath this argument rests an even more shocking one. The AEC has based its entire decision-making process concerning risks and benefits on what it called "acceptable levels" of radiation exposure. Recent research, however, indicates that radiation concentration is *ten times higher* in the thyroid glands of the unborn and newly born than in adults' thyroids. This means that "tolerable" radiation levels in the environment by no means assure that the levels in people, especially little people, are also "tolerable."

> . . . it was not the amount [of radiation] distributed throughout the environment that was so serious. It was the selective concentration in the food chain and then in newly forming organs of the rapidly developing young embryo. Since all higher animals, including man, must pass through this critically sensitive phase, it was clear that, unless the problem was widely recognized and acted upon, man could extinguish himself and all other animals, not through the effect of radiation on the adult, but *through the effect on the weakest link in the chain of life—the unborn and the very young.*[13]

The AEC's incomplete information, compounded by its indifference and the extraordinary power of nuclear technology, becomes a matter of life and death.

Two radiation scientists assert that "present AEC radiation limits could lead to an many as 1.5 million cases of genetic damage per year." Stanford Professor of Genetics, Joshua Lederberg, claims these "genetically determined diseases . . . would mean $10 billion a year in additional health costs." And Nobel-Prize-winner Linus Pauling foresees an increase of 96,000 cancer deaths per year if the general public is exposed to the so-called "acceptable" levels of radiation.[14]

Apprehension has grown within the AEC staff itself, which has begun to realize that their safety criteria, once termed "clearly conservative," may in fact be quite negligent. A trade newsletter, *Nucleonics Week,* reports that even AEC chairman James R. Schlesinger has been "upset" by the upsurge of doubts concerning safety measures once presented as completely reliable.[15]

In this new, complex, technical controversy, it would be surprising if the critics' figures and facts proved to be precisely correct. But their argument stands: *the AEC techni-*

cians are clearly expanding nuclear energy far beyond their own ability to comprehend its impact. As the number of critics increases, so does the number of nuclear power plants, because the technicians dismiss their detractors as being anti-technology, anti-progress, which in turn seems to mean anti-American.

Proponents of nuclear energy argue that emergency safety measures in the reactors are foolproof. No realistic danger is posed to the environment or to man. And (the ultimate technological carrot) newer reactors will be even more efficient and safer—as long as the technicians are allowed to continue research and development uninterrupted. Yet if reactors are so safe, ask the authors of *Toward A Rational Power Policy,* why is there no open debate, and no published research to prove it?

> Despite the projected growth in size and number of nuclear power plants, the AEC has refused to publish a new accident report updating its 14-year-old analysis of the consequences of an accident involving a 100–200 MW [megawatt] reactor. The AEC has, however, conceded that the conceivable harm and damages from an accident involving larger reactors "under some circumstances would be substantially more than the consequences reported in the . . . [1957] study."[16]

As late as May 1972, the journal *Science* reported that, concerning vital safety precautions in reactor construction, "the AEC policy-makers have been studiously ignoring, rejecting, and even discouraging dissenting views from within the agency . . . ."[17]

According to official AEC pronouncements, technical mishaps are virtually impossible. But even they acknowledge that earthquakes, or limited warfare, would make reactor malfunctions likely. Dr. Walter Jordon, Assistant Director of Oak Ridge National Laboratory, estimates the risk calmly by saying: "We and the public should be prepared to face the possibility of a nuclear accident, just as we live with the possibility of earthquakes."[18] (No one mentions the obvious possibility that, if a modern bandit wanted to outdo plane hijackers, a well-placed bomb at a reactor site would be an effective threat not just to the passengers of a plane but to every resident in a given region of the country.) *

There is no easy, administrative answer to this energy debate. Two members of the New York City Environmental Protection Agency (EPA) have recommended that authority on environmental and health questions be transferred from the AEC to the EPA.[19] Necessary as this transfer of regulatory power may be, it is not sufficient. What is needed, to quote the titles of two recent books, is a *"Nuclear Power Rebellion"* against *"The Atomic Establishment."*[20] It would ask the radical question: Should *any* group of experts have the right to make policy decisions without first consulting those whom their decisions will affect?

At last this debate has finally begun. Several groups of citizens have formed organizations to challenge the previously unquestioned right of the AEC to set safety standards and to site nuclear plants. Physicists, ecologists, and doctors have joined with these citizen groups to form a coalition called National Intervenors. Lawyers and activists have begun pressing for more stringent safety requirements and greater funds for safety research. Others have begun to explore means for reducing the demand for electrical power. Still others have begun to consider alternative means of harnessing previously uncontrollable sources of power without threatening either the balance of nature or man's health. (Buckminster Fuller wrote of the Bay of Fundy, for example, that its extraordinary tides could provide "more economically harvestable foot pounds of energy daily than ever will be needed by all humanity." Fuller's ideas would, of course, pose new problems.) [21]

Unless we ask radical questions, we will not find solutions to the impending energy crisis. When government and industry plunge a fortune into fast-breeder reactor research and only a fistful of dollars into searching for alternatives, they will simply not find alternatives to "going nuclear."

---

* In November 1972 such a threat was actually made by a hijacker.

S. David Freeman, former energy expert to President Johnson, warns:

> We should be spending $2 billion a year on research into alternatives. We're going into the future with only one arrow for our bow, the breeder. If it doesn't work out, we'll face a real crisis.

Echoes a British commission on energy problems: "We are committing future generations to a problem that we do not know how to handle."[22]

Abortion and the Atom

At the same time as nuclear technology has been *universally* threatening the very safety of unborn children all over the world, national interest has focused elsewhere. Politicians from President Nixon on down and theologians from Pope Paul have evoked "Nature's ways," and the "sanctity of human life" to attack legislation legalized abortion. By directing the controversy toward this intensely personal question for which no legislation ever has provided or ever will provide a solution, they have conveniently avoided the question of nuclear danger, for which obvious legislative control is possible. Private morality is made public, even as public morality is left to private spheres of interest.

The technician's equation makes a variable out of a child's life even while he is still enveloped in and being nurtured by his mother's body. His growth is measured against the need for more electrical power. The measurements are taken not by the child's parents but by experts whose techniques have given them regal power over human life. Holding positions to which they were never elected, weighing risks and benefits not fully known, playing dice with lives not yet begun—the technicians make poor Solomons. They do not return the baby to his rightful mother, but run off with him themselves.

5.
Childbirth

made or
born

---

*a world of made is not a
world of born . . . .*

e. e. cummings

Just as no one intended to jeopardize the health of the embryo, no one can be charged with conspiring against the well-being of newborn babies. Obstetricians, anesthesiologists, nurses, hospital administrators, and medical researchers pursue their work with the purpose of assuring the success of childbirth. These technicians have nobly sought an obstetrical utopia in which no mothers or babies would die in childbirth and in which mothers could avoid all pain.

Female midwives have been replaced by male obstetricians because only licensed physicians could be permitted to use the newly discovered drugs which would bring this utopia into being. Conscious of their equal rights to reap the rewards of progress, more women sought liberation from pain. Consequently, the medical profession gained in stature and in size, as it found increasing opportunities to use those pharmaceutical inventions which had become its calling card. Not only did they forever banish pain, they also increased the likelihood of successful childbirth by advancing knowledge concerning Caesarian operations for obstructed labor, blood transfusions for hemorrhage, blood types and their compatibility, and of course further drug research.

These discoveries were a revolution. No one, *especially*

that half of the human species which cannot give birth, should minimize the accomplishment.

The issue, however, is that the technicians think their revolution is the final one. Too many of them fail to recognize that this revolution has created new dangers just as it combatted old ones. As Dr. Irwin Chabon writes, describing the effect of the advent of hospital delivery in postwar America, "Childbirth . . . achieved the status of a surgical operation."[1] Medicated women were less able to perform the contractions which expelled the baby, and so the use of forceps became common. Surgery was used more often, and this, of course, warranted further medication. Since the lone doctor could not travel with the full array of drugs and instruments now available to meet emergencies, childbirth permanently entered the domain of hospitals. Over the years more drugs were invented, and more were prescribed. Normal births now took place with less pain, but also under physiological and psychological conditions that would astound those pioneers in anesthesia whose motivation one long century ago was quite simply to free mothers from unbearable pain.

Dr. T. Berry Brazelton, a well known and respected pediatrician, writes in "What Childbirth Drugs Can Do To Your Child":

> I am sure that . . . there are many instances in which medication is necessary or at least extremely useful. I must also add that I realize obstetrics is a complex, sophisticated member of the medical specialties. Finally I want to make clear that I do not presume to know about or see the whole obstetrics picture. My remarks must be seen in the light of my prejudice about the product of delivery. *I am frankly pro-baby. And I do not like what drugs administered to a woman in labor do to her baby* . . .[2]

Drugs:
In the Womb

The most thorough study of the use of drugs in childbirth revealed that anesthetics were used in over four-fifths of the

20,000 deliveries studied.[3] The average number of drugs prescribed to women by their physicians during pregnancy was 3.6, and some took as many as ten during that period.[4] Thus mothers often receive a barbituate, phenothiazine, a narcotic, or some combination of these.[5]

In cases of heavy drugging, the mother is not aware of the birth at all. She receives her baby only much later when, after regaining consciousness, she is shown her child with a numbered bracelet around his wrist and told that this is indeed her child. In cases of lesser sedation, the mother is partially aware of the birth but is unable to receive the baby until the effects of the drugs have worn off.

Despite this heavy input of drugs, it is generally accepted that the mother's physical health is not seriously impaired. But the mother is only half the physiological story. These drugs also reach the infant and affect his development for at least several weeks following birth, and perhaps longer.

The hurried embrace of pharmacological discoveries which have been made over the past two decades have not been accompanied by adequate research into the effects of drugs on the fetus. What research has been done, has led to an "awakening interest in the effect of medication taken in pregnancy and labor on the behavior and health of the infant," according to Margaret Mead and Niles Newton.[6]

In most instances, drugs administered to the mother cross the placenta unchanged and affect the fetus in a fashion very similar to the way they affect the mother, except more so.[7]* While drug dosage has long been varied according to patient size, it is only recently that doctors have begun to

---

* Although not medically prescribed, nicotine is also a drug. Considering the extraordinary promotion given to cigarettes in the media, it is appropriate to note here that "studies indicate that a pregnant woman who smokes is smoking for two: nicotine constricts the blood vessels in her unborn child, cutting down on fetal blood flow, while CO cuts down on the amount of oxygen in the reduced blood supply. The fetus just can't get enough blood or oxygen to grow as fast as it normally would. The babies of mothers who smoke during pregnancy weigh an average of six ounces less at birth than those of non-smoking mothers. Smoking mothers also have more miscarriages and stillbirths . . . ." (Walter S. Ross, "Do You Know What Happens When You Smoke?" *Reader's Digest,* July, 1972.)

appreciate fully the qualitative difference in the newborn infant's response to drugs which are given, with apparent safety, to the mother.[8] Certainly drugs may have unexpected effects during the first weeks of embryonic development, which are characterized by rapid cell division and differentiation; Thalidomide is an example. But a crucial difference between infant and mother remains still later in the gestation period.

The metabolism and excretion of drugs depends on enzyme systems which are not yet fully matured even by the time of birth. The relative deficiency of these enzymes makes the fetal blood cells more susceptible to the destructive aspects of a variety of drugs, and permits the drugs to remain in a developing body far longer than in the adult.[9] A drug that may be safely administered to the mother at a given dosage may not be safe for the newborn.

The immediate effects of these drugs on the newborn infant are carefully documented. Comparisons made between infants born by natural childbirth (which means, among other things, minimal use of drugs) and those born in heavily medicated childbirth have shown that the latter group required more than *twice* as long to begin breathing than their non-drugged counterparts (20 plus seconds versus 5 to 10 seconds) ; required more than *three* times as long to begin to cry (50 seconds versus 10 to 15 seconds) ; and required actual resuscitation *five* times more often (15 percent versus 3 percent). The babies of natural childbirth respond "more quickly to life-stimulus than the others," conclude the researchers, because "the Naural Childbirth baby is born less doped."[10]

Hospitals where heavy sedation is routine find that one out of six newborns needs active resuscitation, and almost every baby needs at least some oxygen at birth to stimulate breathing. In 166 cases of natural childbirth studied, however, *no* babies required resuscitation.[11] Children of the post-technological generation have had to depend on technology's help to overcome technology's harm—all before entering mother's arms.

The story does not end when childbirth is over, however. In cases of relatively heavy usage of anesthesia and premedication, appreciable levels of drugs have been found in the newborn *at least a week after delivery*. These babies, according to Dr. Brazelton, began to breast-feed on the average 48 hours later, and had their first recorded weight gain 24 hours later, than their less drugged counterparts.[12] Because of the baby's enzyme deficiency mentioned earlier, writes Dr. Brazelton,

> [h]is immature kidneys don't excrete depressant drugs very well. And his immature brain stores them for at least a week after birth, concentrating them around the midbrain, which is responsible for much of his behavior. No wonder he is relatively dopey for a week or two after delivery! The real wonder is that he functions at all.[13]

Worried about these difficulties in the first week after birth, some concerned doctors have explored the longer-term effects of these drugs.[14] They discovered in experiments that sensory and motor development were retarded *for at least four weeks* after delivery in babies born under heavy medication. The doctors' study carefully controlled such variables as maternal age, length of labor, socio-economic level, number of previous births, etc., so that it was unmistakably clear that retardation was caused by the heavy use of drugs.[15] Other researchers interested in the development of intelligence subsequent to childbirth have determined that seriously inadequate oxygen intake during the first few minutes of life is statistically related to lower intelligence scores in childhood.[16] Ashley Montagu is so angered by this that he has complained bitterly: "The loading of the mother with sedatives which are known to have an asphyxiating effect upon the fetus . . . have almost certainly done more or less damage to the brain of many a child."[17] The pharmaceutical-surgical method of childbirth thus employs techniques which were designed to assure the mother's comfort and the baby's health, but now pose a threat to the well-being of both.

The Hormonal Stork

We are told that every bureaucratic, surgical, and pharmaceutical innovation that the medical profession makes in regard to childbirth is made with the welfare of the patients in mind. Granted this generous intent, the effects of many technical innovations may ultimately be to hurt those whom they mean to help. A most recent example, reported in *Medical World News* in May of 1970, was the plan by a number of hospitals to set up obstetrical clinics "by appointment." In an article titled "Hormonal Clock Set— Stork Works 9 to 5," the magazine explained that by administering doses of a hormone called oxytocin *in every childbirth,* the time of birth of *all* babies can now be preset. By injecting this hormone, which is the same one that the mother's body produces, the uterus can be made to begin its contractions at a particular time. The doctor can now initiate, with tremendous accuracy, the process of labor which before was initiated by the natural working of the mother's hormonal system.[18]

The purpose is clear. The obstetrical staff can have a good night's sleep; the obstetrician can schedule births at evenly spaced intervals throughout the working day; personnel and facilities can be more efficiently utilized. *Medical World News,* predictably, called the new system "justified." That thirty percent of the women had obstetrical complications; that frequent heavy use was made not only of hormone but of drugs in general; that many of the women were not conscious for the children's birth—all this may be sacrificed in order to devise a more efficiently scheduled hospital wing.

Barry Commoner's "Third Law of Ecology"—that "Nature knows best"—is consistently violated by doctors who would rewrite it: *"We* know best." There are too many uncontrollables in Nature's system for the standards of modern medicine. The doctor whose work led to this use of hormones explained, for example, that the human uterus in the last month of pregnancy . . .

> . . . is a community of about 250 billion cells, which must communicate with each other and work together in harmony to deliver the fetus. The uterus had to learn over thousands of years of evolution how to protect fetal development for 280 days and then suddenly turn into a hostile organ and expel it. This is accomplished with the help of a complex regulatory system, of which thus far we only know . . . four factors.[19]

The advocates of "alarm-clock childbirth" are aware of the complexity of the physiological processes of childbirth; they realize that they do not understand it all. Still, they would attempt to "educate" those 250 billion cells with a syringe of laboratory-produced hormones so that the hospital will run more smoothly.

Such a technique is the inevitable outcome of an approach which assumes from the outset that the problem is one of science and not of persons.

The Natural Alternative

Natural childbirth seeks to resolve the issue of pain during childbirth by human rather than technical means. It begins with the question: *To what degree can women themselves minimize and overcome pain?* To answer this question, we must consider the social and psycological context of childbirth which was excluded from the technician's false frame of reference.

Natural childbirth tries to relieve pain during childbirth whenever possible by education, training, and support, thus lessening dependence on drugs and surgery. As commonly practiced at centers around the world, it involves three learning processes: greater understanding of the physical basis of birth; systematic exercises in breathing and muscle control; and cooperative practice with another person who provides verbal cues and emotional encouragement.

These three factors significantly enrich the experience of giving birth. Women who elect natural childbirth are neither as uninformed nor as fearful as their pregnant friends who are alone and who do not know what is going to happen, nor when, nor why. Erik Erikson has defined clearly the goal of natural childbirth:

> . . . the objective is childbirth without anxiety. The expectant mother will feel some fear because she knows that pain is inevitable. But the fact that the mother has learned, by exercise and instruction, to be aware of the location and the function of the contractions which cause the pain; and the fact that she expects, at the height of the curve of pain, to have the privilege of choosing consciously whether or not she wishes to receive relief by drugs: this entirely judicious situation keeps her from developing the state of anxiety which in the recent past was caused by ignorance and superstition and which, more often than not, *was the real cause of excessive pain.*[20]

Natural childbirth is not "anti-technology," just "pro-baby." Natural childbirth seeks to benefit from the scientific knowledge acquired over the past half-century, so that the benefits accrue to women and not to the experts who nourish the illusion that birth and life could not continue without them.

Although it is difficult to study objectively the relationship between emotional factors and obstetrical complications which require medication,[21] careful psychiatric observations indicate that the self-assurance and sense of cooperation gained from natural childbirth could well lessen the fear and anxiety which magnify normal pain.[22] With these additional, and unnecessary, burdens lifted, the mother is much more capable of using her own strength and autonomy effectively. She is therefore less dependent on the obstetrician's drugs or forceps.

This autonomy means that at the most successful natural childbirth clinics, more than 90 percent of uncomplicated births require no drugs at all. And *all* studies of natural childbirth show that women educated about childbirth require less medication than their unprepared counterparts.[23] Both mother and child are strengthened in their development: the infant is not endangered by the heavy use of drugs, and the mother is "awake and aware" so that she may feel that she actually *gave* birth to her child.

Not only mother and child, but also the family as a whole, may gain from natural childbirth. Many advocate that mothers give birth at home rather than in the hospital. If the mother is in good health and has had thorough prenatal examination, the likelihood of a normal birth is great, and an attending obstetrician would be adequate for the delivery. The mother would be the center of attention rather than simply another patient; and the rest of the family feels involved rather than excluded from the arrival of the newborn. The slim possibility of complication could be met by mobile obstetrical units which could be on call in every community.[24] The mother with a normal birth might once again feel like a pregnant woman rather than a sick patient.

Countries such as Holland which have most births in the home (68 percent in 1968) have some of the lowest infant mortality rates in the world. Dr. G. C. Kloosterman, chairman of Obstetrics and Gynecology at the University of Amsterdam, addressing the 1970 International Childbirth Education Association Conference, explained that the home provides a setting where doctors felt personally responsible for the outcome of the birth. This leaves hospitals better able to deal with the few women who came to the hospital with obstetrical complications.[25] In Sweden, where, as in Holland, childbirth takes place in the home and drugs are used sparingly, paraprofessional women attend to all normal births. Once again, fully trained obstetricians are then left more free to attend properly to births which require hospitalization.[26]

The American medical profession—which consistently uses heavy medication, opposes home childbirth, discourages natural childbirth, and argues against paraprofessional workers—might not be vulnerable to criticism if the United States could claim low infant mortality rates. With their bent for quantification, doctors could then claim that the risk to the infant and the loss to the mother was well worth it, because fewer women and children died in childbirth in America than anywhere else.

In fact, however, the United States is abysmally backward. We rank fourteenth among the nations of the world in infant mortality rate, and twelfth in maternal mortality. The American medical practice often defends itself by attributing our higher death rates to the ignorance and poverty of ethnic groups (though, of course, this is one of the few times the American medical profession has ever shown much concern for these groups*). However, excluding the number of infant deaths per thousand births for nonwhites (41.1), which is shockingly higher than that for whites (21.6), our "whites only" infant mortality rate is still more than half again higher than Sweden's (14.2).[28] Dr. George Silver, Deputy Assistant for Health and Scientific Affairs at HEW, told a conference:

> I feel that the situation at the present time is so urgent, so fraught with difficulty and dire possibilities, that every step and every opportunity must be taken to influence as many as possible in the professional field. . . . Our infant mortality in this country is a scandal, and for many parts of the country it is worse than a scandal; it is a crime.[29]

When Men Define Women

Although America has much to gain from the advocates of natural childbirth, our medical profession has responded coldly. In Communist nations and many European countries its use has become widespread. After Pope Pius XII endorsed the method it spread quickly to the heavily Catholic Mediterranean countries and to South America.[30] Exponents of natural childbirth around the world speak of the tremendous joy in consciously experiencing and actively giving birth to a baby, but in America such an idea finds little circulation among medical men.[31] The whole question of the psychosomatic aspects of childbirth has been of much greater interest

---

* Jonothan Kozol writes: "In certain neighborhoods of the United States the childbed death rate for black women is now six times the rate for white women. . . . The figure for newborn infants nationwide is estimated to be as high as 40,000. These infant deaths occur primarily in the rural slums and in the Northern ghettos. These 40,000 infants are the victims of social, professional, and institutional murder."[27]

to European obstetricians and psychiatrists than to Americans. While on this side of the Atlantic research and money are devoted to pharmacological methods of controlling pain, physical, psychological, interpersonal, and nutritional aspects of control are ignored.[32] Even when the most thorough analysis of the psychology of childbirth concludes that the less drugs are used the better,[33] the easy use of drugs is still widespread in America.

Sensitive and systematic interviewing (by women obstetricians) have shown that mothers who received no general anesthesia or analgesia were more likely to have positive feelings about their experience giving birth.[34] Nevertheless, American obstetricians (who are predominantly male) have become so reliant on their techniques that they want to assume the opposite—namely, that women really don't *want* to be "awake and aware" for childbirth. One obstetrician writes:

> . . . the progressive obstetrician has believed, all this time, that he was rendering a distinct service to the mother sparing her the psychic trauma of a physically painful experience. . . . Instead he is now being accused of having denied the mother that vital experience necessary to provide for a healthy emotional relationship with her child. This is not an easy pill to swallow—nor is it a convincing one, especially when thousands of women *awakening* from their delivery have remarked, "This was wonderful, how soon can I have another baby?" In fact, it is no secret that some of the largest obstetrical practices in America have been built upon obstetricians' reputation for "knocking his patients out cold."[35]

Armed with the assumption that the women want to be "out cold," the obstetrician has no difficulty in imposing himself as the key figure. One modest doctor proclaimed at a symposium that, aside from the presence of a "wise obstetrician," "all else amounts to little more than irrelevancies."

The assumptions of the technicians' false frame are: that women prefer to be unconscious during childbirth; that pain is entirely unavoidable and uncontrollable; that husbands do not want anything to do with childbirth; that childbirth drugs are not injurious to the infant until specific deformities emerge (as with Thalidomide). Only if more doctors and mothers radically question the technicians' false assumptions will the false frame be broken.

The medical profession earlier in this century had an essentially captive audience. Its new techniques were applied without much question. Seeking to carve out their niche in a competitive economy, ambitious fathers willingly left the whole affair of childbirth to the medical profession. Uprooted from the traditional setting in which childbirth once took place and mesmerized by the idea of progress, women adapted to practices which were intended to free them from pain.[36] Mothers rarely knew the intricacies of medicinal chemistry and physiology. As the use of drugs grew, the medical profession did not try to inform them. In the 1970s a group of young men and women, members of the Health Policy Advisory Center, found it necessary to write:

> . . . for American women, pregnancy and childbirth are just another harrowing, expensive medical procedure. The doctor does it; the woman is essentially passive. Even in large cities, women have to go from one obstetrician to another before they find one who approves of natural childbirth. Otherwise, childbirth is handled as if it were a surgical operation, even to the point of "scheduling" the event to suit the obstetrician's convenience through the use of possibly dangerous labor-inducing drugs.[37]

The Mother Revives

Radical creative men and women have had to learn to educate themselves. A surge of women in the past few years have turned away from the brave new world of modern obstetrics.* In 1970 the International Childbirth Education Association heard an address by Dr. John Miller in which he shared his surprise:

---

* The use of "brave new world" is not a metaphor, but rather, it seems, merely a news report. Cf. "The Obsolescent Mother," in *The Atlantic*, May 1971.

> I have witnessed in the last few years on the West Coast a change in the childbirth scene so dramatic and so drastic from anything that could have been foreseen just a few years ago, that I am hesitant to talk about it, because whatever I say today may be hopelessly dated a few weeks from now.[38]

This dramatic change, Dr. Miller explained, was the sharp and unexpected increase in the number of requests for childbirth at home with minimal or no use of drugs.

More and more young women are rejecting the guaranteed painlessness, effortlessness, and unconsciousness of drugged childbirth. They know that it will require an investment in time and will, but they consider it worthwhile if their children are to enter this world, as Erikson says, "less drugged, and more ready to open their eyes."[39] Women no longer want to delegate their first task of motherhood to a physician, no matter how "wise" he may be. They consider it their inviolable right to be as active in giving birth to their children as they plan to be in giving them a chance to grow.

If the full development of the next generation is our goal, it is certainly not an arbitrary decision to begin with their birth. No social system can continue without the births of healthy children. As Erikson said many years ago: "If we want to make the world safe for democracy, we must first make it safe for the healthy child."[40]

And children must not only be born healthy, they must also be cared for.

6.
Feeding

putting milk into babies

---

*There is no finer invest-
ment for any community
than putting milk into
babies . . . .*

*Winston Churchill
March 21, 1943*

Until the end of the nineteenth century, hygienic conditions on farms were so poor that cow's milk was used only by impoverished mothers, if then. The babies of lower-class mothers who could not provide enough breast milk often simply died. Well-to-do parents of the nobility and middle class (which was still small) often gave their infants to wet-nurses. Frequently, the wet-nurses moved into the homes of their monied employers rather than keep the nursing infant in their own homes.[1]

The controversy about breast-feeding extends across the centuries from Plutarch to Rousseau, a "running war" stretching over two thousand years.[2] In pretechnological eras, however, those who found breast-feeding unrefined or "beneath" their status were few in number, and those children not breast-fed by their prudish mothers were fed by another less prudish one—*not* by a bottle. By hiring the breasts of a poor woman, the rich woman's were freed for other pursuits. The child of the poor wet-nurse was the loser. Also seeking her milk, her own children were often bumped aside by their rich competitors whose parents could buy the breast at a better price.

With improved hygiene and greater affluence, bottle-feeding rapidly began to replace the custom of wet-nursing. This practice, which became increasingly common in America throughout this century, "freed" the mother. She did not have to worry if she was providing enough milk (the bottle was an easy measure). She could get more rest and be gone from home longer (someone else could bottle-feed the baby, and since formula feeding often fills up the baby more, there could be longer intervals between feedings). And she could feed in public (the breast-feeding mother, on the other hand, was supposed to be publicly invisible in modern America) .[3]

Again, this is less than half the story. As with drugged childbirth, the baby's health is jeopardized by the universal acceptance of bottle-feeding. First, mother's milk is more digestible than cow's milk. In his panoramic book on human physiology entitled *The Body Has a Head,* Dr. Gustav Eckstein sums it up neatly:

> Cow's milk has too much protein, not for the cow, but for us, and in cow proportions, and since human infants do not grow as fast as the calves that are hurried off to market, and since protein is the stuff of growth, there is the practice of diluting cow's milk for our babies, never completely satisfactory because, diluted, the protein is still cow protein and still in cow proportions.[4]

Differences in the amount and kind of fatty acids between human and animal milk may later be related to cholesterol levels and hardening of the arteries. Also, according to many doctors, human milk contains certain antibodies which probably protect them against various infections. Cow's milk does not contain these same antibodies.[5]

From Flesh to Plastic

If technology can pretend to educate the body's hormone system, it can also pretend to produce a "better" milk product in a more "practical" container. Although the primary component of any ecosystem is the food chain, the technicians are so mystified by their own expertise that they intervened in just this most basic ecosystem of mother, milk, and child.

The growth of mother and child is not only biological but psychological. Bruno Bettelheim lectures to his bottle-fed graduate students:

> In feeding, more is happening than just satisfaction of the baby's hunger. The mother is relieving the pressure, which is often painful, of milk in her breasts. Although the baby is fed, the baby experiences not simply that she is satisfying his need, but also that he is satisfying hers.[6]

Erik Erikson terms this human process mutuality: a relationship "which can be depended on to activate my begin as I can be depended on to activate theirs."

> As the newborn infant is separated from his symbiosis with the mother's body, his inborn . . . ability to take in by mouth meets the mother's . . . co-ordinated ability and intention to feed him and to welcome him. At this point, he lives through, and loves with, his mouth, and the mother lives through, and loves with, her breasts. . . . For the mother this is a late and complicated accomplishment, highly dependent on her development as a woman, on her unconscious attitude toward the child, on the way she has lived through pregnancy and delivery, on her and her community's attitude toward the act of nursing and caring —and on the response of the newborn.[7]

The conditions for successful breast-feeding are perilously lacking in America today.[8]

Both radical women[9] and distraught professionals[10] have complained about how much modern hospital arrangements and obstetrical practices militate against any mother's attempts to breast-feed. Drugs are once again involved: only half as many heavily medicated mothers breast-feed effectively in the first days following childbirth than those with little or no medication.[11] For at least the first four days after childbirth and sometimes longer, drugs impair *both* the mother's ability to feed and the baby's ability to be fed.[12] Hospital personnel are more than ready to jump in with full or supplementary bottle-feeding during this period, so that from the start the baby becomes accustomed to something other than his mother's breast, and his sucking response is impaired even if the breast is later offered.[13]

Careful studies of different hospitals indicate that the attitudes of doctors markedly affect the number of women who do or do not breast-feed. This is why it is so disturbing to learn that medical personnel in the United States and England are more likely to discourage than to encourage natural feeding.[14] Just as the medical profession assumes that most women "can't" really manage childbirth, they also assume that most women "can't" breast feed. Again, it is largely men who occupy the seat of judgment on this singularly feminine matter.

Their judgment, however, is disproved by history. Virtually *all* American women breast-fed in the year 1900. A University of Minnesota researcher in 1921, for example, followed almost 3,000 infants through their first two months of life, during which 96 percent of them were fully breast-fed.[15] How and why, then, did only 38 out of every hundred women leave the hospital with a nursing baby by 1946? And how is it that by 1956, on the threshhold of the "affluent," "technetronic," "great society," the figure had dropped to 20 out of 100? In two generations, America had "achieved" the lowest percentage of breast-fed children of any major country in the world.[16] The generation which created the student revolution also has the unique distinction of experiencing less breast-feeding than any preceding generation.[17]

It would be simple, but not true, to explain this incredibly rapid historical change simply in economic terms. The production of bottles and of formula ingredients is big business, admittedly. The dairy industry quite logically lobbies for bottle-feeding, and zealously convinces many adolescents and adults that, by some evolutionary quirk, man is the only member of the animal kingdom which requires milk *per se* long after nursing is over.* And milk from another species at that!

---

* Following close behind in the race to exploit the baby market is the billion-dollar diaper industry, which now wants not only the minimal profit of making cloth diapers and of washing them, but the maximal profit of

Breast Milk:
Purchased and Polluted

Although industries often do profit when a human ability is undermined, this in itself does not explain the rapid decline in breast-feeding. The explanation is far more complex than the profit motive. Having been geared for a society in which technical creative thinking was in demand, postwar parents allowed its false frame to penetrate not merely their public, economic lives, but their private, interpersonal world as well. Industry was being transformed by greater technical efficiency—"the maximum productivity with the minimal expenditure of human energy."[20] Urban and suburban Americans naturally applied the supremacy of technique to their homes also. Only in the large rural sections of the country did significant numbers of women continue to breast-feed; in fact, the *smaller* the town in which a mother herself was raised, the *longer* the time she was likely to breast-feed her child.[21]

Today's urban mothers may never have seen a breast-feeding mother, either human or animal. A sight with which any rural child is intimately familiar has become a rarity in the cities and their metropolitan areas. The omnipresence of strangers in the city made public feeding uncomfortable, and the ubiquity of the mass media enshrined the imagery of bottle-feeding in every woman's mind. The medical profession, which should have offered mothers discriminating advice in the midst of this public propaganda, instead offered the same worship of technique that was predicated on women's incompetence.

Women became convinced that most women *inherently* lacked sufficient milk; that the tension which surrounded breast-feeding was *inevitable* and would make feeding diffi-

---

selling disposable paper diapers.[18] Considerations about a baby's skin or the gigantic addition to the nation's refuse are hardly mentioned. Last but not least is the detergent industry, which willingly prescribes, for the mother who still washes diapers and clothes, approximately *ten-times* the necessary amount of washing detergent, according to the scientist who developed "Tide" for Proctor and Gamble.[19] Ten times more detergent is used, ten times more phosphates pollute the waterways, ten times the profits: the technically creative mind is at work again.

cult; that the *normal* anxiety about having produced enough milk was not worth the trouble; and that, after all, the doctor's formula was *better* for the child anyway. Doctors argued that as high as thirty percent of women are not able to breastfeed, but failed to explain why almost one hundred percent could breast-feed only fifty years ago.

The medical profession cannot account for the astonishing drop in breast-feeding in physiological terms because it involves the psychology of human development. Just as giving birth can be made less painful by awareness, training, and support, so can breast-feeding be made easier, and more enjoyable, simply by providing mothers with encouragement and the example of other mothers doing so. Precisely the opposite is provided in most American hospitals.[22]

So vast is the scale of technology that it has now created circumstances which could subvert even the resolve of women who are determined to breast-feed their children. Informed women have known since 1969 that mother's milk now contains *two to four times* the level of DDT permitted by the Food and Drug Administration in cow's milk.[23] By feeding "naturally," women might endanger their baby's health more than by using animal milk. Such is the bizarre world in which they are asked to raise their children.

The heedless use of DDT might have continued unchecked in American agriculture had it not been for Rachel Carson's *Silent Spring,* which documented the inadequacy of restrictions on this dangerous pesticide. Hounded by mass-scale food producers, who appreciate DDT's efficiency, and by the chemical industry, which does not want to lose the market for its profitable product, the government long continued to allow wide use of DDT for what it crazily termed "essential" uses.[24] Mothers are thus often left wondering if nurturing their child at the breast does not ultimately endanger their child's health more than bottle-feeding him.

Nevertheless there are significant signs that young mothers in greater numbers are realizing what the *La Leche League* (Spanish: "milk") and courageous mothers before them have been saying for some time: that with support from other women who have freed themselves from society's ingrained alienation, almost all women can successfully breast-feed and thereby add to their own as well as their children's well-being. If in the past a single determined woman could spark changes in the way a hospital treated new mothers who wished to breast-feed,[25] certainly a great number of organized mothers can effect wider changes and greater awareness. Just as the plight of the impoverished mother too malnourished to produce milk for her child should become a thing of the past, so should the plight of middle-class mothers who want to breast-feed but don't.

7.
Eating and Infancy

the mechanization of
taste

*The mechanization of the world could never proceed
very far while taste, even the taste buds, remained
uncorrupted, because in that case most of the products
of the machine would be simply unwanted . . . . But
in modern Western man the faculty of mechanical
invention has been fed and stimulated till it has
reached almost the status of an instinct.*

George Orwell

*One lazy gesture with an automatic can opener;
spoon the stuff into a pan; heat it, and the meal is
ready. Thus an entire generation has been raised,
from infancy to maturity, chiefly on processed, prepared, canned and packaged factory foods. Most of
such foods have been cooked, peeled, shelled, ground,
sliced, minced, tenderized, pasteurized, or in some
other manner deprived of their wholeness before they
went into packages or cans. The consumer does not
have the entire food put before him, but only such
portions as the food processors decide to include in
the finished product.*

Helen and Scott Nearing

Before a child ever reaches school, even nursery school, his brain should reach 90 percent of its full weight. If, however, he does not receive sufficient food during the prenatal and postnatal period, his mental and emotional development can be impaired—no matter what later measures may be taken. This is precisely the risk to *millions* of children from poor families throughout America.

Of 50 million school age children in 1967, six million came from poor families. Only 18 percent of their families were assisted by food programs; and only 30 percent participated in any free-lunch programs at school.[1] "The biggest deficiencies at the Federal level," testified Dr. Mayer before the Senate Committee on Nutrition and Human Needs, "are the underfunding of practically every [food assistance] program, particularly . . . the school lunch and breakfast programs." His testimony was followed by Mrs. Marion Wright Edelman's:

> If we are not human enough or moral enough to feed hungry children unhesitatingly and swiftly, how will we respond to the "bigger" issues of life facing our society? . . . If this country cannot solve hunger, what can it do? . . . If somehow we have not managed in four years to get food to the people, to stop

crippling children, to provide the minimum elementary assistance to our children, I am not sure what we *can* do . . . .[2]

Tang and Wheaties are paraded across our TV screens,
supported by million-dollar advertising budgets, yet America
remains a nation where "substantial numbers of newborn,
who survive the hazards of birth, die before their second
birthday from causes which can be traced directly and primarily to malnutrition."[3] This is the conclusion of the Citizens' Board of Inquiry into Hunger and Malnutrition in
the United States. Introducing the report in 1968, Senator
Robert F. Kennedy said, ". . . in the wealthiest nation in the
history of the world, millions of men, women, and children
are slowly starving."[4]

The Brain:
Poverty and Poison

Protein deficiency can inhibit brain growth during infancy
and result in stunted development in children. In particular,
children from poor homes suffer from nutritional deficiency
anemia, a condition which results in the decreased production
of oxygen-carrying red blood cells, and which often has
serious irremediable effects on the child's ability to grow
and learn.[6] Here the cycle and its myriad political myths
begins: a "'vicious cycle," says Nobel-prize-winning chemist
Joshua Lederberg, "of malnutrition, mental retardation,
indolence, and unemployability," which in turn destines
these children's children to the same despairing fate.[7]

The Department of Health, Education and Welfare may
announce that the children of the poor are far sicker than
the children of the rich;[8] *The Congressional Record* may en-
shrine in history's memory the fact that, despite their illness, 60 percent of poor children have never seen a doctor,
and 90 percent no dentist.[9] But the situation continues.
Speaking to pediatricians, Senator George McGovern cried

out against the distorted national priorities that permit this outrage to continue.

> Does it make sense to allocate $10 or $25 billion to a highly doubtful missile defense and then permit bad diets to render 15 million Americans defenseless against hunger? What price are we paying for the brain damage to unborn infants caused by the malnourishment of the mother? What is the cost of retarded intellectual and emotional growth resulting from bad infant diets? Can it be true . . . that half of the mental retardation among the poor families of this nation is caused by malnutrition! If so, has not our missile defense system already been penetrated by a deadly and dangerous foe?[10]

These questions fall outside the range of the technicians' decision-making. The technicians boast that there are only half as many hungry people in this country now as there were ten years ago. Even if that statement were true, it would remain ethically meaningless. *If making it half-way to the moon would be national failure, why is feeding half the hungry children supposedly a national accomplishment?* The sad truth is that for many policy-makers such abstractions as "national commitment," or "communist aggression," or the "challenge of space," are more real than malnourished American children.

Those most deprived by the technological state, the children of the poor, are also deprived of the physical energy and mental ability to change their lives. They live in a democracy, yes, with many constitutional freedoms. But if these defenseless children have been robbed by that same democracy of the capacity to use those freedoms, then what meaning do they have left?

An estimated 80 percent of retarded children in America are believed to be handicapped, not because of genetic or other inborn physical causes, but because of socio-economic causes. "While genetic, chromosomal and hereditary causes occur with about the same frequency in all racial and economic groups, retardation of unknown origin is nearly ten times more likely to occur among the poor, black, and Spanish-speaking in the US than among the white and affluent."[11]

If an adult is going hungry, he may steal, or beg, or leave town, or seek welfare assistance. A hungry infant, however, can only cry, or eat things that aren't food. Like paint.

The lead-pigment paints in old, low-quality housing begin to peel after years of wear. Hungry infants, attracted to the sweet and sticky chips of paint, often chew them as they flake off the walls near their cribs or fall near where they are crawling on the floor. Eating small amounts of lead causes mental deficiency or behavior problems often manifested only later in childhood; larger amounts may cause serious brain damage; while long-term lead poisoning can cause paralysis, convulsions, and death. Known clinically as "plumbism," high lead absorption affects high percentages of children in all urban areas.[12] According to a neurologist's statement at a meeting of the Lead Industries Association, ". . . lead does something to the growing brain which is different from what it does to the adult brain." The same could be said of mercury, cadmium, and nitrite as well.[13] But because the children who are victims of poisoning do not constitute a block of voters or an economic interest group, public health officials and medical researchers for many years have had little interest in the problem. The lead in the diets of inner-city children comes not only from paint on the walls, but from dirt in their yards and playgrounds. Forty-nine members of Congress have urged the Environmental Protection Agency to order all lead removed from gasoline because automobile exhaust has created alarmingly high levels of lead in most major cities. So high are the levels, the congressmen charged, that a normal child could consume dangerous amounts of lead simply by sucking his thumb or failing to wash his hands before meals. (The first signer of the report was Senator Philip A. Hart, chairman of the Senate Commerce Committee's Subcommittee on the Environment. "In view of the facts," said Hart, "it is not melodramatic to suggest that our choice is between higher gasoline prices and mentally retarded children.")

Passing the Buck

Both malnutrition and lead poisoning sound far off to the suburbanite technician who believes that his hard-won affluence has assured his children of good nutrition. A technician himself, he seems to believe the boasts of other technicians about fulfilling the growing child's food requirements. He trusts that these technicians have assumed responsibility for the overall quality of our diet, but this is not so.

The food technicians show off their technical creative skills in dreaming up new kinds of commercial products. But when it comes to creating an overall healthy diet, they wipe their hands clean. The following comments of a food industry executive interviewed by the Citizens' Board of Inquiry are an eloquent statement of technical creativity.

> We, like most other food companies, are specialists in certain segments of the very broad spectrum of foods. While the products that we produce fit into a balanced diet, we don't profess to offer a balanced diet within our product lines, nor should we invade the realm of the medical profession in recommending balanced diets.[14]

Yet if we consult "the medical profession" to whom this food executive has transferred responsibility, we find doctors who think their job is only to diagnose illness and recommend treatment. The doctor does not want to "invade the realm of the business profession" and recommend what products should be sold. Occasionally, the medical and business professions will even get together and pass the buck jointly to federal agencies such as the Food and Drug Administration. And of course the government, relying on medical specialists and sensitive to industry lobbies, passes the buck right back. What gets lost somewhere in the shuffle is our health.

And what gets found is profit. The sugar industry, for example, actually hires opinion researchers to convince food producers such as Gerber and Heinz to use sugar in their baby products. The researchers produce polls which show that the majority of Americans do not think that enormous quantities of sugar they ingest is injurious to their health.

The polls neglect to point out, of course, that the populace's mistaken ideas about nutrition are largely due to the millions of dollars spent on misleading advertising by the very industries that paid for the polls in the first place.[15]

The Baby Business

To develop healthily, babies should have human milk and well-prepared food. Unfortunately, the practice of grinding or mashing normal adult food for infant consumption has disappeared just as surely as the practice of breast-feeding. By the same principle of minimal expenditure of human energy and flashy advertising which sold bottle-feeding to America, the corporate technicians have created a vast new "baby-foods" industry.

The search for new markets always seems to require men who usurp parents' bio-psychological functions and make a profit-making venture out of them. Having pharmacologically altered childbirth and mechanically replaced breasts, the remaining task for the technicians was to put a combination of ingredients into small, expensive jars and convince parents that these jars were better than anything they could ever prepare themselves.

Ralph Nader's investigators decided to focus on the case of baby foods as the most critical illustration of the food industry's malpractices. If the food industry would not police itself in the production of a foodstuff so vital to early human growth, the investigttors felt, then it could not be trusted at all. Their findings merit reading verbatim and at length.

> The story of the purposeful and economically motivated pollution of baby-foods by their manufacturers should dispel all beliefs in food industry self-regulation. If baby food producers are not motivated to police themselves, it is unlikely that any food producers are. Twenty years ago a jar of baby food contained a given amount of fruit, vegetables, or meat. As the costs of these ingredients rose, baby-food companies began to replace part of them with starch and sugar—each of which is less expensive than the ingredient it was replacing.

Naturally, food thinned out with starch or sugar tasted blander or sweeter than the originals, so the baby-food makers began adding salt and monosodium glutamate to please mothers who tasted their babies' food. Then it was discovered that the starches added to the food would break down and become watery if a mother fed her baby some of the bottle's contents and let the remainder sit, even in the refrigerator, overnight. The baby's saliva, which got into the food on the spoon the baby was fed with, was "digesting" it. The answer provided by the baby-food companies was to find a starch that saliva could not break down and add it to the bottle's contents. So now baby-food contains not only added sugar, salt, and monosodium glutamate, but also added modified starch which baby saliva does not break down in the jar or the mouth and which some researchers fear may not be completely digested even by the rest of the baby's system. None of these additives in the food for purely economic reasons has been proven safe for consumption by babies.[16]

Not only have these ingredients not been proven safe, they have been viewed as potential health hazards by many capable doctors, including Dr. Jean Mayer, former nutrition advisor to the President of the United States. Sugar is seriously questioned because it has no nutritional value, is unnecessary, and establishes in the infant conditioning for its taste. The salt in baby foods, says Dr. Mayer, is "proportionately *higher*" than in foods for adults, and "enormously higher" than in breast milk.[17] And monosodium glutamate was denounced by Dr. Mayer in an address at the Women's National Press Club in Washington in the wake of incomplete but highly suggestive research demonstrating a relationship between monosodium glutamate and brain damage in infant mice.[18]

Only under a barrage of angry criticism did Heinz, Gerber, and Swift remove the monosodium glutamate. The salt, sugar, and modified starch remain unaltered. The baby food giants have stuck to their false frame of analysis. In a letter to his share-owners, Dan Gerber complained that all the pressure to remove MSG was unwarranted because no one had proven *conclusively* that MSG was harmful. If it is economical for us, and "convenient" and "tasty" for you, argue food technicians, then we are going to put it in our products unless somebody proves absolutely that it is dangerous. Ralph Nader, testifying before the Senate Committee on Nutrition, challenged this logic by asking bluntly what possible reason for adding MSG the baby food industry could have other than *greater profits*. It has no nutritional value and babies cannot even distinguish its taste. Mothers who do the buying are the ones who are to be attracted by the taste. Why on earth take the risk of adding this potentially dangerous ingredient, demanded Nader, without thoroughly studying its short- and long-term effects on children?

Drugs:
At Breakfast

Having hooked kids as babies onto their products, the food technicians are not about to let go of them as they become older. What does the child in a well-to-do family, having outgrown bottles and baby foods, eat for breakfast? Chances are he begins with a manufactured dry cereal which costs far *more* than the original grain it is made from but contains *less* protein. These cereals represent such nutritional extortion that those who defend the cereal industry against critics have now fallen back on the argument that since "95 percent of breakfast cereals are consumed with milk," and milk is a nutritious substance, the bowl taken as a whole does indeed provide a wholesome food. As Sidney Margolius says sarcastically in *The Great American Food Hoax,* "If milk is the main nutritional value in eating dry cereals, then obviously there are easier ways to drink it than with a spoon."[19]

Constantly exposed to the $80 million dollar yearly advertising of the processed cereal industry, the child probably knows by name the twenty-five variety of cereals (sold by Kellogg, Nabisco, Post, General Mills, and Ralston) in which sugar is first or second in percentage of total ingredients. Senator Moss of Utah may tell the US Senate that "The Breakfast of Champions, or Tony the Tiger's favorite cereal, may be letting us down." Such pronouncements never penetrate the orb of advertisements with which the $80 million have successfully surrounded the preschool child. Senate hearings are not televised during Saturday cartoons, but large corporations' commercials are.

When the average American child makes his toast with the "enriched" white bread to which he has been exclusively exposed in advertisements, he is receiving only a small portion of the original minerals and vitamins present in whole grain. Mechanical processing destroys far more elements in grains than are ever replaced. According to Dr. Henry A. Schroeder of the Dartmouth Medical School, the milling process as performed by modern bread manufacturers

> removes 40% of the chromium, 86% of the manganese, 89% of the cobalt, 68% of the copper, 78% of the zinc, and 48% of the molybdenum—*all trace elements essential for life or health* . . . .[20]

A generation brought up on this conditioning process learns to consume whatever the food industry produces in its search for increasingly mechanical processes and ever greater profits. It is, writes Jacques Ellul, as if the consumers, by an unconscious reaction, "adapted their taste to the type of bread which corresponds exactly to the demands of mass production."[21]

The child will also be encouraged to finish his orange juice because outstanding ad campaigns have made such encouragement a standard component of American motherhood. Yet how many kids are actually drinking orange juice? Breakfast drinks such as the Coca Cola Company's "Hi-C" have been advertised as being made from fresh fruit and containing "lots of Vitamin C." But as one alert FDA official has explained:

> The 10% o.j. 90% water drink is hardly even fit to drink. What makes these products palatable? It is the addition of substantial and noticeable quantities of pulp, orange oil, acid, sugar and color. These "incidentals" are what make the product. . . . To add water in the cannery, and dress it up with orange essence, added pulp, color, acid, etc., has only one function. It fools the public.[22]

Such items in General Foods' product line as "Tang" and "Awake," consist mainly of sugar, flavorings, and artificial colorings. Vitamin C is added to the mixture, of course, but at far greater cost than the equivalent vitamin pills.

"Food tastes and habits are largely the product of cultural determination," writes Ralph Nader, "and in the United States this means largely the policy of the food industry and its determined effort *to shape those tastes that maximize its immediate projects and sales.*"[23]

The nutritional bankruptcy of this breakfast is alarming enough without the further threat of food additives. Supposedly the FDA regulates chemical additives to ensure that only those fit for human consumption appear on supermarket shelves. The bureaucratic and heavily-lobbied FDA, however, is hardly equipped or motivated to test thoroughly the hundreds upon hundreds of additives that industry has introduced willy-nilly into the nation's diet. And even if it were equipped and motivated, the FDA and its technical advisers would have to alter their reasoning on two important matters.

First, extraordinary differences in human tolerance for drugs and in human metabolism generally render suspect any judgment concerning the safety of additives. Sodium nitrite or monosodium glutamate may be safe for *most* people, but what about the others? Where do *they* buy their bread or soup? And how, in the first place, do they learn that they are members of this nutritional minority?

Second, myriad artificial substances now flow through the human body simultaneously: compounds in purified water; diverse ingredients of petrochemical smog; medicines for colds and allergies and chronic illnesses; food and beverage additives; nicotine; etc. No one even claims to have studied the interactive impact of this technological potpourri on the human body. The way it stands now, one requires an advanced degree in chemistry to understand an average American meal.

In fact, preservatives, stabilizers, sweeteners, emulsifiers, flavor enhancers, coloring, etc.—all of them chemical additives—have been built into processed foods with such recklessness that the expansion of nuclear power looks cautious by comparison. The result: a "food pollution" which may well prove to be as serious as environmental pollution.

The food industry rightly claims to provide the middle-class child a greater than ever variety of food (distribution) which can be stored longer (preservatives) and prepared more easily (processing and packaging). The only costs to the child are his parents' money, and his own health.

While real incomes were far higher in 1965 than in 1955, those ten years witnessed a *decline* in the number of house-holds that had adequate diets! This is not the conclusion of mischievous muckrakers but of the United States Depart-ment of Agricluture![24]

During this same period of time, the sales of the food industry grew enormously. The chemical industry's sales of food additives more than doubled.[25] And, since 1950, the processors and distributors who rely on those frequently un-safe additives gained an increasing percentage of the profits.

Twenty years ago Americans spent $45 billion a year on food, of which food producers received half and food proces-sors and distributors the other half. Today, with the nation's food bill doubling to $90 billion and families staggering to make ends meet, the farmers only get $30 billion, while the technical middle-men make $60 billion.[26] Thus, while our diets deteriorate, those who *grow* food make less, while those who *process* it make more. Our per capita consumption of fresh fruits and vegetables steadily declines while our intake of processed sugary food soars![27]

The technicians are proud of this efficient agri-business which has transformed the family farm into a mechanized, chemicalized conglomerate. They have removed themselves from the process of growing food to such an extent that their children no longer have any idea of where supermarket food comes from.

A Revolution In Eating

Many young men and women who have looked closely at the technicians' menu have decided that they and their children will eat elsewhere. Some have changed their diets out of simple fear: they are unwilling to take the risk of eating food laced with chemicals which industry found expedient to use. These young people have removed from their refrigerators and cupboards as many processed foods as they could, and replaced them with fresh and whole foods wherever possible.

Other young people, often with training in the biological sciences, have changed their diets for *medical* reasons. Their parents, unaccustomed to affluence, ate whatever money could buy, especially those foods which before they could not afford. Their children too adopted a diet symbolized by TV food advertising: a diet revolving around soft drinks, sugary treats, pseudo-cereals, and other nonessentials. But as young people, they began to feel the cumulative impact of this distorted diet on their own bodies, and to witness among their elders the phenomenal rise of circulatory disease and other ailments due in large part to severely unbalanced eating habits.

When young food activists said, "Eat less meat and dairy products," the experts called them "faddists." But then, more recently, President Eisenhower's personal physician, the renowned Dr. Paul Dudley White, called for "a Children's Crusade" in eating habits. White is convinced that without a fundamental change in diet beginning in childhood, circulatory and other ailments will continue their meteoric rise. Then, at last, the technicians listened. As with the Vietnam War, the kids argument had become "respectable."

Still other young people have challenged the American diet on *ecological* grounds. They have argued that Americans are not only violating the requirements of the human body by submitting themselves to the products of the food industry—they are also underwriting agricultural practices which seriously damaged the soil and water on which future generations must depend for their food supply; that pesticides and chemical fertilizers, the technical crutches of mass farming, have threatened wildlife and polluted streams and lakes in even the most rural, picturesque areas of the country; that unless agriculture returns to organic methods, which seek to utilize science to maximize the productivity and quality of natural processes and minimize the reliance on chemical intervention, America might well destroy the natural resources which provide us with the only *real* food it has.

Taking these medical and ecological arguments one step further, a group of young people have emerged who oppose the "food-industrial complex" on *economic* grounds.[28] Their simplest criticism is that consumers are paying too much for too little nutrition, and that labeling and advertising are misleading, incomplete, and occasionally fabricated outright. Some of them have set up food cooperatives, organic food stores, wholesale food distribution networks, and farming communes, while others have begun to pressure industries to improve the quality of their products and the accuracy of their promotion.

But the *political* criticisms go still further. Given malnutrition in America and worldwide starvation, it seems highly inappropriate to these politicized food critics that 85 percent of all our grain is fed to animals. In 1968, US livestock (excluding cows) were fed 20 million tons of plant protein primarily from sources that could be eaten directly by man. What is outrageous about this is that that plant protein did not produce an equivalent 20 millions tons of animal protein, *but only 2 million.* This is because livestock must be fed eight pounds of protein to produce one pound of animal protein for human consumption. As a result, in 1968 alone 18 million tons of protein were "lost." This amount, according to the book *Diet For a Small Planet,* is "equivalent to *90 percent of the yearly world* protein deficit."[29] As one aware official in the US Department of Agriculture put it: ". . . the billion people in the developed countries use practically as much cereals as *feed* to produce animal protein as the two billion people of the developing countries used directly as food."[30]

America is operating a "protein factory in reverse." If the success of our food industry were judged not by the accounting criteria of profit, but rather by the nutritional criterion of protein, it would have to be considered utterly bankrupt. Food activists consequently think of a thick steak as a nutritional Cadillac: a status symbol which wastes the limited resources of our planet at a time when those resources must be used with greater efficiency, and compassion.

Young people and other activists have only begun the difficult re-examination of this food fiasco and the possible effects on future generations of kids. Their reaction is incomplete, sometimes inaccurate, and sometimes even faddist. But some reaction is essential if the next generation is to grow at all. Today in our overstuffed nation, we sit entranced at the spectacle of moon exploration while our children wither of malnutrition or gorge themselves on sugary, chemical concoctions. No wonder the post-technological generation, which was Bottle-, Gerber-, and Froot Loop-fed, has begun to re-examine their culinary upbringing.

8.
The Family

children are the people I dig

. . . somewhere inside me, you know, I've always wanted to be a father . . . . I'll be even more responsible, because—you see children are really the people that I dig. I remember a period in my life when I was really hung up on talking to children. I knew a girl once who had some little children. And I noticed that she never talked to them. She always screamed at them and she would treat them as though they were stupid. I looked at her little boy, and the cat was uptight, and he was like enraged. Every time I saw him he seemed to be enraged, and I wondered what was wrong with him, you know? I observed the situation, and it occurred to me that it was just because no one talked to him, that he was being treated as though he couldn't think or that he wasn't a sensible person, and that they seemed to be waiting for him to be geting older, and then he would start thinking. So I started talking to him. And it was very clear to me that you could hold an intelligent conversation with the child. I brought this to her attention and I made her start talking to the cat, you know, and he just changed, because he was being communicated with.

> Eldridge Cleaver
> Former Minister of Information
> Black Panther Party

In 1971, cases of child abuse, many of which resulted in death, were reported in the United States in excess of *60,000*. (Unreported cases may well double this figure.)[1]

Approximately 600,000 minors ran away from home in 1970, double the number seven years earlier. (Authorities expected this wave of run-aways to diminish once campus revolt waned, but instead this wave has grown to tidal proportions.)[2]

The proportion of ten to eighteen year olds arrested for serious drug abuse doubled between 1964 and 1968 and has continued to grow since.[3]

The National Commission on Drug Abuse estimates that *1.5 million* adolescents have used heroin.[4]

If the rate of juvenile delinquency continues to rise at its present rate, *one out of every nine* minors will eventually stand in juvenile court.[5]

Half of all major crimes are committed by those under eighteen years of age.[6]

"The war against crime," writes James Miller in *Life,* "has necessarily become a war against children."[7]

Such trends as these will "continue to grow," forecasts one juvenile court judge, "until the nuclear family is reestablished or reoriented."[8] And indeed this is the most frightening fact of all, a fact for which we have no numbers: that beneath this tangible legal evidence rests a deeper social crisis in the American family, a crisis which threatens the growth of all children—rich and poor alike. The "fortunate" technicians' families, snuggled in the suburb or in comfortable city apartments, are also responsible for producing some of the children for whom play grew into crime, and for whom learning was replaced by addiction.

Where Do The Children Play

We busy, busy adults, with the vanity of maturity, see everything as work. Without continued effort and application to our jobs, we would have no health insurance, pay raises, savings plans, or retirement benefits. Yet somewhere in our deep forgotten past, perhaps late at night as we drift into sleep, we must recall that what we now proudly call work was born in child's play.

How a preschool child plays will be one crucial determinant of how he works as an adult. Because an adult's creative power is rooted in early emotional attitudes toward learning and experimentation, the quality of a generation's work depends greatly upon the kind of preschool environment their parents provide. More and more psychologists today believe that as much as half of all human intelligence is developed by age four.[9]

Quite able to move about and to ask questions, the preschooler can sense what kind of living experiences his mother and father and siblings are having inside and outside the home. At this age he is able "to visualize himself as being as big as the grown-ups" and "to understand what roles are worth imagining."[10] Family members represent to him possibilities of his own future. Before he ever enters a classroom, his growth is profoundly influenced by the way his caretakers—whether parents, relatives, guardians, or institution personnel—act around him and toward him. For example, if they react to "errors" with severe criticism, the once playful learner will realize that it is more important to be conventional than to be imaginative. The child will learn to perform assigned tasks with caution and precision, but he will not learn to explore beyond the prescribed range of alternative activities.[11]

If, on the contrary, caretakers seek to develop children who "can be critical, can verify, and not accept anything they are offered," they will make available a wide range of tasks of various levels of complexity. Teaching at its best, argues Piaget,

> *means creating situations where structures can be discovered; it does not mean transmitting structures* . . . . Children have real understanding only of that which they invent themselves, and each time we try to teach them something too quickly, we keep them from reinventing it themselves.[12]

Of course what is too quick for one child, is too slow for another. Therefore, if each child is to develop his independent curiosity by exploring the world at his own pace, he must be treated flexibly and individually, not just as a stereotyped "three-year-old."

Another important aspect of the preschool learning environment is playmates. Some children may be cooped up all day alone in an apartment with their mother and the television. Other children are fortunate enough to live in a setting where they may play with others. A four-year-old is ready not only to learn how to work on things, but how to work on them with others. Cooperation "is an essential factor in intellectual development," writes Piaget.[13] A preschooler can learn in a rudimentary way that one's actions in the world may be other-enhancing and self-enhancing at the same time.

If the setting in which a child spends his first five years of life will indeed influence the type of creative person he becomes later, then the question must be asked: what kind of "home" facilitates a child's full development?

A once possible alternative was the traditional, extended family. Gesell and Ilg—who, along with Spock, redirected postwar child-rearing—recall the rural farm with in-laws and grandparents all combined into a functioning economic unit:

> . . . the world of nature and human relationships expanded in a rather orderly manner, keeping pace with the maturity of the child. The home was large, the membership of the family numerous . . . . Someone was always near to look after the preschool child and to take him by graduated stages into his widening world, step by step, as his demands gradually increased. There was free space around his home—a field, a meadow, an orchard. There were animals in the barn, pen, coop, and pasture. Some of the fellow creatures were young like himself . . . .[14]

As these child psychologists realize, however, the preindustrial rural home was not all bliss. There was loneliness, poverty, and endless manual labor. Transportation was poor, education negligible, and drought, flood, or blight disastrous.

Spurred on by salaried industrial jobs, men rushed to the city. In place of the extended rural family emerged the nuclear urban family. Unfortunately, this new family is even less suited to a child's needs than its rural predecessor. The nuclear family evolved to meet the needs of industry, not of children. Its *raison d'être* was not human development, but technological development. As Alvin Toffler puts it in *Future Shock,*

> . . . "extended" families were well suited for survival in slow-paced agricultural societies. But such families are hard to transport or transplant. They are immobile. Industrialism demanded masses of workers ready and able to move off the land in pursuit of jobs, and to move again whenever necessary. Thus the extended family gradually shed its excess weight and the so-called "nuclear" family emerged—a stripped-down, portable family unit consisting only of parents and a small set of children.[15]

While abstractly expanded by space-defying technologies of communications, the child's world has concretely shrunk to the confines of an apartment or urban house. He has contact with sidewalks, automobiles, and televisions, of course, but not often with growing life, with other children, or with a variety of adults.

Think for a moment of the child's world before the advent of Ford. Almost any two- or three-year-old child go could anywhere he wanted as soon as he was able to walk. His playground was wherever his legs could take him and his sense of direction guide him. Whatever restrictions were imposed were human—his body's strength or his parents' wishes—not technological impositions. Older children soon became the equals of adults as far as mobility was concerned: in cities, street cars and horse-drawn buggies; in the country, horses, buggies, and boats; and everywhere, walking and running.

Today's world is made for adults with cars. The child's environment consists of a dangerous asphalt grid, criss-crossed by steel–cement super-highways. The three-year-old—even the ten-year-old!—cannot just "go out and play." Not more than a few seconds walk from almost all front doors, even at a toddler's pace, is a ton of sharp metal hurtling down a road. Unsupervised children must be told to "play inside," or to "stay in the yard." At best they are given elaborate instructions and ultimatums about where and how to move about, while every mother spends half her day anxiously glancing through the window to make sure her child has not become a statistic.

There seem to be two outstanding reasons behind this insanity.

First, the cityscape evolved during the technological era so as to serve the private passenger automobile, not to serve children ready to explore the world. Due in good measure to the Highway Trust Fund and the highway–auto–petroleum complex, public transportation which is safe for and accessible to children is nearly nonexistent,[16] as are bicycle paths along major city roads. In transportation terms, the technological revolution has made children second-class citizens. Driver's licenses, as every child knows, are not obtainable before the age of sixteen or eighteen. Until then life is an interminable negotiation, as every parent knows, about who will take whom where when—if at all.

Secondly, the technicians wanted for their families not only a private car, but also direct road access to a private driveway, and a private garage adjacent to a private home on a private lot. They reasoned, it seems, that this apparent privacy meant personal control and convenience. What it really meant was the devouring of children's space in favor of the automobile, and the endangering of all areas adjacent to roads. For all but the very rich, private yards became too small for even a decent game of whiffle ball. Small children were confined to an area with which even the most docile farm cow would be dissatisfied.

Child psychologists now express concern over the stripped-down family. Fearing that the child will soon have no playmates whatsoever, they complain that "the preschool child was not meant to live alone."[17]

A Lonely Cast of Characters

Despite all the talk about shorter working hours, most upper-middle-class fathers in fact work *more* than the normal forty hours, according to Galbraith, since this is what the corporate job ladder requires.[18] While a father's identity revolves around his work, the children are left to mother and to teacher. Father expresses his responsibility for his family by providing the food, goods, travel, schooling, and neighborhood which his income permits. Most important of all, the father is *gone*. Unlike rural family kids, children today have little or no personal contact with their father's work. The scale of technologized industry is so enormous that its workers must congregate in giant installations, which are off limits to both their wives and their children.

While fathers no longer produce anything in the home, neither do mothers. The noble claim of the technicians—that what before was made could now be bought—has transformed the modern child's home. He almost never sees anything being made—neither in the home, the barn, nor the fields. Meanwhile the technician's wife is "the consumer," cast by the male-controlled media as a chronic over-spender who constantly nags her husband for more things. Men, of course, are ultimately in charge of what shall be consumed, whether the product be soap or soap-opera. While the "primary" tasks of producing wealth and controlling power are for males, "secondary" matters like home-making or raising and educating children are left to women.

The technicians leave their children to women, but only until their children approach the age when they too can become technicians. Then the men want control. In elementary schools, 85 percent of teachers are women; in high schools only 50 percent; and in college, only a tiny fraction.[19] University departments of education and social work are flooded with women, while the fields on which industry depends—business and commerce, economics and engineering—maintain their over 90-percent-male membership.[20] The message of the technological revolution to women is painfully clear: the crucial tasks of civilization are reserved for men. Women should derive meaning vicariously through their husbands' careers and their children's achievements.

In this way the worlds of the two sexes have been increasingly separated. The technological revolution has caused the integrated tasks of farm or family shop to be split irrevocably into specialized labor. Once the father may have grown wheat and the mother made bread, but now parental roles are unrelated. A wife may never have visited her husband's office, nor may she understand the technical, political, or economic issues that impinge on his daily activity. And the husband may see his wife primarily on weekends (if he's not away on business), and even then his briefcase is full of reports to be read. He does not feel he is neglecting his children; on the contrary, he is providing for *their* future by advancing *his* career. This is not conjecture but statistical truth: the post-technological generation has spent less time with their parents than any generation before them.[21]

Since the technological revolution requires a certain kind

of father and a certain kind of mother, we should not be surprised that it also requires a certain kind of child. The target of a technological society is the play age. Bruno Bettelheim, who has spent a lifetime helping the troubled children that our society produces, says quite plainly: *"We are stealing childhood."*

> If we don't stop it, we are going to kill each other off. Every decade we raise our expectations: we want sooner intellectual development in children, sooner and more complex. The post-Sputnik generation has been geared from childhood for productivity, and they are missing something because of it.[22]

With their faith in the supreme value of specialized training, the techncians have decided that more children should be made to learn, and the sooner they can learn the better. So they reduced the play age, as Eda LeShan puts it in her book, *Conspiracy Against Childhood,* in order "to teach more children more facts faster."[23] *College Begins at Two* reads the title of one recent preschool primer for parents; and news magazines, in articles with headlines like "Never too Young to Learn," announce that accelerating preschool learning is "education's hottest trend."[24] As usual, few adults ask if all this is in the interest of children's long-range development. The technicians are in the foreground, asking their perennial questions: "Can it be done?" and then, "Who can do it better, at less cost?"

The social factors which impinge on the family are far more complex than those involved in childbirth or feeding, yet a similar pattern emerges: just as we "choose" the childbirth and feeding which coincided with the requirements of technology, so did we "choose" the nuclear family structure, which fits those same demands.

Both the daughters and sons of the technicians have suffered. The divorce rate, which dramatically increased among the technicians' generation, is merely the legally documented part of their children's fragmented sexual inheritance. Whether or not their parents are legally separated, the children of the technological revolution can see that their parents have been socially separated. As Marx said long ago, *"from this relationship man's whole level of development can be assessed."* Only a few months after marrying his childhood sweetheart, Marx wrote that the relationship between man and woman "is the most natural relationship of human being to human being," a relationship in which the sum of man's development is "sensually revealed, reduced to an observable fact."[25] The technicians conveniently devalue the importance of lasting love relationships, for otherwise they would have to face the naked fact that, amidst all the technological splendor, the man–wife bond is disintegrating.

At least some people feel there is no cause for alarm in the number of "broken" families. With quiet quasi-objectivity, Alvin Toffler describes the "options" or "alternative scenarios" of tomorrow's family. Like him, we could simply avoid the problem by adopting no values of our own. We could just let things happen and choose whichever brand of family we like best in technology's supermarket. We could have our children raised by "professional parents" whose job was to care for children. We could have "serial marriages," a quick succession of new mates and new sets of children resulting in an "aggregate family." Toffler argues that these are likely possibilities because, in a technological society, the odds are heavily against love which last until "death do us part." As a result of technology, he observes dispassionately, a family unit based on an unbroken man–woman relationship will soon be a relic of history.[26]

We do not know whether Toffler has any ethical values against which he measures the merits of these alternative futures. For him, things are simply less likely or more likely, not better or worse. On the other hand, certain groups of women's liberationists have quite explicit criteria. Writes one group: "We ask not if something is 'reformist,' 'radical,' 'revolutionary,' or 'moral.' We ask: is it good for women or bad for women?"[27] On what grounds should the family be restructured . . . For the needs of the technicians or for the needs of these women's liberationists? For the financial convenience and sexual pleasure of adults, as described in Robert Rimmer's *The Harrad Experiment?* Should we simply pick out whichever of the futurologist's scenarios suits our whims?

The present debate about the family seems to be focused on the role of women. Perhaps, for the moment, it should be. Blind allegiance to technology has left the nonworking American woman with an "identity" which does not hang together, with a "home" that cannot survive.

Despite the legitimacy of this debate, it must be refocused. It is already clear that women will soon work with men, and earn men's pay, and wield men's power. Aldous Huxley knew this over thirty years ago when he depicted men and women in *Brave New World* as completely equal automatons. The real debate today must focus on what will happen to our children. Will the liberation of women lead to a revitalized family and the creation of communal space where children can play among loving adults? Or will it lead to the institutionalization of two-to-five-year-olds who from birth onward have been a virtually anonymous part of a mass-produced generation?

Family Liberation

"We recognize the rights of adults," wrote Maria Montessori decades ago, "but not those of the child. We recognize justice, but only for those who can protest and defend themselves . . . ."[28] How painfully true this still is in the present debate about the future struggle of the family.

Because the technological revolution destroyed many of women's traditional functions yet gave them nothing in return, this "second sex" has given rise to a vocal, politically active group calling for women's liberation. Even before this organized opposition was born, women were trying to escape the "air-conditioned nightmare" of the isolated home. Married women in ever greater numbers (one of three in 1965) [29] joined the work force. They did not want to be mere helpers to decision-making men, but equals who worked in men's institutions and were paid men's wages.

Women's liberation has taken these legitimate demands one step further. Tired of male lawyers running divorce proceedings and male doctors deciding the legality of birth control and abortion (only 3 percent of lawyers and 6 percent of doctors are women),[30] angry women have called for "equal numbers of men and women in all institutions." Tired of being confined to the "unfulfilling" tasks of child care, home-making, and lower-level teaching, they want to participate in the political, scientific, and economic institutions which are the core of the technological society. To enable them to do this, they have naturally demanded publicly financed day-care centers so that their preschool children can be supervised while they are at work.

Since the men's world appears to be the only "meaningful" sphere of activity, women want to join it. They too have the right to think like men think and do what men do. As Simone de Beauvoir said long ago in *The Second Sex*, the liberated woman *"accepts masculine values*: she prides herself on thinking, taking action, working, creating, *on the same terms as men."*[31]

As any reader of Aldous Huxley's *Brave New World* knows, the danger in this reshuffling of sexual roles is that the technological system may gain workers while children lose parents. This point must be raised because, in all the debate about sexual differences, one trait men and women have in common is rarely mentioned: *neither adult sex seems to be as concerned about children as it is about itself.*

If the women's liberation movement is to free children as well as women, it must *transcend*—not accept—masculine values. The mere acceptance of masculine values would do nothing to challenge the impoverishment of the home, the inflexibility of the forty-hour week, or the specialization of child care. If women do not challenge those values, they may achieve their "liberation" by sacrificing their children's.

If we are to act on our children's behalf, we must revolutionize the family quite differently. We must not start by demanding a publicly run day-care center in order that mothers could join fathers for nine-to-five workday.* After all, who would staff these centers but *other* women? And not "liberated" women either, since they would by then have become executives, etc. Specialization would not be overcome, but merely extended from industry to include the family. The child–staff ratio would be as high as that in the present public school systems. If now both men and women decided to leave child care to "somebody else," children would simply enter overcrowded, understaffed, and underfinanced, public institutions at the age of one or two rather than in kindergarten.

Are we to believe that, by some bureaucratic miracle, two-to-five-year-old children will be treated with sufficient flexibility and individuality that they will develop independent curiosity? Why should child-care centers be any less joyless and mind-numbing than the public schools which Charles Silberman so carefully described? Is it not far more probable that, as presently envisioned, day-care centers will simply begin to "steal childhood" at an unprecedentedly early age?

To avoid a bureaucratic day-care center we must change the work week. As perceptive women activists have pointed out,[32] it is an unnecessary violation of human freedom for industry to require inflexibly forty hours a week of labor. The essential step toward liberating both men and women, as well as their children, is to establish varied, flexible, part- and full-time work schedules.[33] Then, if both husband and wife wish to work, they would have a number of ways of integrating their working hours for the benefit of their children.

Equally important, husband and wife could share in the excitement and hardships of both home and work. Instead of increased separation within a marriage and further fragmentation in sexual roles, a husband and wife could choose the respective roles in work and home which allow each of

---

* The day-care center was initially conceived for women who had no economic support and therefore *had* to work rather than take care of their children. Even in this limited application, the day-care center concept is not radical. It is far more radical to seek adequate welfare for dependent mothers. Then a mother is free to choose whether or not to work.

them to find the balance of life styles that best fits their marriage. Writes Michael Rossman:

> We must be directly involved in what and how our children learn, for no one else can represent our interest in the future . . . . Our parents were forced to abandon their children to the part-time uses of the State because they were integrated into its economy and culture, because they saw no alternative, because they were isolated in marriage and in privacy and could not organize their lives to be also a school . . . . To free our young many must come together, to share their powers in critical mass and intimacy. We believe it involves all entering equal as children into the school of the larger Family.[34]

Getting Together:
Home

The future of the family also rests upon the imperatives of population. If there are too many children, nothing we may wish to do on their behalf will succeed. Many young Americans have decided to have no more than two children. However, while having a small family assuages the adult's conscience regarding population control, it also removes a child's traditional playmates—his brothers and sisters. Instead of several siblings of varied ages who can care for each other, there is literally a two-generational family: two children of about the same age, and two parents. It is hardly surprising that children raised in such families would readily think in terms of generation gaps, because that is literally all their nuclear families are.

To decelerate population growth, and yet at the same time to assure preschool children of accessible playmates, it is essential that groups of families assume joint responsibility for the care of their children.* *Communal child care*—an independent association of several families living together, in adjacent apartments, or in separate homes, who can

---

* If families do not, business or government will. As *Newsweek* reported, entrepreneurs who franchise fried chicken stands or auto-transmission repair shops are ready and willing to apply their expertise to the day-care center market.[35]

flexibly arrange their work days—can create an informal, intimate, "day-care center" controlled exclusively by the parents. With communal child care, children would have a small group of friends with whom to play, yet a group large enough for diversity. Unlike the child in the isolated nuclear family, they would have a setting in which cooperation is possible. Also, they would be exposed to many adults of both sexes, each of whom would bring different skills and experiences into the preschooler's world. Unlike the public day-care center, the child's caretakers would not be anonymous or arbitrary. They would all be friends of the child's parents and parents of the child's playmates.

For the children of the poor, of course, the further step of financial assistance must be taken. But this should not be in the form of a federally-run day-care program which subjects poor children to preschool institutionalization while rich children frolic in suburban play centers. On the contrary, federal aid to working and dependent mothers should be made directly to the mother for each of her preschool children. "It would save money in the end," Dr. Spock concluded years ago, "if the Government paid a comfortable allowance to all mothers of young children who would otherwise be compelled to work." Not only would it be economical; it would be better for the child.

> Between the ages of one to three . . . is the least advisable period for the mother who has always taken care of her child to go off to work for the first time, or to make changes in the person who takes her place . . . . This is the age when he comes to depend for security on one or two familiar, trusted people, and is upset if they disappear or keep changing.[36]

With their combined child-care–welfare money, poor mothers could join together to set up responsible, child-centered day-care facilities without relinquishing parental control of their children's lives to the municipal or federal government. It could be, as William Shannon has written in the *New York Times*, "a radical, direct, simple, utopian alternative to day-care centers."[37]

To organize such communal child-care, the home would once again become a center of creative day-time activity. The home would no longer be impoverished. It is not "liberation" from the technological society to escape from a dying home, but acquiescence to it. The very idea of a home is radical in an era when private identity, to use Marcuse's phrase, is being absorbed "by the function of the individual in the state—by his public existence."[38] Nothing is grown or made (or, as we have seen, born) in the modern home. Clothes, bread, furniture, games, vegetables, dishes, music, entertainment: all are purchased and imported.

This is not meant to deny that complex industrial products can be made most dependably and efficiently in mass production. But dependence on technical specialists has gone so far that "the home" has little vitality or individuality left. If the home remains a minimal producer and a maximal consumer, it remains a slave to external authorities. It must rely on food technicians to decide what is biologically "safe." It must rely on TV networks for "entertainment." Indeed, for every chore, whether unclogging a drain or fixing a table or treating a sore throat, the home must hire a man who is too busy, who charges too much, and who really doesn't care.

The consumption of the impoverished, isolated home verges on insanity. As father (and/or mother) works to pay the bills, every half-acre plot has its lawnmower; every child his discarded toys, bikes, and clothes; every living room its television; every laundry room its washer and dryer; every garage its cars. Countless expensive appliances could be used more economically if shared by a few families rather than used by one.

When families are stripped down into isolated nuclear units with only one or two children, their structure is inevitably more uniform, and their function inevitably more dependent on mass public and professional services. Too heavy a burden is placed on each relationship within the structure —whether husband–wife, parent–child, or child–child—and too little connection is maintained with those outside.

Several families associated in a small social group, or commune, can create a viable, intimate home free from the rigid impersonality inherent in large institutions. They cannot be everything unto themselves—doctor, plumber, potter, musician, decorator, carpenter, mechanic, gardener, midwife, seamstress, minister—but that should not be the goal. The goal is not to escape altogether from society's network of goods and services, but rather to benefit from that network and to grow within it.

In an environment of interlocking, cooperative relationships, both men and women could have responsibility for child care and for employment. Neither sex would be the standard against which the other must measure itself, for each would be involved in the common challenge to "transcend itself" by learning "to feel and to represent the concerns of the other." Just as women share "masculine" traits, writes Eriksen, "so real men can partake in motherliness . . . ."[39] Nothing can justify prejudices, he concludes, "which keep half of mankind from participating in planning and decision-making, especially at a time when the other half, by its competitive escalation and acceleration of technological progress, has brought us and our children to the gigantic brink on which we live."[40]

Women are obviously needed in medicine, on hospital boards, in pollution control panels. (After all, it is *their* babies whom men deliver, and *their* milk that men's pesticides poison.) They are clearly needed in the food and drug industries. (It is hard to imagine sugary, starched baby foods if women and children ran the Gerber industry.) Radical women are also desperately needed in the communications industry. (The insulting advertising and insipid programming of afternoon television could be put to an end.[41]) Perhaps it will finally be a woman who will summon the courage to run a political campaign on the platform that *all* children should be fed and clothed before we fly to the moon. The same need for women is present throughout society: in urban planning, scientific research, school reorganization, budget allocations, etc.

The women's liberation movement will be radical only if it refuses the "equality" which male technicians will gladly offer. If women seek "equality" only, they will become the technicians' allies in a joint betrayal of their children's true needs. Radical women must stand up for the child-centered values which men have all to willingly pushed aside as they devoted themselves to technical progress or martial grandeur. If women defend themselves *and* their children, perhaps men will realize that rearing children is not a solely feminine, but a jointly parental, responsibility.

9.
Television

hearing any casual tales

And shall we just carelessly allow children to hear any casual tales which may be devised by casual persons, and to receive in their minds ideas for the most part the very opposite of those which we should wish them to have when they are grown up?

Plato

American children, who, on statistical evidence, spend from three to six hours a day absorbing the contents of television, whose nursery songs are advertisements . . . will be able only by heroic effort to disengage themselves from this system sufficiently to recover some measure of autonomy.

Lewis Mumford

The technicians who had taken over creative productivity for industry's use were ready and willing to take over creative amusement and thought as well. Corporations seeking to increase demand for their products adopted television quickly as their avenue of communication. Their investments enable television to expand financially from fewer than 175 thousand households in 1947 to over 40 *million* just ten years later.[1] In 1970, when few homes are without TV, a remarkably small number of corporations (such as Proctor and Gamble, General Foods, and the motor companies) control an enormous part of viewing time. The industrial system, after impoverishing the home, had offered to replenish it with its own culture.

Each expansion of the industrial system since the 1900s has further invaded the child's world. After the industrial revolution, proper men and women condoned child labor as an unpleasant but inevitable condition. Now, following the technological revolution, their successors consider as bothersome but unavoidable the outright manipulation of children as consumers and learners.

Indentured to Industry

In nineteenth-century England, where the industrial revolution was at first most advanced, children were hit most cruelly. Child-labor legislators had to fight for such statutes as the law of 1833 which declared that "children from age nine to thirteen were not to work more than 48 hrs. a week."[2] Even such primitive measures were adamantly opposed by mill and mine owners who considered child labor an unparalleled economic asset.[3] Factory owners were so powerful that reformers, such as the determined Earl of Shaftsbury, were compelled to defend themselves from mass criticism and to be grateful for the most insignificant successes. Advocates of rapid industrial development denounced proposals for child-labor reform on the grounds that they would halt economic expansion. Only a few radical reformers argued that "progress" which required the manipulation and destruction of childhood was insane.[4]

The first decades of the twentieth century still found child labor flourishing in America. Radical men and women known as "muckrakers," tried to arouse public awareness of the cruelty of child labor by writing impassioned essays and novels. The industrial exploitation of children was well documented by such men as John Spargo, in his *Bitter Cry of the Children* published in 1906.

> Many times I have heard fathers and mothers . . . say that they did not want their children to work, that they could have done without the children's wages and kept them at school a little longer, or apprenticed them to better employment, . . . but they were compelled to send them into the mills to work, or lose their own places.[5]

Others described the agony of children not yet into their teens who spent over twelve hours in the black pits of coal mines, or operating silk-frames or cotton speeders in the mills. Because of their youthfulness, children suffered far more frequent accidents than older workers, while their workdays were bought at far less cost to the economy-minded owners.[6]

The owner classes in America had learned the justification for barbarism that English "robber barons" had used for so long: "Why should I invest my scarce capital in machinery," they would argue, "when I would accomplish the same work at less cost with child laborers? My competitors, still using cheap child labor, would undersell me and I would lose my business!" Edwin Marham, in 1907, wrote an article titled "Spinners in the Dark," and reports his conversation with a "mill-baron of the better sort," who told him that "I deplore this business (of child labor) as much as you do. But I am part of a great industrial system, and as long as that endures I must run my mills as others are run."

The industrial revolution is now long past, and many comfortable adults feel they can reflect on the exploitation of children as a horror story which has ended. Society today is in the throes of another revolution, however, for which terms such as "technological," "technetronic," "postindustrial," "knowledge," "consumer," or "communications," have been applied. Just as the previous revolution provided the means for mass production, this revolution is providing the means for ever-increasing mass consumption. Owners of large enterprises now offer hollow apologies not for their callous use of the child as a worker, but for their manipulative use of the child as a consumer. Like Markham's mill baron, competing firms defend their massive advertising geared at children by explaining that they are part of that same "great industrial system," and, as long as it continues, they must further escalate what in the mid-fifties Vance Packard had already called the "pseudo-seduction of children."[7]

This steadily deteriorating situation has now produced its Earl of Shaftsbury, Senator Moss of Utah, who has asked for federal action to patrol the content of billions of dollars worth of advertising directed at young children. Followed by groups of mothers and consumer unions, Senator Moss and others have decided that affluent America should be able to entertain itself without allowing any corporation with a wad of bills to inundate millions of children with any message of their choice.

In the preschool years, when "the child is at no time more ready to learn quickly and avidly, to become bigger,"[8] advertisers can lead the child to the attitude quite early that "I am what I can own or buy." Human growth is reduced to a succession of ever more grandiose possessions which he can learn to use—and pay for. The child in this way may develop an attitude toward life by which he relates to activity through the products it involves. (Who would gain anything by telling him of activities which involve no products? Even yoga, a quiet exploration and enjoyment of one's own body, becomes peripheral to the "Yoga-Tites" and "Yoga-Mats" which the advertiser seeks to sell.) No one tells a child how to make a toy or game himself: if he does that, no cash registers click.

The postwar generation now of college age was exposed during their preschool years to TV's *Ding Dong School* "principal" who would intone the alphabet and Wonder Bread with equal sincerity. The "principal" came under the scrutiny of educators and doctors only when, perhaps attempting to compensate for the nutritional deficiencies in the bread, she told her three-to-five-year-old viewers how to swallow the yummy little red pills that have all the vitamins boys and girls need, and urged them to get their mothers to the drug store to buy them. Only then, points out Vance Parkard in *The Hidden Persuaders*, were some doctors moved by professional ethics to voice their objections. They argued that TV should not encourage the pill intake of toddlers, not only because such a decision is a medical one, but also because such small children are unable to read labels.[9] The Ding Dong School was clearly teaching not only the three R's, but the rudiments of mindless consumption.

Black & White, Good & Bad

Criticism of TV commercials is nothing new. When something is so crass and insipid, critics are not hard to find. Analysis of television programming is more difficult, however, because programming appears to have constructive potential.

Shallow plots and biased reporting notwithstanding, television has created a new environment. Perhaps TV cannot live up to Marshall McLuhan's billing as the electronic Trojan Horse, carrying in its belly the "revolutionary" values of an electric age. But there is no doubt that it is an essential component of the "global village," capable of bringing the then-and-there to the here-and-now with breathtaking immediacy. It is both classroom and courtroom: transmitter of information to remote towns and impoverished regions, and witness to the angry charges of dissenters and the proud counter-charges of officials. Both an electronic blackboard and jury, television has been a catalyst for much that is valuable in modern life.

Recognizing TV's achievements should not mean ignoring the immense power its entertainment and news programming possess over all members of society. Through the Fifties and Sixties, children from six to sixteen on the average spent 22 hours per week in front of the TV, over 50 percent more time than British children spent in the same occupation. For sixth-graders, the average was 28 hours per week—almost as much time as spent in school. Although adults may glorify the world-shrinking wisdom of Zenith and RCA or admire the sales power of Saturday cartoons, children may experience less than edifying effects from this electronic magic box. For the child, reality and fantasy are hard to separate in this flickering environment. As the White House Conference on Children and Youth explained in 1950, the early years of a child's growth are

> . . . a period of enterprise and imagination, an ebullient creative period when fantasy substitutes for literal execution of desires and the meagerest equipment provides material for high imaginings. It is a period of intrusive, vigorous learning that leads away from the child's own limitations into future possibilities . . . . [C]hildren now begin to feel guilty for mere thoughts, for deeds that have been imagined but never executed . . . . [S]ince [the child] does not always distinguish clearly between actuality and fantasy, his overzealous conscience may disapprove of even imaginary deeds.[10]

The White House Conference states quite strongly that the child of four or five wants to find out what kind of a person he can be.

> To be any particular kind of person, he sees clearly, requires being able to do particular kinds of things. So he observes with keen attention what all manner of interesting adults do, . . . *tries to imitate their behavior, and yearns for a share in their activities."* (Italics added).[11]

In the light of such statements twenty years ago by the nation's foremost psychologists and educators, television broadcasters might well have reexamined their responsibility for this new medium of communication. Since television intertwines fantasy and reality and offers the child scores of "interesting adults" as models for imitation, TV executives might have considered developing programming based on criteria other than those used by sponsor corporations searching for a cheap way to reach millions of consumers. Unfortunately, as in the era of child labor, childhood had few defenders, while the industrial system had many.

TV "entertainment" is captivating for the small child because it appeals to his fantastic imagination. As the White House Conference reported, ". . . fantasy substitutes for literal execution of desires." The child can imagine himself in the roles of a vast array of television models whose behavior, if imitated, would lead to punishment. Thus the child only imitates them in fantasy. However, because "his overzealous conscience may disapprove of even imaginary deeds," he experiences unnecessary guilt for having conceived of himself doing things which his parents would abhor.

In this way, the inner mental life of a generation of children is directed into mass-produced fantasy situations. Potentially, this could enlarge the child's world and increase his awareness of people, places, and ideas which otherwise would have been beyond his grasp. Indeed it could be a revolutionary tool if used with children's full growth as the guiding aim. Instead, the programming continues to be characterized by stereotyped roles and violence.

Television's fantasy characters influence the child so as to counteract precisely the growth which at this time should be fostered. Wrestling with his newly gained "conscience," trying to be a "good boy" or "nice girl," the child viewing TV is faced with show after show in which the good guy and bad guy are divided by a chasm which cannot help but baffle him. For reasons which never emerge from the inner circuitry of the television box, Matt Dillon is honorable, kind, just, and victorious, and the parade of rustlers, killers, bandits, thieves, are, for some equally impenetrable reason, consistently cruel, lazy, wily, and vanquished. The star of the show—whether a private eye, a doctor, a policeman, or a reporter (the shows are interchangeable)—is always virtuous. His opponents are always vile, usually for reasons which are completely out of view and out of context. The outlaw or criminal is, in the vast majority of episodes, inherently bad, and the hero inherently good. Matt Dillon and Perry Mason are admirable because that is how the producer cast them. What better indoctrination for cold-war political stereotypes?

Children are not cast, however. They must grow. Unlike the endless television reverie, real growth is painful because it is pervaded by ambivalence. Mother feeds you and takes care of you, but she also scolds and makes you do things. Father brings you things and takes you places, but he also sometimes leaves you and won't pay attention when you want him to. How inviting to spend one's hour with television: some people, Mighty Mouse or Davy Crockett or Napoleon Solo, can be completely admired, and the bad guys completely despised. With mother and father everything is complicated, unclear, and constantly changing. But on TV the feelings are simple, the stereotypes clear. Bad and good are separated. There is not a balance of traits in all men, only one-dimensional portrayals of dichotomized types.

The appeal of such escapism has been confirmed in a later period of childhood by experiments showing the relationships between IQ and television viewing. The experiments took a group of sixth graders and divided them into low-, middle-, and high-IQ groups. At the time these three groups showed relatively little difference in viewing habits: each group had two-thirds to three-fourths heavy viewers. But between sixth and tenth grade, a remarkable change occurred. The higher-IQ children, who at this level of schooling are likely to be more interested in school and have more significant relationships with teachers, fall out of the ranks of the heavy viewers in great numbers, while the lower-IQ children cluster in the heavy-viewing category. By tenth grade there are more than twice as many heavy viewers among the low-IQ groups than among the high.[12]

Television's dualistic world of fake people represents a dead-end escape for the child who faces critical tasks in his own development. He may escape his fear of inferiority by living in a staged environment where no one criticizes him or competes with him. He can avoid facing the task of finding out what he can do well; he can avoid developed self-motivation. In this electrical utopia he may be whoever he wants to be simply by flicking the channel-changer. The cruel inequality of these children's illusory utopia, however, is that the most disturbed children with the *least* satisfying human contact are the *most* vulnerable to television's gray glare. Those who most need to focus on the tasks of growth are the most distracted. So the weak are made weaker.

Anger and Apathy

Perhaps even worse than TV's stereotyped roles is its endless violence. The reasoned thinking of responsible adults must accept the premise that, at an age when fantasy and reality are difficult to distinguish and models for imitation are being searched for, hours of exposure to fantastic cruelty, violent relations between man and woman, "sadism, murder, private eyes, gangsters, more violence and cartoons"[13] might well harm the inner lives of small children.

The television industry, despite the experimental proof, continues to deny any such harmful effects. Middle-aged TV spokesmen would rather defend their own vested interests than open their eyes and ears to their children's lives.

Research has established with a variety of methods the fact that *exposure to violence in the media is related to increased violent behavior in children*. Experiments in which children watched the behavior of other persons found that those children behaved more violently than other children not exposed to the destructive behavior. The same was true when children were exposed to the film of a person acting violently, and a film in which a cartoon animal (a cat) behaved violently.[14] These experiments posed such a threat to the medium that the Television Information Office issued a statement attempting to discredit their conclusions. But the debate only served to spark further research which confirmed the original experiments: children who were rated most aggressive by the individual judgments of their classmates were those who watched television programs involving a high degree of violence.

Numerous reports document children's real-life imitation of violent tactics used on television shows. In a classic study of the effect of TV on children, Wilbur Schramm maintains that children often confuse "the rules of the real world and the rules of the television world."

> . . . [T]o young children television is terribly real . . . . [A]s long as violence is so prominent in the fantasy world of television, and movies, and comics, there will always be the possibility of confusion between fantasy violence and real-world violence.[15]

Television seems to stimulate extreme behavior: if not aggressiveness, then the opposite, apathy. Research has shown that *heavy exposure to television is related to isolation from other people*. In one test, upper-middle-class New England children who did not get along with their parents, or who faced a great deal of parental discipline, spent considerably more time with television than did other children.[16] Children with unsatisfactory social relationships tend to retain longer, and daydream longer about, the fantasy they get from the mass media.[17] Children who watch television frequently

> do so (particularly the intelligent ones) because they have difficulties in making friends or problems in their family rela-

tionships . . . . A vicious circle is then set up whereby the ready access to television aggravates those problems of the children which led them to view heavily in the first instance.[18]

Some cautious critics of television argue that only *disturbed* children with *abnormal* social relationships will be adversely affected by television. For example, psychiatrist Lawrence Freedman argues that the "average child" would not "confuse the 'as if' of the pretend world with the real experiences of his personal family relations. Most youngsters find the immediate personal relationships more compelling and rewarding than the animated, pictorial substitutes."[19] Analyses such as these are based on the hope that only few children watch TV by themselves, without a parent with whom to share their experiences. But, as Schramm points out, in modern America

> [m]ost parents don't have time to give children all the home experiences they need to ensure these "happy, secure" relationships . . . . [P]arents are inclined to be grateful to television as a baby-sitter rather than to treat it as something that requires much of their *own* time if it is to be used healthfully.[20]

Thus, it would be far more accurate to assume that more and more children are finding those "pictorial substitutes" more compelling and rewarding than their "immediate personal relationships." They spend more time with the tube than with their parents. As Urie Brofenbrenner argues, the parents of the TV generation spend less time with their children than ever before. Most importantly, Brofenbrenner points out:

> The primary danger of the television screen lies not so much in the behavior it produces as *the behavior it prevents*—the talks, the games, the family activities and the arguments through which much of the child's learning takes place and his character is formed.[21]

An Electronic Teacher

Now, with the arrival of "Sesame Street" and its offshoots, television is starting to educate as well as entertain. From one perspective, these shows constitute a step forward. They are certainly more humanely motivated, and more "educational" than virtually every other show. And, like day-care centers, they provide an educational equalizer for lower-class families which allows the preschooler in the ghetto comparable access to training in the basic skills of literacy.

The Children's Television Workshop, which produced Sesame Street and which is now seeking to produce a series in reading instruction for the elementary grades, has as its admirable aim "the production of an entertaining television program with sound educational content that would teach the pre-schoolers useful knowledge, skills, and attitudes."[22] This aim certainly sets it apart from the mass of shows watched by young children which provide little besides shallow hysteria and fast-moving combat. Follow-up studies on children who were exposed to the show demonstrated that, for both disadvantaged and middle-class children, reading and counting abilities were more developed than were those of children who had not seen the programs. Ratings showed that Sesame Street reached more than half the nation's 12 million three-to-five-year-olds, and that the more they watched the more they learned.

Dr. Lloyd Morrisett, chairman of the board of trustees of Children's Television Workshop (along with its president Joan Cooney), worked diligently to guard their brain-child from the swarm of advertisers anxious to find a place among the kindly Muppets for their particular flaky cereal or mechanical contraption. Financial assistance from the Ford and Carnegie Foundations, the Office of Education, and additional grants from corporations enabled the program to expand their television time to reach larger audiences. Because of the outstanding quality of the program, it received the enthusiasm of critics and producers, and numerous other groups are now experimenting with other types of instruction to be broadcast nationally. Dr. Morrisett believes that, given the increasing number of students and limited resources,

> [t]elevision, or computers, or some combination of other technologies may help overcome reading failure . . . . [C]omputers

may give individual reading instruction to beginning readers, with each student proceeding at his own pace, and receiving as much remedial instruction as he needs . . . . I think the promise of computers and cassettes, of cable television and programmed instruction, films and games, is great.[23]

Because of Sesame Street's humane intentions and outstanding success, it is all the more important that we examine it critically.

What step in the evolution of TV do programs like Sesame Street represent? At first, parents gave TV the task of providing creative activity in which the child could participate (since the parents were doing nothing creative in the home). Now, parents in all social classes are giving TV the task of teaching their children the earliest, most fundamental skills of literacy. Thus the box is becoming not only baby-sitter, but schoolmarm.

If Sesame Street has brought enormous talent and money to this task, why should a parent not be willing to have the program instruct his or her child? It saves the parent time and energy; it might well teach skills more effectively; and the children obviously enjoy the Muppets and the music far more than their parents' uncertain, and perhaps sometimes irritable, attempts to teach. Why is it so important that this preschool learning process take place between a parent and a child?

During this stage of childhood, the rates of change of intellect, of the emotions, and of bodily control must maintain some degree of mutual balance. This basic balance is inherent in the groundplan of development because normally growth in one sector leads to, or is based upon, growth in another. Learning to walk, for example, will probably lead both to emotional issues (going where he has been forbidden) and cognitive gains (learning what mother is doing in other rooms). Without the advance in body control, these encounters would have remained outside the scope of the child's experience. Of course, this internal balance is always in moderate disequilibrium, for the various lines of development are always jumping a little "ahead" or lagging a little "behind."

But one striking imbalance has become so common in the technological state, that many psychologists and educators have felt compelled to comment on it. Anna Freud describes children with such an imbalance as having "exceptionally high verbal intelligence quotients which are coupled . . . with exceptional backwardness on the lines toward emotional maturity, toward companionship, toward body management."[24] Normally this imbalance is only minor and tends to be regulated by the everyday encounter with a caring parent who can sense such a disparity and respond to it. However, when instruction in cognitive skills is performed by a television, the normal tie between cognitive and emotional development in the three-to-five-year-old is severed.

The child learning counting or the letters of the alphabet from a family member must learn at the same time basic ways of *communication*. He must learn how to know what he is feeling (for example, that his mother is going too fast) and to know how to express it. Needless to say, no communication is required of him by the television. In fact, if his parents found him talking to the television, they would think something was wrong.

Learning with his mother, or with an older brother or sister, also requires *cooperation*. The child must be willing to concentrate when his "teacher" has the time, or to tell the other person that this is not a good time. He must deal with his feelings of not being as smart as his "teacher" and must be willing to learn from that person even though he is sometimes angry with him. He must behave in such a way that if he enjoys his "classes," his "teachers" will have them more often. The television, on the other hand, requires nothing and responds to nothing. It simply repeats, in verse and song and game, its lesson plan. No matter how entertaining it may be, it does not help the child develop his abilities to work together with another person, because it will continue to say its lines and go through the motions of its skits whether the child is asleep, impatient, participating, crying, or gone.

Learning skills with another person underscores for the child that he needs care and attention to meet the challenges of growing up and that, by facing those challenges actively, he makes the caring person happy. This is *mutuality,* "a mutual affirmation that others can be trusted to activate my being just as I can be trusted to activate theirs."[25] The learner does not feel passively taught, but actively engaged. He sees the "teacher" find pleasure in his response to her efforts, and realizes, as does the feeding infant, that by receiving one may give. As a result, he knows that he is a loved person in the eyes of others, *regardless* of how he spells or writes or counts.

A good number of educators and authorities believe that television makes children passive. Dr. Eugene Glynn, in his chapter of the volume *Television's Impact on American Culture,* states this position boldly:

> . . . passivity, receptiveness, being fed, taking in and absorbing what is offered . . . [t]hese needs of the child should be outgrown [as] his relationship to his mother changes. Basically, this growth depends in great part on the mother's attitude toward the child: her encouraging him to greater activity and self-reliance, the lessening of her feeding functions.[26]

Dr. Glynn argues that if the child continues to enjoy watching television, these traits may not be outgrown but remain unchanged, and that the long-term effect of TV viewing will be "passivity and dependence in multiple shapes and forms." More cautious analysts of TV's effect on children state not that television makes a child passive, but that it merely "encourages and reinforces those tendencies *when they exist in dangerous amounts.*"[27] This might be a worthwhile distinction among older children. But preschoolers are having their *first* encounter with the skills of literacy when they are exposed to TV. How passive or active they will later be in exercising these skills may well be largely determined by the setting in which they are first taught.

Learning from a machine at the preschool age tends to separate the learning of communication, cooperation, and mutuality from the learning of cognitive skills. Perhaps at this age no disastrous results manifest themselves. But we must see this as the begining of a long process, the next phase of which occurs in the classroom. For the first time in the history of man the preschool child can achieve basic cognitive growth, which ultimately leads to *technical* or *intellectual productivity*, without making commensurate progress in emotional growth, which is the basis for *interpersonal* and *introspective sensitivity*. If this mechanical procedure is continued, boys and girls may be raised to be economically productive without ever being able to ask any fundamental questions about their own or their society's experience.

Turn On Homes, Turn Off TV

Most frequently, attempts at TV reform focus on improvement of programming. The excitement about reforming television rests on the legitimate desire to free the airwaves for interests and programs which may not be shared by the top one hundred corporations. Young producers and directors, eminently successful in the movie industry, have already established a number of alternate media groups which are ready to spring into action as soon as the air time becomes available, either on the present networks or on cable TV.[28] Young lawyers have begun to investigate the diversity and decentralization possibilities of cable TV programming.[29] Radical mothers who founded Action on Children's Television (ACT), have demanded that the FCC ban all commercials from children's shows.[30] And John Holt has called for a radically new children's programming which, unlike Sesame Street, would not adjust children to existing schools but rather inspire children's curiosity so that present educational methods would be rendered obsolete.[31]

These actions for radical change are long overdue, and we should welcome and support them. But no matter how "child-oriented" or "well motivated" television might become, one further question must be asked. Might not less exposure to television, *no matter how exemplary its content*, be better for the growing child? Must we confine ourselves to asking how we can improve the quality of programming that our children watch bleary-eyed, for two, three, or four hours a day? The average child, by the time he reaches sixteen, has watched from 12,000 to 15,000 hours of television—that is, *about one and a half solid years, twenty-four hours a day!*[32] Our cultural memory is so short that, after only one generation of television, we have apparently lost the ability to question whether those three special hours every day of childhood might not be better spent.

Too many parents who see their children simply flock to the television do not ask if it is indeed best for the child. If children find it more interesting than anything else, they reason, it can't be that bad. This reasoning fails to proceed beyond the convenient assumptions of the technologists. Even when parents criticize television, they criticize its contents alone, not its false frame of reference.

The industrial system has pulled people into tightly-packed spaces, separated them from open land and swimmable water, isolated them in nuclear families and transient neighborhoods, taken the father out of the home for the entire day, and convinced mothers that they are not worth much unless they too are out there producing and consuming. Moreover, it has seen to it that not much of anything goes on in the home which interests the mother, much less the small children there. Then, and only then, did technological innovation bring the family television. When children willingly sit mesmerized by the screen, entranced by anything that the networks have deemed profitable to broadcast, they do not sit there because there is nothing else in the world that they would rather do. They sit there because there is nothing else in *their* world that they would rather do.

What if a child was allowed to have a few years of childhood in which to freely explore the interplay between his body and mind and the world of nature? What if he lived together with other children, of different ages, all growing and learning about the world? What if the domestic space he lived in was filled with several lively adults, all narrating their day's joys and sorrows? If this child were attracted to television at all, the attraction would be highly discriminating. Compared to *his* world, television would be a bore: its excitement shallow, its characters unreal, its plots repetitive, its laughter canned.

Fortunately, a growing number of parents have placed other things in the center of their living rooms—and their lives. They have realized that impoverished homes *require* TV; they could not have survived without the invention of television. If children just learned from each other, they might see through the TV hoax. But as long as they pay daily homage to the technological icon, such enlightenment can be forestalled, and perhaps prevented altogether.

No matter how liberal, open-minded, fast-moving, or child-oriented TV programming may be or become, the most important experiences with fantasy and learning during the early years of childhood should remain within the context of loving *human* relationships.

Radical parents should not automatically and without explanation supply their children with a television. They should let their school-age children ask for a television, and perhaps even require them to exert some kind of will, initiative, or desire in acquiring it. And, when their children reached the proper age, they would discuss the commercial basis of television and the particular psychological qualities of the medium with them. They would, above all, retain sufficient independence to decide that their home should be a creative *human* world in which all the members, especially the newest ones, may first encounter real and loving persons before they meet TV's concocted characters.

10.
School

an apprenticeship to gadgetry

One speaks to planners, designers, teachers, administrators: one hears about schedules and modules and curricular innovation—new systems. It is always 'materials' and 'technique,' the chronic American technological vice that murders as it saves. It is all so smug, so progressively right— and yet so useless, so far off the track. One knows that there is something else altogether . . . that lies at the heart of all yearning or wisdom or real revolution. It is that, precisely, that has been left out.

Peter Marin

Education . . . is being oriented toward the specialized end of producing technicians; and, as a consequence, toward the creation of individuals useful only as members of a technical group . . . . They will be servants, the most conformist imagineable, of the instruments of technique . . . . And education [will be] an exercise in conformity and an apprenticeship to whatever gadgetry is useful in a technical world.

Jacques Ellul

Teenagers who have been going to school for nearly a decade gain a new legal status when they turn sixteen. They become "voluntary" participants in the educational process. To learn is no longer their obligation, but ostensibly their right. Still, although sixteen-year-olds may legally leave school, they have been convinced socially and psychologically that they must stay longer.

Since the technological system requires specialized training, it exhorts young people to continue their education. Through all the available media it hammers home the idea that unless they do continue, they will find themselves jobless, friendless, and obsolete after graduation. Particularly for the half of the generation who do not continue on to college, the failure to receive a high school diploma is graphically depicted as a personal disaster.

Not only is a diploma necessary, but so are good grades and recommendations. Holding all the aces in this game of economic poker, the schools have traditionally succeeded in pulling off their bluff. They convince a generation from nursery school to graduation to play a game and play it enthusiastically, even though the rules and rewards have already been set in favor of the technological dealer and the real goals cannot be questioned. "You can't just ask: 'Well, what's the point of it?'" one high school student told Charles Silberman. "The point is to do it, *to get through* and get into college. But you have to figure the system or you can't win, because the odds are all on the house's side."[1] We may question, this student is saying, but we may not question too deeply. The ultimate penalty is that one may not get dealt in and thus never receive that cap-and-gown send-off into the world of the knowledge workers. Once the student is willing to apply his creative energies without question, he is on the way to becoming the technical-creative producer the system has groomed him to be.

Since the beginning of this century, it has been clear that schools were supposed to serve the industrial system. The "industrial era school," to use Alvin Toffler's phrase, was as necessary an invention as television, because not only new kinds of consumers, but new kinds of workers were required.

> Mass education was the ingenious machine constructed by industrialism to produce the kind of adults it needed . . . . [T]he whole idea of assembling masses of students (raw material) to be processed by teachers (workers) in a centrally located school (**factory**) was a stroke of industrial genius. The whole administrative hierarchy of education, as it grew up, followed the model of industrial bureaucracy. The very organization of knowledge into permanent disciplines was grounded on industrial assumptions. Children marched from place to place and sat in assigned stations. Bells rang to announce changes of time.[2]

As early as 1910, business practices began to provide the unquestioned models of administration on which the schools were run.[3] The schools became the reflecting mirror of the industrial system's changing image: once patterned on the factory model, now they are being made to fit the image of technical, corporate organizations. A decade after Robert McNamara introduced his "accountability" analyses into the Pentagon bureaucracy, it was thrust upon the schools. A few years after computer systems for management decision-making were devised, they were adapted to the schools. This mimicry reveals an educational system based not on the growth of the child, but rather on the growth of the economy. The child-learner of today is spared the physical violation of the child-laborer, for the advanced "technetronic" system does not need so many bodies. What it needs is more trained minds.

In their blind devotion to specialized training, the technological revolutionaries obscure a basic truth about learning. Albert Einstein wrote, on education:

> The same work may owe its origin to fear and compulsion, ambitious desire for authority and distinction, or to loving interest in the object and a desire for truth and understanding and thus to that divine curiosity which every healthy child possesses, but which so often is weakened early.[4]

But educational technicians, set deeply in their false frame of technique, can see only the product.

Technology in the Classroom

Today a high-powered promotion is underway for the classroom application of TV, filmstrips, tape cassettes, programmed instructional materials, and, finally, multi-million-dollar computers. There is a compelling logic for the introduction of this technology into the classroom. Because the overwhelmed and often poorly prepared teacher cannot cope with her thirty to forty pupils, the technicians argue, she deserves whatever technical assistance is available. This most recent technology has appeared precisely when most school systems face a formidable array of economic and human problems: demands for more individual instruction, understaffed schools, teachers' demands for pay raises, rising building costs, and, finally, taxpayers voting down bond issues for education.

In this setting, the advocates of "Computer-Managed Instruction" (CMI) and "Computer-Assisted Instruction" (CAI) find an ideal situation for yet another technical solution to human problems. "Step closer folks," computer salesmen are saying across the country, "let me show you what I have here. This machine, for only 35 cents to 50 cents an hour, can teach your children most of the basic skills, and many of the more complicated subjects too. It's cheap, never strikes, never demands higher wages, and never reports sick. And best of all, it will teach your child with more individual attention and with greater success than a human teacher."[5]

This is the pitch which many schools are hearing, and to many it sounds enticingly simple. They are promised a device which will match or even outperform the "good teacher"; "any average program" will provide the sensitivity and intelligence which, until now, have only been provided by the few outstanding teachers. With CMI, the student never comes in direct contact with the computer itself. On the contrary,

> . . . student–teacher interaction is maintained in the classroom. The student utilizes currently available instructional materials. The computer is brought into the program behind the teacher as an aid. The computer becomes an informational system which records the students' learning and academic history and his program of studies, scores the tests and examinations, and furnishes on a retrieval basis this information back to the teacher. The computer monitors the day-to-day progress of the youngster through the program.[6]

This excerpt from a promotional booklet describes a CMI system called PLAN (Program for Learning in Accordance with Needs). If the school system can afford this system, maintain the developers, it will allow the teacher to use her time most effectively, by enabling her to treat each child with greater knowledge of his individual abilities.

The PLAN
Is Invisible

When technicians interfere with a human process, they disguise their external control in the language of progressive liberalism. Project PLAN announces that its "individualized instruction" assigns "appropriate learning tasks to students according to their needs," and defines "appropriate ways of accomplishing these learning tasks." It prides itself on its use of the "systems approach"—the technical creative planner's form of *hubris.*

> By systems approach, it is intended to indicate that *all* the relevant factors in the situation are considered, not just selected aspects. In other words, the *whole* educational program of a student, rather than just specific parts of the program is treated . . . . Project PLAN also deals with guidance aspects as well as academic aspects. We are talking about a computer-managed system of individualized instruction which accounts for the *total* educational activities of the youngster.[7]

All the teacher must do is to code the instructional materials as required by the computer so that it can "monitor" a given student's progress. PLAN takes it upon itself to develop "Teaching–Learning Units" (TLU) which "prescribe various learning activities by which the youngster may accomplish the assigned objectives." TLUs not only assign the objectives, but evaluate the student's performance "relative to the educational objectives." The computer then recommends one of two alternatives for the student: he is either "advised to go on to the next set of objectives," or he is "re-cycled until he masters the objectives originally assigned."

PLAN advocates repeatedly stress the flexibility of their program. But as always there is a catch. Choices can be made "within limits." And activities may be selected "in terms" of the prescribed TLUs. What is objectionable here is not that there are limits and terms to the learning process, since *any* instruction would have some sort of framework, but that the limits and terms are not openly specified and explicitly acknowledged either to the students or to the teacher. The limits and terms are determined not by a teacher who stands in front of the class, and not even by the elected school board, but by the requirements of the computer and the objectives of the programmers.

The PLAN planners are committed to developing "independent learners" as long as the learners do not become so independent that they want to decide themselves how they want to learn. Their definition of "independent learning" is devious and self-serving. Although PLAN claims to put the responsibility for learning "back on the student" (as if it had ever really been anywhere else), it keeps the ultimate responsibility for itself. PLAN's designers assert dogmatically that the more "independent" a learner becomes, the more important the instructional materials become. By definition, "the student learns through the activities provided by the instructional materials." In short, PLAN seeks to make students learn more effectively what someone else assigns while convincing them that they are doing it "by themselves."

The PLAN designers have their own peculiar philosophy of education. The teacher, they willingly explain in the language of progressivism, does not teach but "facilitates learning." What this really means is that "students actually don't learn from teachers; *they learn from materials* in much the same way that sick people don't get well from doctors, but rather from medication."[8] This statement by a proponent of computer instruction is probably the most eloquent description of technical creativity that we have yet encountered. This single sentence renders the concept of education (as well as the concept of health) utterly mechanical. Anything which the computer cannot process—for example, growth in critical thinking and self-direction which leads the student to question the sequence of operations the computer requires him or her to perform—is simply not education.

Long before computers became commonplace, Maria Montessori wrote that self-control, determination, and cooperation are traits which require interpersonal relationships. It would be impossible to develop such qualities, she wrote, "by keeping children motionless, seated side by side; under such conditions 'relations between children' cannot be established. . . ."[9] A half-century later, in 1964, the New York World's Fair presented the "School of the Future" (an exposition of "modern" educational method now being implemented in many schools), in which each student becomes what Lewis Mumford calls a solitary "learning grub" . . .

... in a closed compartment, appropriately egg-shaped, in which information would be processed and fed to him from a central station .... The isolation cell, one of the cruelest forms of punishment ever devised ... is now proposed as the standard school equipment.[10]

Computer hucksters do not only want profits. They know they are part of an enormous industry which will double by 1975 and, it is prophesized, will surpass the oil and auto industries in total size before the year 2000. But they also believe they are fulfilling a historic role: the transformation of "the character of civilization," to quote *Time*'s panegyric of the computer industry.[11] Their progressive intentions are negated, however, by their own technique.

The CMI system of computerized evaluation may merely confine the student's mind, but CAI systems, such as that described by Mumford, actually chain it. With CAI, students are not only evaluated by the computer, but taught by it. The learning process takes place in front of its screen. The passive student no longer asks: "Is this going to be graded?" in order to decide how hard he should try. Now he must ask: "Is this on the computer program?" Perhaps to convey a sense of the program's ultimate wisdom, the computer designers have modestly named one of the most advanced CAI projects PLATO.

PLATO is Programmed

Developed at the Computer-based Education Research Laboratory (CERL) at the University of Illinois, *Pro*grammed *L*ogic for *A*utomatic *T*eaching *O*perations stresses its progressive aims just as the CMI promoters did. The expected applications of the system must be enormous, for the federal government has already massively subsidized the CERL computer installation. Indeed, the goal sounds humane when explained by CERL's head: to provide "individualized instruction tailored to the specific preparation and motivation of a given student." Students, teachers, and administrators are all enthusiastic about PLATO, claim its programmers, because the student "may proceed at his own pace and can exert considerable choice in the selection of alternative teaching strategies and methods of presentation." The PLATO proponents are even interested in encouraging "critical thinking":

> To encourage development of critical thinking skills, *the author sets up the teaching strategy and presents the students with questions or problems* so the student must think about what information he needs, about possible solutions to the problems or sources of information, interpret the data gathered, and test his solution. The computer immediately provides an appropriate feed-back to the open-ended questions, thus reinforcing a correct approach, or in the case of an incorrect response, encouraging the student to a new approach.[12]

The only problem with this "critical thinking" is: *whose* problem is the student trying to solve? *whose* information is he using? and *whose* "correct approach" is the student being reinforced to adopt?

By replacing the student–teacher interface with a computer–student interface, the concept of "critical thinking" is rendered conformist. It completely loses the creative quality of truly liberal education. Unlike students taught by progressive human education, computer-taught students cannot explore the assumptions and values on which the choice of subject matter and style of instruction is based. As Robert Boguslaw has noted in a thorough critique of the technically creative "systems analysts," we can accept that the computer can "think" faster than human beings and might even devise a "better" system of values. "But they wouldn't be ours. And they wouldn't be the machine's. They would be [the programmer's]. And that's the rub."[13] The pseudo-objectivity of PLATO programmers' values becomes most evident when they extend their domain into the social sciences, in which even computer programs cannot avoid dealing with man. Those who praise PLATO would have us believe that, as in the Athenian gardens, a dialogue between a wise man and inquisitive students is occurring. Nothing could be further from the truth. Two examples of PLATO's programs reveal that beneath the technical platitudes lurk some dangerous ideas about what learning and critical thinking are.

The Politics
of the Machine

The first of these two programs is a lesson in future social and technological developments called "Delphi." Its repressive features are shared by most programs in these fields.[14]

> DELPHI is an exploration in possible future technological and social developments. Examples of developments are intelligence drugs, credit-card economy, manned lunar base, air-cushion vehicles, synthetic food production, and US involved in limited war. Using his keyboard, the "explorer" forges ahead into the future investing the resources allotted to him in the development he considers most desirable. The computer calculates the constantly changing probabilities of the developments on the basis of the investments made and the way that the developments are interrelated.

The range of possible future developments in this program is predefined; the developments that *are* explored reveal the programmer's values. Among the examples one does not find social developments such as the conquest of poverty and malnutrition, nor more equitable medical care, nor more humane schools. The computer does not raise these scenarios of the future, one supposes, because the programmer didn't feed them to it. *But what if they concern the student?* And what if the student thinks he should invest his resources in such goals regardless of the computer's assessment of which investment will bring the most "return"? The computer leaves the student in the position of a low-level bureaucrat: he can make all the unimportant computations while the "boss" does the thinking. A student who accepts this as education is like the demented prisoner who thinks he is free because the warden tells him he can wander anywhere in his cell.

The second example of a PLATO program, called POLIS

I, places the student in the role of a police chief in a small town. He is expected to make decisions "consonant with current interpretations of the US Constitution" as he seeks to deal with the various factions in his town, such as the mayor, city council, militants, etc. By definition, the computer wants trainees for the *status quo*.

> In making his choices the student can ask his "city attorney" for clarification of numerous concepts, such as "clear and present danger," and will be provided relevant excerpts from court decisions . . . . [H]e must make a decision which is defensible by constitutional standards. . . . [F]eedback is limited to informing the student (through the city attorney) why unconstitutional choices are unacceptable and suggesting that he reconsider his decision.

The computer (which means, of course, the programmer) is the anonymous judge, since the data bank makes the crucial decision as to which legal cases are relevant to a given trial. The computer has even less difficulty that did Sheriff "Bull" Connor in deciding that "unconstitutional choices are unacceptable." Martin Luther King and his marchers, though heroes in the history of human freedom, are merely aberrations from this particular program. We can only be grateful that they, and the US Supreme Court justices, were not educated with the "individualized instruction" now available. If the PLATO apostle is correct in concluding about DELPHI and POLIS I that "teaching computer might to some extent do for social science what the microscope did for biology," we can only shudder at the absence of critical thought in that future of social science.

The computer salesman feels his program is educationally successful if students learn more facts and retain them longer than do students taught by people. Measuring only the product rather than the process of education, he will take any steps necessary to make children learn more efficiently. The false frame he wants educators to accept is that learning consists only of what can be measured. Thus, in essays with Skinnerian titles like "Feedback Procedures in Programmed

Instruction," programmers report on experiments designed to find the optimal "reinforcing" method.

The central question in these experiments concerns the concept of "knowledge of correct response" (or KCR). The debate within the educational computer industry has focused on which is best: KCR feedback immediately after the student has answered the computer's question, delayed KCR, or no KCR at all. Since present data indicates that computer-taught students remember more facts with immediate KCR, programmers have deemed that immediate KCR should serve as the criterion of the best instruction method.[15] These programmers conveniently forget that, to complete any *independent* project which requires originality and self-reliance, perhaps the most important character trait is *will*, the ability to choose a goal oneself and to have the necessary self-confidence to achieve it. Carl Rogers refers to this ability when he speaks of internal rather than external evaluation as a basic component of any creative act.[16]

If in the modern school the children will receive immediate acceptance or rejection of every answer they make to each small question in a geometry proof or Russian translation, they will have become part of an assembly-line verification process. Doubt and uncertainty will have been abolished; but so will determination and self-confidence. The student will never learn to live with the self-doubt that is the constant companion of any creative person, whether a painter or an innovative businessman or a revolutionary. This reinforcement ritual will make the student a storehouse of information, but will leave him ever in need of outside authority and external validation for any action he takes. The system seems designed for producing the archetypal spineless bureaucrat who is able only to carry out orders sanctioned from above. These technical educational devices undermine the human potentials which, if permitted to grow, can lead to creative men and women. Computer education establishes school for the child who is, in Montessori's terms, "weak of will," and who will "readily adapt himself to a school where all the children are kept seated and motionless, listening, or pretending to listen."[17] A generation which accepts the technicians' schools, will also accept their jobs.

The Teaching Business

Technical-creative education wants measurably defined objectives. When education is defined as "what can be easily expressed and measured,"[18] then *accountability*, a cost-efficiency analysis which seeks to achieve higher test scores with a minimal expenditure of money, becomes inevitable. The industrial revolution brought bureaucratization and rationalization to the economic process. The technological revolution is now bringing bureaucratization and rationalization to the educational process. When this transformation is complete, the child-laborer will have become the child-learner.

The most concrete invasion of the classroom by the industrial system is exemplified by *performance contracting*, a practice of contracting out to private firms for the instruction in public schools and paying them according to the number of children who achieve the test performance level specified in the contract.[19] On July 14, 1970, the Office of Economic Opportunity selected six companies to teach reading and mathematics in 18 school districts, with contracts totaling $5.6 million. Nixon's man at OEO, Donald Rumsfeld, decided that the way to compensate for years of neglect of urban schools was to push accountability.[20] Because of this high-level support, learning-corporation heads are estimating no fewer than 250 performance contracts by the early 1970s. Charles Blaschke of Education Turnkey Systems has suggested a hundred-fold increase in the performance contract market, from $250,000 in fiscal 1969 to $250 million in fiscal 1971. Obviously, this rate of growth makes the teaching of children into a promising market.

Since in performance contracting the profit a firm makes depends on whether students score above or below the test performance specified in the contract, measurement of results stands at the core of the enterprise. Often the contracting educational firm itself designs the test by which the performance of its pupils will be measured. The firm first defines education in terms of its own test, then shows how normal educational methods do not meet the terms of that test, *then* shows how its own methods will meet those terms.

That one of the first firms awarded a performance contract, Dorsett Education Systems, actually taught their pupils specific parts of the test by which the success of their firm's instruction would be assessed did not trouble many educators. Despite this corporate cribbing, the "success" of Dorsett's activity has stimulated excitement across the country. It appears that no limits can be placed on the instructional methods employed to achieve the desired measure of performance; these firms are legally bound to care only for the child's skills, not for the child himself.

When a contracting firm enters a school, it naturally takes along its own machines. Since often the contracting firm also manufactures computers or games, it gets to use them free of charge, and gains free publicity among the captive student audience. And in the long run, a wide range of corporations other than the contracted firms stand to profit from the classroom industry. IBM's Science Research Associates, the Xerox education division, the GE–*Time* venture called General Learning, Westinghouse Learning Corporation, the Raytheon Educational Company, are some of the giants. These firms were temporarily disappointed in the mid-Sixties because teaching children was not as easily operationalized as making stoves or computers, and the response to their sales pitch was disheartening.[21]

But the federal government now provides a powerful ally. Dr. Leon Lessinger, former Associate Commissioner of the Bureau of Elementary and Secondary Schools at the US Office of Education, enthusiastically reports that the nation of accountability is being accepted by leading government officials so quickly that schools will never be able to return to pre-accountability days. Noting that the Nixon Administration heartily endorses performance contracting, Lessinger envisions the government utilizing its federal aid to promote industry management of schools, a move which would create a potential market of $1 billion or more.

The growing alliance of cost-minded government officials,

computer sellers, education corporations, and beleaguered and underfinanced school officials has cast the whole question of schools and schooling into a false frame of technical creativity. The questions this alliance asks are threefold: Will schools be able to raise enough money for computer hardware? Will computer producers be able to lower their prices enough so that CAI and CMI will be more efficient than human instruction? And will advances in computer technology be rapid enough that performance contractors will be able to measure pupil achievement of assigned objectives? The technicians would like nothing more than to seduce everyone into debating the financial efficiency of computer instruction and performance contracting. Others have already willingly confronted them on this issue.[22] But few critics have challenged them by asking: *what happens to the child?*

That computerized education is technically feasible and economically efficient does not mean it is humanly beneficial. The claim that computers will do better and faster what is now being done poorly and slowly is admirable, except that "much of what we are doing now in education is wrong," writes Emmanuel Mesthene. "If technology helps us do it very efficiently, it may lead us beyond the point where we can detect and correct our errors."[23]

All the computer pushers' claims boil down to this: "You can't live up to your ideals of education with one teacher for thirty or more students. And you don't have the money to get more teachers. So we have some hardware which will leave the impression that you are really providing the individualized instruction which you always claimed was your goal, although in fact the instruction will be more impersonal than ever before."

Whether intentional or not, the computer technicians are fostering a concept of education by which energy, money, and talents will be spent on mechanical and electronic equipment at the expense of the genuine education of teachers and students. Teachers will not be freed for the pursuit of humane educational goals by their mechanical servants. As Michael Wallach explains:

Given the overwhelming commitment of our society to science and technology as a prime value, and given a growing industrial commitment to the propagation of automated instruction . . . teachers will not be on top of the pyramid, freed from disagreeable chores by labor-saving devices. Rather, on top of the pyramid will be the educational engineers who fashion devices and programs for automated instruction, and the educational administrators who route the students through these devices and programs.[24]

Viewed from the child's perspective, writes Wallach, professor of psychology at Duke University, all this hardware "may well constitute an anachronism." Instead of a human revolution in the development of both the educators and the educated, we support technological innovation—and then call it progress!

The Classroom Marketplace

To voice such criticism is more than rhetoric. It is an essential counterforce to an overwhelming barrage of technical double talk. So deeply has the panacea of technique penetrated educational strategy that even teachers do not protest the mechanization of the classroom. Writes one trainer of teachers in *Teacher,* a professional magazine:

> . . . technology is really the only salvation for today's hard-pressed teacher. For admit it, no matter how dedicated we are, no matter how willing, or how industrious, there's a limit to our time, our skills, and our talents. We can regroup our children and departmentalize each other and objectify learning behavior until we're blue in the face and we still won't be able to provide the kind of truly individualized, educational program we now know our children need. *We've simply got to have help . . . . We've got to get together with the producers of the hardware, the writers of the software, with our administrators and supervisors to communicate our thoughts and hopes . . . .*[25]

Conceiving of themselves as the neutral instructor of some body of fixed knowledge, such teachers are alienated from their own resourcefulness. They think themselves unable to relate general areas of knowledge to the specific needs and interests of the students.

Raised themselves in the industrial-era school; trained by schools of education working on the same principles; bound by a curriculum and certification regulations which are impractical, mismanaged, and archaic; school teachers all too often join the administrators in welcoming antiseptic, "teacher-proof" educational methods. Underpaid, understaffed, and overwhelmed as they are, they let the responsibility for humane education be lifted from their weary shoulders by the high-sounding phrases of those technicians who speak of "individualized instruction," or "creativity," but define it in terms of their techniques rather than in terms of the growing teenager.

Whether it is a professor with a new textbook or a computer seller with a new program, the aim is to bypass the inept teacher. Teachers need no longer teach, but can simply administer the materials—like the doctor whose drugs are far more important than he himself.

In the vacuum created by the disappearance of a real teacher, the technicians enter. In full-color three-page magazine ads, such monoliths as AT&T provide a frightening answer to the perennial education question: "What do you do when a child gets lost in the crowd?"

> As a teacher, you worry: Will Mary quit trying, because she can't keep up with the class? And what about Mark—is he bored because the pace is too slow?
>
> The practical reality of teaching children as a group makes it difficult to give each one the individual attention he needs. Students at both ends of the scale, with totally different rates of learning, suffer the most.
>
> Faced with this perplexing challenge, many educators and administrators have sought ways in which newly developed teaching tools may help to individualize instruction. One such teaching innovation is Computer Assisted Instruction, in which a computer is put to use drilling, testing, and reinforcing concepts which heretofore required the efforts of a teacher . . . again and again and again.[26]

One of the most difficult educational issues, the technicians explain, is really very simple. *When Mary or Mark get lost in the crowd, you remove the crowd and give them their very own machine.* So AT&T pushes its wares, feeding the dangerous illusion that children educated via machines will make better human beings, all beneath the picture of a small black boy with a big grin on his face and his arms warmly embracing a computer console keyboard. "We could not afford to give you a concerned human being," our society has told this little boy. That message will not be forgotten.

AT&T is not alone. Electronics outfits and steel companies have a vested interest as well. Aware that all hardware in classes means new markets, Republic Steel ("You Can Take the Pulse of Progress at Republic Steel") finances full-page ads which proclaim that "someday a single computer will give individual instruction to scores of students," and that such "individualized instruction" will spark "independent thinking." Their ad closes: "The long reach of steel from Republic is probing into every area where man's imagination needs it—from schoolroom . . . to defense." With such powerful merchants propagandizing for the mechanical classroom, each radical voice raised in opposition is that much more needed. Yet education journals and "concerned" periodicals raise few criticisms; and when they do, it is within the false frame of costs and techniques that the industry itself has defined.

Generally regarded as a "conservative," Bruno Bettelheim argues that beneath today's angry college youth's concern about Vietnam and pollution is a deeper feeling that

> youth has no future because modern technology has made them socially irrelevant, and as persons, insignificant. . . . It is modern technology with its automation and its computers that seems to make man and his work obsolete, seems to rob him of his personal importance in the scheme of things . . . .
>
> It makes sense that much of their battle is fought in and around the school, for it is education that prepares us for our place in the work of society. And if education today prepares us only to be replaceable items in the production machine, to program its computers, then it seems to prepare us not for a

chance to emerge in importance as persons, but only to serve the machine better.[27]

When Bettelheim described the horrors of Nazi Germany, General Dwight D. Eisenhower made his description required reading for all officers on the European front. But when he describes the American classroom, his advice is ignored.

Because human solutions are so alien to their way of thinking, the technicians cannot bring themselves to leave power and control in the hands of free individuals. By their reliance on technology, they limit themselves to solutions in which a few experts have disproportionate control. Resources poured into machinery and materials create a self-fulfilling prophecy of anonymous, alienated individuals skilled enough to run a machine but powerless to redirect it.[28]

In classrooms which cultivate such individuals, children are naturally frustrated. True to form, the technicians come up with a frightening antidote for the very restlessness their world has caused.

Drugs: in School

Last Fourth of July [1970], after a day of celebrating their inalienable rights to liberty and the pursuit of happiness, Americans were jolted to learn from the Huntley–Brinkley program that doctors in Omaha, Nebraska, are giving hundreds of school children so-called behavior modification drugs, to "make them behave better in school . . . ."[29]

Something seemed to be ailing a large number of children, something called hyperkinesis, a strange inability to concentrate and sit still which leads to compulsive movement and excessive "disturbance." This condition affects perhaps one million school children. Estimates of its frequency run as high as ten out of every hundred kids.[30] Amphetamines and amphetamine-like drugs can control this disorder, some doctors say, by blocking out the neural messages which make the child fidgety, rendering him quieter and more able to do "his work." Medical support for the use of these drugs comes from many quarters, including the American Medical Association's Council on Drugs. Most parents of the Omaha children support the sanctioned drug use; the AMA's *American Medical News* summarized their position by asking "What's all the fuss about?"[31]

The "fuss" was created by men and women who feared that these drugs, if not already grossly misapplied, would soon become like computers: a slipshod, artificial cover-up of human problems which our culture is determined to ignore.

Establishment drug "pushers" know very well that comprehensive medical diagnosis of hyperkinesis is still lacking. And they must also know that complaints about a child's behavior come initially from a harassed teacher who is tired of dealing with especially difficult children when there are thirty other children begging for her attention. Trusting the teacher's judgment, and without interference from parents, doctors prescribe their drugs, brushing out the door the one crucial question: *where do all these troubled children come from?*

The list of possible explanations is endless. Are these children products of overdrugged childbirths? Are they malnourished? Do they lack the necessary trace chemicals for normal brain functioning?[32] Are these trace elements the same ones that are lost in food processing? Is the condition environmentally caused? Or a product of urban living? Why do more poor children have this "physiological" disturbance? Have the children whose behavior appears hyperkinetic been thoroughly examined by a neurologist to confirm the lay diagnosis—and if suburban kids were so examined, what about kids from the inner city? Are they perhaps simply bored? Is this physiological behavior the result of dehumanizing conditions in the child's classroom and in his community?

Once the use of drugs is accepted, *any pressing reason to ask these questions will have been removed.* Whatever cause lurks behind these children's behavior—physical, educational, social, psychological—may remain undiscovered. Behavior in classrooms will not have inherently changed, it will simply have been deadened by mind-affecting drugs.[33]

School environments must provide space for children to

explore if they are to prevent boredom and frustration. Urban schools particularly fail to provide such space. In one urban school, typical of many others, children spend the noon hour in their classrooms with sack lunches, supervised by a small fraction of the faculty, so that the teachers may take a well-deserved lunch break. The understaffed supervisors cannot risk taking the large number of children outdoors, so they all stay inside. The gym teacher at this inner-city school customarily deals with misbehavior by requiring that all the children sit still and not talk, causing them to forfeit their gym period. The school has encountered a number of hyperkinetic children, to whom drugs have been prescribed. To sum up the picture as presented in this school: hundreds of children, whose counterparts a few generations ago would have been punished for being too "idle," are now being asked to sit stock still for most if not all of the day.[84] Those who do not, or cannot, comply may be drugged.

An elementary school child, facing the joint decision of his teachers, parents, and physician, will hardly know enough, or have courage enough, to rebel against drug treatment. (If he did, it would probably be considered simply more evidence of his affliction!) As Edward T. Ladd, professor of education at Emory University, argues, this practice raises not only medical and educational issues but legal ones. Echoing the call for a "fetal advocate" by concerned obstetricians, a "consumer rights commission" by worried nutritionists, and a "certified education accountant" by opposition educators, Professor Ladd asks for a "medical lawyer" to be attached to all public schools to protect the rights of children.[85]

It is children, the most defenseless group in our society, who suffer most from the alienation of the technicians' society. And when they demonstrate in growing numbers that we have given them a physically or mentally unbearable world, we respond like mindless technicians by dosing out drugs to *make* it bearable. Indeed, this is how adults have been trained to treat themselves. Over 225 million prescriptions for psychoactive drugs were filled by pharmacists in 1970, as compared with 166 million five years before. Conflicting estimates of the percentage of American adults using mood- or mind-affecting drugs hover around the one-third mark, but all agree that whatever the exact figure is, it is rapidly going up.[36]

More and more adults are using these drugs, true-life "opiates of the people," as a defense against the pressures of the technological society. A group of concerned doctors and psychologists maintain in their book *Mystification and Drug Misuse* that mind-affecting drugs do not

> reach the source of the anxiety or misery and do not remedy the unfavorable social and interpersonal arrangements and personal circumstances which generate anxiety or unhappiness . . . . To decry the use and misuse of drugs by young people while paying so little attention to the growing use and misuse of psychoactive agents in general . . . is highly misleading and unproductive.

Irrational drug use, they say, is not a medical question "but a social, political, and economic one."[37]

One need only pick up the medical journals, whose very existence depends on drug company advertising, to realize the drugs are now being peddled to deal with "the anxiety that comes from not fitting in," for the "difficulties that Susie experiences when she goes to college," and for all "the common adjustment problems of our society." No wonder school children are now being asked to join this pharmaceutical Russian roulette! It is simply another manifestation of what Dr. Selig Greenberg calls our "overmedicated society" which is now in the throes of an "epidemic of irrational prescriptions." Like all technically creative solutions, it breeds greater dependence on its own methods. The estimated 1.5 million hospitalizations per year in the US due to adverse reactions to drugs require, of course, higher health bills and more medication.[38] Instances such as this, multiplied many times in other areas of medicine, have created a health-care system which Senator Edward Kennedy has called "the fastest growing failing business" in the US.[39]

Irrational drug prescription is deadening the capacity of

human beings, especially small children, to react to the de-humanizing conditions which the triumph of technology has bequeathed. From childbirth, through school, into adulthood, and even in nursing homes for the aged (where excessive use of tranquilizers make caretaking much easier) [40]—life is being oiled, the stages of life streamlined. When the human parts of the machine fail to work smoothly with the technical, they are reshaped and relubricated until at last they do.

In this way, the circle closes in upon itself, and a colossal rigidity is imprinted on the cycle of generations. Alienation before labor can become so complete that, when a generation enters the laboring world, it will lack the human strength to rebel against the conditions the system imposes. That generation's children will then be left utterly exposed, and technology at its zenith may make of them anything it wishes.

Alienated Learning

The old adult dispute between management and labor was "Who decides what we *earn*?" Now the generational dispute between high school administrators and students is "Who decides what we *learn*?" If someone else decides when, where, and how the student is to focus his mental energy, then the student is alienated from his own potentials for self-direction, just as the worker is alienated from his labor. Work now done in public schools, explains Professor Philip Jackson,

> entails becoming engaged in a purposeful activity that has been prescribed for us by someone else, an activity in which we would not at that moment be engaged if it were not for some system of authority relationships. . . .The teacher, although he may disclaim the title, is the student's first "Boss."[41]

If the machine's conception of freedom triumphs, the computer-bred generation may well lose the ability to ask "Who decides what we learn?" They will have been told for years that they are "free to study those things that are of most interest . . . within the broad limits set by what materials have been prepared by the computer."[42] Students up to now have been taught by teachers with visible fallibilities undisguised by shiny chrome. These students must feel that what they are studying matters, if only to themselves. The teacher must do his part to convince the student of the value of the material. If the student rejects the material, he knows that the teacher must respond to his rejection in one way or another.

The problem is not merely one of relevance, though even today American students are still stuck in course sequences about the lineage of the English Kings. The problem is seeing that students relate directly to the subjects being studied. Current teaching techniques disassociate a body of knowledge from its roots and applications. Biology classes spend weeks on leaf collections and only hours on the ecology of the students' environment. Health classes enumerate anatomical terms, but do not comment on the effects of drugs upon the body. Home economics transmits some recipes, but does not discuss where food comes from or what happens to it when it is processed. Physical education glorifies popular team sports, but offers no counsel on physical activities that can be carried on outside the school environment.

To require knowledge of fashionably relevant subjects instead of the traditional high school curriculum is obviously not the solution. It is arrogant and dangerous folly for administrators to decide unilaterally what students should learn, no matter what the subject. Teachers are then placed like foremen over the laboring students, and they themselves become pawns in the hierarchy of the knowledge factory. These bought-off teachers (who in some performance contract schools are actually called "managers") tell young people what they are supposed to learn whether or not students want to know it.

The classroom is predicated on the child's lack of will and self-knowledge, and the school is structured on this same repressive idea. When after years of this schooling children have indeed become apathetic to anything but grades, educators point to their resulting low motivation as *cause* for the original educational approach.[43] How this contrasts with the educational philosophy of someone like John Holt, who believes that only the student himself can choose what knowledge he needs most! "He may not do it very well," Holt points out, "but he can do it a hundred times better than we can."[44]

Marx is most often thought to have been referring to an industrial, material product when he wrote that "the object produced by labor, its product, now stands opposed to it as an alien being, as independent of the producer." But Marx also recognized the possibility of a person's alienation *before labor* involving "the products of his own brain."[45]

Having lost all interest in the activity itself, alienated school children do their work merely for its *exchange value*: they pursue topics and reply to answers and conform to methods of inquiry which have been chosen by the manager of the classroom. Like the worker who cannot leave his job because he needs the wages to feed himself and his family, high school students are convinced they cannot abandon the classroom or its manipulative teaching processes because they need their diploma to find labor in the knowledge market.

The mechanization of the factory required that every motion of the worker's body conform precisely to the pace and pattern of the machine. The introduction of standardized, programmed materials adapted to computer technology represents the extension of this process into the classroom. In education, the minute specification of the child-learner's activity is aimed at mental rather than physical operations. Machine instruction breaks down all learning into the smallest possible steps and strictly orders the sequence of those steps. Individually Prescribed Instruction, yet another example of the programmed instruction being pushed by the US Office of Education, defines each operation the child is to perform so narrowly that Charles Silberman felt compelled to complain that "what is crucial to the system . . . is not the adjective 'individually' but the verb 'prescribed,' "[46] just as the Soviet Union's "democratic centralism" is a good deal more "centralized" than "democratic."

We may choose to call this "education for docility," as does Silberman, or "authoritarian education," as it was termed by the old progressives, but none of these terms improve upon Marx's concept of *alienation*. For Marx, alienation is the condition of the man who fails to achieve "self-realization," and cannot therefore achieve "true freedom." The development of human power "is its own end," argues Marx, while in alienated labor

> . . . the product of labor, the commodity, seems to determine the nature and end of human activity. In other words, the materials that should serve life come to rule over its content and goal, and the consciousness of man is completely made victim to the relationships of material production.[47]

When someone or some*thing* else decides for them what matters and how much it matters, students become alienated from their own capacity for decision. These students have knowledge (technical proficiency), but they have no will. They have skills, but no independent values.

Some high school students have begun to see through the sophisticated forms of control that authorities try to exercise and are beginning to recognize what is being done to them in the name of "acquiring knowledge."[48] The calculus class, unquestioned in the immediate post-Sputnik years, is no longer sacrosanct. Neither is unquestioning preparation for the College Boards.[49] A wave of students determined to escape the knowledge prison guarded by education-measurement experts will not be put off by allusions to the promised land of high achievement.

Getting Together:
School

At last we must create schools based on people, not machines or techniques. When only a fraction of the people who should be involved in education of the next generation participate in it, then education must inevitably resort to dehumanizing techniques.

Once *every* parent was a teacher. Every mother and father taught their children the skills of the field, the shop, the hearth. After the industrial revolution, the father was gone from the home, and mother could not provide the technical training which society required of children. So mass education became the domain of professionals, and parents relegated yet another of their social functions to a bureaucracy. Mute and timid, men and women permitted the industrial system to transform the relationship between generations so that it would fit the system's needs.

All the rhetorical liberalism of computerized "individualized instruction" stems from one fact: there are too many children for too few teachers in our public schools. Reformers may play with ideas such as flexible scheduling, open classrooms, independent study, and so forth, but the same dilemma remains: teachers, good and bad alike, do not have enough hands, eyes, energy, or emotions to care individually for over ten times the number of children in the average family. Unless we accept the bizarre prospect of a computer network instructing and evaluating our schoolchildren, we must infuse the classroom with more human energy. *We must change the pattern of human relationships in education.*

We have already mentioned the importance of parental participation at the preschool level. This participation must continue throughout the school years. Many mothers with high school and college degrees sit idle and bored in their homes, or at luncheons, thinking it too late to start a career. Their teenage children, meanwhile, sit idle and bored in the school classroom because their teachers do not have the time or energy (even if they have the will) to care for the oversized, adopted "family" with which they have been left. Parents—the original educators—have abandoned education to the professionals and limited themselves to PTA or school board meetings. Perhaps one reason so many women feel the meaninglessness of motherhood is because the educational system, with the machinery it acquires to replace women, has excluded them from their rights and responsibilities.

Mothers could refresh their education by becoming immersed in the process once again. Contact with the children of other families and neighborhoods might help them understand their own children better. Already in British "informal schools," mothers are invited to drop by and help out, and they often do. In those schools, which are now being experimentally adapted in a number of American school systems, no materials are as crucial to the program as "simple talk"—

> spontaneous and companionable conversation, storytelling, play-acting, communication with interested adults. From such experiences, both reading and writing grow—an insight which clashes sharply with traditional restrictions on talking in the classroom.[50]

When children start doing, rather than just sitting, no single teacher can offer her two or three dozen children the interest that they want. Although some may prefer computers to assist the teacher, for it has the shiny glitter of progress *and* it creates a new market, it is far better to seek to interest mothers. Education can then remain decentralized, and not only the students will grow but, perhaps, their mothers too.

As the women's movement rightly asks, why only women? The reasons for involving fathers in education are compelling. Students, particularly those in their early teens, have begun to visualize themselves in specific adult roles, and are questioning their own abilities as well as the relative value of various occupations. Since the modern urban child hardly ever shares in the active working lives of men in varied occupations, men should be encouraged to participate occasionally in the classroom side-by-side with mothers and teachers. These working men (and women) could bring to the appropriate classes some idea of their working experience. Employers permit their employees to be absent for jury duty; it would be strange if they would not also permit them to participate in raising their community's children.

Perhaps the calculus class is uninspired because most of the students have never met or talked with a man who uses higher mathematics daily in his occupation. Bringing such men into math classes may interest students more in the field, or it may well convince some that such professions do not attract them. Rather than postponing decisions until college, students could begin the "valuing process" by which they learn to determine their own futures.

Chemists, making both napalm and life-saving medicines, in the chemistry classes; social workers in sociology; mechanics and designers in shop; computer designers and data processors in physics or math; city government officials, or militant blacks, in political science; bank clerks, bank presidents, or housewives in economics classes; obstetricians, ecologists, or sanitation workers in biology; any worker in any class which interested him. The classroom *can* be opened in fact as well as in name. Students *can* become engrossed in their studies as whole persons, emotionally as well as intellectually, if these studies are rooted in the "real life process" of adults with whom they share experiences, and not relegated to abstract, contrived textbooks.

This intergenerational classroom should certainly include those men and women whose lives span the widest range of history, and in whose consciousness the contradictions of technical progress are engraved most deeply. Old men and women who have survived sixty or seventy years of turbulent history can bring to school-age students a flesh-and-blood curriculum that no new technique could ever provide. And, given the mutuality inherent in all human relationships, these grandparents, now put out to pasture in ever earlier retirements, or shunted off to nursing homes notorious for their inadequacy, might also gain from sharing their abilities and experiences with the young.

The most recently educated group of potential teachers—college students—can provide a perspective quite different from that of the older generations, but equally valuable. Thousands of college students who are searching for involving activity in social problems are concentrated in those large urban areas which could profit most from additional teachers. Searching for relevance, many college students in all fields would be willing and even eager to spend several hours a week in public schools. Two physics majors willing to assist could enable the regular high school physics teacher to use an exciting experimental method of instruction rather than rote textbook memorization.

Mothers, fathers, the retired, working men and women, college students—all would make the classroom a more authentic learning environment. Teaching "standards" would not be undermined, as some high priests of the education establishment self-servingly tell us. On the contrary, a beginning could be made toward our ideals of democratic, humane education—education not just for the few children of the rich in progressive preparatory schools, but for *all* children.

The purpose of these new human relationships would be to create a *community classroom*. To be sure, these community citizens would inevitably bring contemporary, controversial issues into the students' world. But that is what is needed. Should we instead follow the National Education Associations dictum that "it is better to risk boredom than pandemonium,"[51] when the boredom has become deadly?

We should also not neglect the education that takes place among the students themselves. Students capable of teaching themselves can also teach each other.[52]

A student who is one year ahead of another, whether in actual grade level or only in mastery of a subject, has freshly learned the material that his fellow student is still struggling with. Can they not also become assistants to the teacher? Children's with "learning problems" or "low IQ's" are said to slow down the intelligent, capable children in the class. Behind this rests an assumption which the technicians fail to make explicit. They assume that they know where and when their students are going and how they are going to get there. A student's destination, they would have us believe, has nothing to do with any human attributes besides technical intelligence.

In what sense would a high school freshman, who completes his algebra or his English in record speed, be "slowed down" by being given the responsibility *to understand* why one of his classmates is lagging far behind? Chances are that he will not only learn something about human interactions by working with his fellow student, but that he will also gain a deeper understanding of the mathematical or grammatical principles involved. The "student-teacher" would be slowed down only in the sense that he would not acquire the maximal amount of math or grammar in the minimal amount of time—thus postponing his technical productivity.*

There can be no more challenging task in any classroom than understanding, communicating with, and helping another student. If the teacher viewed the classroom as a community rather than a mental factory, he would not conclude that the bright student was being "slowed down" by sharing his abilities with a classmate, but rather that the community was being strengthened. The full growth of *both* the fast and slow student could be enormously accelerated.

Unlike computer-taught children, who could not possibly gain the foggiest idea of what it means to understand and communicate by teaching, students in the community classroom can become teachers as they learn.

No new jobs, no new products, no new techniques, no new markets. Just new people.

---

* The tragedy of the traditional classroom is that the bright student's progress was significantly slowed down *even though he did not help his slower classmates*. He simply sat bored while the teacher explained again and again to the laggards, or scolded the trouble-makers. So convinced was the traditional teacher that he or she was the repository of all teaching abilities, and so obsessed with the need for complete order and control, that never did students pair off in sensible teaching–learning units.

11.
Youth

America, save your children

Allison Krause, nineteen years
  old,
                 you're dead,
for loving flowers.

There's a small on earth
of a universal Dallas . . .
America, save your children!
         Yevgeny Yevtushenko

Between the conception
And the creation
Between the emotion
And the response
Falls the Shadow
            T. S. Eliot

To some it may seem paradoxical to emphasize the
importance of the life-giving process at a time
when the earth appears to be facing a future with
impossible conditions of overcrowding. But precisely
at such a time in history, it is all the more
important to become sensitive to the preciousness
of life. We must shift the task of our species from
a commitment to quantity in reproduction to a
commitment to quality in childbearing.

      Arthur and Libby Colman
      Pregnancy: The Psychological Experience

At some point in a young person's growth—when his education ceases to be a compulsory activity, when he moves away
from home to go to college, or when he starts to earn part of
his own living—he begins to question the values he was
brought up with and to consider how he wants to live as an
adult. From that point on until he sets about pursuing the
vocation or set of goals he has decided upon, he exists in a
transitional identity-shaping period which can be referred
to as "youth."[1]

During youth the individual becomes able for the first time
to establish an independent identity out of his multiple and
conflicting identifications with authority. He is no longer
satisfied to perfect specific skills, but searches for worthwhile
values to which to dedicate his work. He must think beyond
adults' explanations because he is practically an adult himself:

> in youth the tables of childhood dependence begin to turn: it
> is no longer for the old to teach the young the meaning of life
> . . . it is the young who, by their responses and their actions,
> tell the old whether life as represented by their elders and as
> presented to the young has meaning.[2]

Youth is different from any of the stages of life dealt with in earlier chapters. A child's choices are always severely limited by the schooling and supervision which he must receive for the first sixteen years of his life. Young people, however, can make basic choices for themselves.

Once we become young men and women, we must stop blaming our parents, our teachers, our doctors, or our "technological, materialist, capitalist" society for what we become. The stage of youth gives us a greater freedom, but also a greater responsibility—*to choose*. We may be as controlled by our historical circumstances as are B. F. Skinner's conditioned rats, or as free as Herman Hesse's Siddhartha. Our collective childhoods may leave us with a legacy of weaknesses, by which society may bribe, manipulate, or overwhelm us. But we will have strengths too, which during youth may be consolidated and renewed.

There are no easy generalizations about youth. Young people are no longer forced to attend school if they do not want to. They can, at least nominally, select for themselves the road they wish to take.

Indeed, young people do take widely divergent roads. Some go to school to receive technical training for a year or two; some swell the ranks of the unemployed: a large minority goes to college; others join the Peace Corps, VISTA, or other social action groups. The technological system exacts its toll from all young people, and perhaps most particularly those who do not directly participate in it: the high school dropout who cannot find a job, the juvenile delinquent made more delinquent by an inhuman correctional system; the stranded veterans of Vietnam (whether jailed and resisting, or returned and forgotten, or dead). But the system also exacts a critical, if less visible, toll from the very children it prizes most.

"Youth" has undergone revolutionary changes in the past half-century. Education, widespread affluence, and mass culture have laid the basis for a much extended period of youth affecting more and more young people. A few generations ago, "youth" was a short, almost unidentifiable stage of life wedged between the dependence of adolescence and the responsibilities of parenthood. Now it has become a major life stage for most of a generation, a time one may try out various adult roles and activities without actually bearing the responsibilities of adulthood.

The increased importance of this stage of life can have a vital, liberating effect upon society as a whole. If society allows a generation of young people the time to work out their own identities independently, it will foster creative, autonomous individuals who will bring purpose and commitment to their adult lives. But postwar American society has tried to develop young people with "creativity" without granting them the autonomy to use it. They have wanted technicians, not radicals—though in cultivating the former, they have often inadvertently created the latter. The means of "radicalization" for more than a few of these young men and women has been college.

The University

The growing segment of the youth generation entering college has assumed unique importance in the technological order. Away from their parents, without children, and usually financially supported, college students are the technocracy's favored sons and daughters. To them it gives the greatest freedom, and of them it asks, ultimately, the highest loyalty. This is the group which has access to the skills, and thus to the wealth and power, which run America. As they begin to ask en masse *which* skills are truly needed, and for *whose* benefit they should be used, they begin with these questions to reorder and revitalize the established institutions.

If universities became dedicated to fostering creativity among their students, society might be revolutionized as these students became citizens, workers, and parents. But the university is not interested in creativity, as the political testament of the Sixties shows: when radical and creative students emerged, it was more often in opposition to, rather than in sympathy with, the education they were experiencing.

"Knowledge" today does not mean "truth," in the sense of "the truth shall make you free." Knowledge has come to mean a commodity, a concrete thing. By accepting this reified concept one can indeed define the university, as does the University of California's dean of planning, as a "system for storing, retrieving, processing, disseminating, and creating information."[3] The university is thus quite literally a "knowledge factory," where the prized producers of knowledge, the professors, are up for grabs to the highest bidder.[4] One can then speak of the professor as enterpreneur, as has Clark Kerr.[5] Not only physicists, engineers, chemists, computer developers, and business managers, but also linguists, psychologists, anthropologists, statisticians, etc., produce knowledge essential to the economy, and are paid for this knowledge by the industrial system (both public and private) "to the point where they may have a larger income from consulting outside the university than from teaching and research inside."[6]

Under this system, higher education tends to become mere job training for the present system of production and administration.[7] As technical knowledge becomes the key growth factor in the economy,[8] the forces of production and consumption extend their domain to the learning process. More "knowledgeable" people are wanted than ever before; but only people with a certain kind of knowledge—technical-creative knowledge. These students are asked to innovate, but within certain strict limits. They are to create new forms and new systems, but they are never to apply their creativity to the basic values which underlie the systems.[9]

If the sole responsibility of the university were the "storing, retrieving, processing, disseminating, and creating [of] information," then today's universites would be, if not perfect, at least adequate. But universities are not in fact the producers of neutral, impartial knowledge. American higher education, like American secondary education, is the servant of the productive system. As such it has become, like managing a business or running a war, a *technical* operation. Its

basic principle is the transmission of more knowledge to more
students at less cost, so that they may in turn apply that
knowledge to the range of problems specified by the technicians. This new ideology of education is based on "systematic
investment" of "human capital" as part of a rationally-
calculated "educational overhead" in a "knowledge-based
economy."[10] The terminology, as much as anything else, indicates how knowledge has become a product of great political importance.

Because education is defined only in measurable and
monetary indices, it does not include creativity or the process
of full human development. These qualities are considered
"too vague and general" to be included as reasonable goals
for higher education. When the university does not provide
room for the development of real creative abilities, and goes
so far as to inhibit their growth at the very stage of life
when young men and women are seeking new commitments,
a reaction is bound to occur. This is why, precisely one generation after the triumph of the technological revolution,
the college campus triggered a crisis in the American political
system.[11]

A Time to Decide

If universities and colleges become oriented more toward
the real human needs of society and less toward the gadgets
and weaponry of technology, they may indeed become the
birthplace of creative adults. Essential to this creativity is the
time between childhood and adulthood which college provides for young people. Without it, most "youth" would be
tied down to work and families immediately after high
school.

Mass higher education, despite its faults and the necessity
for basic change, *has* contributed to the maintenance of
youth as a major, liberating stage of life. Affluence may also
be called the "father of youth" since, without it, the young
would have to take their place immediately beside the old
in the nation's factories, offices, and laboratories. The mass

media as well has contributed to the emergence of "youth culture," since it was through the media of film, television, radio, stereos, and print that the existence of a viable "counter-culture" became more than an illusion.

The growth of mass education, affluence, and the mass media, all dependent on technology, have played important roles in making youth a distinct stage in the life cycle. But another technology, equally sophisticated and complex, has enabled the private basis of youth to keep pace with the public. This new technology is hormonal contraception—the Pill.

Contraception is not new. Withdrawal, rhythm, and primitive condoms and foams—all have been available for generations; even diaphragms are over one hundred years old.* What is new about contraception is, first, that population control is being recognized as an essential social goal; second, that contraceptive devices have been legalized; and third, that the level of affluence and education has been raised so that most young men and women can afford to and know how to use various contraceptive methods. These three related developments represent human progress of crucial importance.

Despite the roots of the word, contraception can be lifegiving. It liberates parents from the tyranny of numbers and of chance, and assures children—at least in theory—of being wanted. The act most against life is to give life to a child whose parents and society refuse to be lovingly responsible for his growth. That which prevents the never-born from entering life also permits the born to have a better life. *Contra*ception thus can serve *pro*creation.

Young people want sex but they do not want children right away. Having children would mean the sacrifice of a

---

* This section deals primarily with the use of contraceptives by young people. The IUD (intrauterine device) will not be discussed here because it is not suitable for women who have never been pregnant, which is to say the vast majority of young women. Also excluded is the cervical cap, which is more difficult to insert and less effective than the diaphragm; its use would be indicated only when anatomical reasons prevent the use of the diaphragm. No mention is made of male sterilization since most young people plan to have children eventually, or at least are not positive that they do *not* want to have them.

great deal of their personal independence and so, in a very real sense, the end of youth. In so far as "youth" includes both having sexual relations and not having children, it depends on contraception and, when necessary, abortion. With them, youth becomes a life-stage where one can choose to have children or not, a time when one may lead an active sexual life without the social responsibilities of child-rearing. Birth control pills seemed to fit perfectly the prescription for maintaining this stage of life.

Drugs:
To Postpone Parenthood

Just as pre-anesthetic childbirth or pre-computer schooling were not perfect, so were previous forms of contraception far from ideal. *Coitus interruptus* mars the mutual pleasure of intercourse; the rhythm method is highly ineffective and requires periodic abstinence; the condom is a latex rubber sheath, unpleasant to put on and wear; and the diaphragm, though highly effective, also requires insertion prior to intercourse. *None* of these contraceptive methods are 100 percent guaranteed baby-proof; and *all* of them require of man and/or woman some responsibility just before or during love-making.

The unreliability of those contraceptive methods set the stage for another debut of technique. Technology promised to substitute reliable technical control for all-too-individual human responsibility. After analyzing the problem, the technically creative mind devised a startling new solution: don't try in vain to block those thousands of swimming sperm; suppress the egg instead. Instead of trying to prevent the climax of a process already in motion, manipulate the process itself!

Enter the Pill, the would-be hero of technology's sexual revolution. When taken orally each day, the synthetic sex hormones contained in the Pill mimic the activity of a woman's natural hormonal system. Their purpose is to fix the pill-taker's body in perpetual early pregnancy. By so doing, no egg is released. There is nothing for the sperm to impregnate. Absolutely effective contraception is achieved.

Unlike the diaphragm, which is somewhat less effective and which requires careful preparation and insertion before or during love-making, the Pill gives everything and asks nothing in return. Or so the advertisements read. Dubious claims have been made for the Pill, such that it increases sexual desire or keeps women "forever feminine,"[12] but the Pill's overwhelming triumph is primarily due to its greater effectiveness and antiseptic "convenience."

Let us critically consider the relative advantages of the Pill over the diaphragm, away from the heavy public relations campaign which surrounds oral contraceptives. First, regarding effectiveness: Dr. Robert W. Kistner, a staunch supporter of the Pill, indicts the diaphragm by citing an alleged 12 percent failure rate; Dr. Louis M. Hellman of the FDA puts it at about 10 percent; another study indicates a failure rate between 2.9 and 4.5 percent; and other medical authorities put the rate at less than 1 percent. Which rate actually applies depends on how conscientious the women in the study are. A careful diaphragm user, properly fitted, should recognize that the lower rates are relevant for her. By publicly citing the higher rates, Drs. Kistner and Hellman and others scare women from the diaphragm and do a selling job for the Pill manufacturers.[13]

Second, as to convenience: the Pill's advantage here is quite ambiguous. Unlike the diaphragm, which need be attended to only when actually having sex, the Pill must be attended to daily, no matter what. For unmarried women with infrequent sexual relations, taking the Pill "for no reason" is often an unpleasant and negatively charged responsibility. Also, the Pill is not effective during the first month of its use, whereas the diaphragm is immediately effective. The Pill, moreover, should be periodically stopped for a few months every two years to give the woman's body a chance to resume its normal function. This is advocated even by Pill advocates like Dr. Kistner.[14] The diaphragm can be used without interruption.

The advantages of the Pill in regard to effectiveness and convenience, though real, are not as significant as public opin-

ion might think. And these small advantages are overwhelmed
by disadvantages, when we consider the health and safety
of the pill taker. Like high-altitude aerial bombardment, the
Pill's method of waging war against unwanted pregnancies
may be more effective than anything else, but it also raises
more biological, ethical, and legal problems than anything
else. The Pill, unlike other contraceptives, often serves against
procreation. When a woman who has been on the Pill does
decide to have a child, the long-term effects of the drug may
jeopardize not only the health of the mother-to-be, but also
the growth of her child. Although the judicious use of estrogen–progesterone therapy may sometimes be indicated for
medical reasons, the (1) long-term ingestion of (2) synthetic
hormones by (3) healthy women for (4) the sole purpose of
preventing pregnancy when (5) other methods of contraception are available, can only be seen as another example of
our idolatry of technology.

Any able doctor knows that the diaphragm represents far
less danger to the health of a woman than synthetic hormones. While the diaphragm and spermicidal jelly affect only
the adjacent tissue, oral contraceptives affect every organ of
the body. According to the World Health Organization, they
cause "an increase in glucose tolerance" (with consequent
risk of diabetes mellitus), and "an increase in coagulability
of blood" (with consequent risk of blood-clotting), "and liver
disturbance." They also affect carbohydrate and cholesterol
metabolism, and are suspected of increasing the likelihood
of heart disease, cancer, and many other diseases.[15]

The link between the Pill and these serious diseases has
not been conclusively proven: *nor has it been disproven.* "For
all the interest and energy that companies are putting into
developing oral contraceptives," wrote the trade journal
Chemical & Engineering News, ". . . nobody knows fundamentally how the drugs work."

> . . . the biochemistry of inhibiting conception by taking drugs
> remains one of reproductive physiology's most fogbound re-
> search areas.
> And little wonder. Each woman who uses the pill is daily

swallowing tablets containing various synthetic formulations of
sex hormones . . . . [B]eing biochemically pseudopregnant,
therefore, she fails to ovulate. Failing to ovulate, she can't
conceive. When faced with comprehending this biochemical
interplay of brain, glands and genitalia, most scientists turn to
work that leads to quicker publication . . . .[16]

Medical experts delight in engaging laymen in highly
technical disputes in order to convince doubters that the
Pill is "reasonably" safe for "most" women. Most circum-
spect specialists will admit, however, that to test reliably the
impact of continuous doses of synthetic hormones on the
female body would require studying several thousands of
American women who had taken the Pill for several years.
As Dr. Hugh J. Davis, Professor of Obstetrics and Gynecology at Johns Hopkins University School of Medicine, testified before Senator Gaylord Nelson's hearings in 1970, the
use of the pill by over 9 million American women represents
"a massive endocrinological experiment which has given rise
to health hazards on a scale previously unknown to medicine."[17] The Pill's avid supporters in the medical community
call such critics "alarmists" or "irresponsible." But the critics
are rationally arguing that the Pill supporters do not yet
know—indeed *cannot* yet know—the ultimate effects of the
Pill. "All studies of women on the Pill are for a relatively
brief period", said Dr. Charles Lloyd at the 1969 annual meeting of the American College of Obstetricians and Gynecolo-
gists. "The main problems may not appear for twenty years
in women who began taking the Pill when they were
young."[18]

The Pill is more dangerous than the diaphragm not only
to the women who take it, but also for her unborn children.
Wrote the Food and Drug Administration's Advisory Committee on Obstetrics and Gynecology in 1969: "It is not yet
possible to draw definite conclusions about their [oral contraceptives'] effect on the health of women and infants . . .".[19]
Reacting to the committee's report, the *New York Times*
issued a stinging editorial about "the ignorance that exists
about the long-term impact of present birth control drugs

upon the health of the women who use them and of the infants they have after ceasing to take these anti-pregnancy chemicals . . . ."[20] What effect these hormones would have on the development of "pill babies" cannot be determined until a reliable sample has grown up and had children themselves—in other words, sometime around 1984.

The Business Rationale

The Norwegians, with no more "facts" than we, banned the Pill over a decade ago. The Soviet Academy of Medicine also prohibited the Pill, choosing instead to promote the use of IUDs. According to the *Medical World News*'s Moscow reporter, "They favor a mechanical device over a chemical one because its effects are limited to the uterus . . . . They are proceeding cautiously in many directions. Meanwhile, the Western world is their guinea pig for the Pill."[21] Why did we Americans rush into this pharmaceutical swamp? To distinguish ourselves for our technical gutsiness?

We can better understand why so many young women bought the Pill only if we understand how it came to be sold. J. D. Searle & Co. introduced Enovid, the first oral contraceptive, to the American drug market in 1960. A conservative chorus forewarned that promiscuity would become rampant, and orthodox Catholics officially vowed to boycott this violation of God's domain. But the Pill producers, infatuated with their ingenuity, dismissed these detractors as prudish vigilantes, the Luddites of the sexual revolution.

Dr. John Rock, the inventor of the Pill, promised American women that oral contraceptives neither disturbed menstruation nor "damaged any natural process".*[22] And Searle, anxious about the public image of its controversial new product, published a pastel-colored pamphlet on the "Story of Enovid," referring to "the quiet revolution" taking place in contraception. The pamphlet played down the Pill's potential

---

* Dr. Robert E. Hall of Columbia University, reviewing Rock's book for the *New York Times Book Review*, called it "medical fantasy."

dangers, hiding behind the fact that no pertinent, long-range studies were yet available.[23]

The contraceptive "revolution" is a profit-making enterprise. The financial journal *Investor's Reader* wrote in 1961:

> One of the hottest items to come out of Searle labs in recent years is Enovid . . . . Enovid has undoubtedly captured the financial public's fancy. The 4,425,000 shares of Searle stock (51 per cent held by the Searle family) have doubled in the last year."[24]

Political intrigue was involved as well. The FDA permitted the sale of Enovid based on a clinical study of only 132 women who had taken the Pill for over a year—a study moreover, which examined the effectiveness of the Pill, but not its safety. (This and other facts were not revealed until a 1963 Senate investigation of the FDA headed by Senator Hubert H. Humphrey.) [25] Too short in duration, too few in number, too narrow in scope—this study opened the American market to Enovid.

Within about a year, Enovid-users had reported over one hundred cases of blood clots. A major conference was called to discuss the safety of the Pill—sponsored, strangely enough, by the prime manufacturer, J. D. Searle, Inc. In convening the meeting at 9:15 A.M., President John G. Searle asked the assembled scientists for a "true, honest answer" to this "serious problem." The conference passed a resolution at 4:15 that afternoon, with only one opposing vote.*[26] The statement maintained that no evidence was available that pills caused clotting disorders. The Pill had weathered the first

---

* The vote was cast by Dr. Stanford Wessler of the Harvard Medical School. It was followed by this dialogue with the conference chairman:

CHAIRMAN DEBAKEY: You are not in favor of the resolution. Will you tell us why you are not?

DR. WESSLER: The point at issue that disturbs me is that a decision is being reached on a statistical basis, yet the pertinent statistics aren't available.

DEBAKEY: You do not think we have enough statistics?

WESSLER: I am not referring to the quantity of statistics. I am referring to their pertinence . . . .

storm of dissent, and has survived to this day. The FDA forecasts that over 50 million women will be using the Pill by the mid-1980s.

Economic and political factors have played their role, but the Pill has triumphed ultimately for more personal factors. Although the decision-makers on corporate boards and government agencies spearheaded the contraceptive revolution, it was the millions of interpersonal decisions made in thousands of doctors' offices and in millions of bedrooms that made this technological revolution a "success."

The Bedroom Rationale

Medical science has approached the fertility of women as a clinical problem, to be solved by the best technique. If one considers the woman's reproductive system apart from the woman as a whole, then it is undeniably true that hormonal contraceptives are superior to anything else. Just as the car was superior to the horse (if one ignored pollution), and just as the bomb was superior to the gun (if one ignored civilian casualties), the Pill is superior to diaphragms (if one ignores the woman's health). This, after all, is technical creativity at its best: isolating a problem from its context and examining it under controlled laboratory conditions, attacking it in the most direct, scientific fashion, and ignoring how the solution may alter the original overall condition. This way of thinking was so useful with machines, that it was applied to the human body.

While doctors approached women as a clinical problem, men approached them as sexual objects. From this point of view the Pill is also superior to anything else. Men, especially young men, could be sure they would not have to deal with the "problem" of pregnancy. They would not have the interruptions and distractions from spontaneous sexual pleasure. As members of the "now" generation they could publicly express enlightened views on the war or ecology, while privately acting as self-serving lobbyists for the Pill. But "improving" sex while impairing health—*her* health—is a dehumanizing potency, a bedroom version of the counterfeit power all around us. Males, the proverbial defenders of the "weaker sex," thrust the responsibility for contraception upon women and even told women which method to use. They wanted to have all the fun, and none of the worry, all the while depicting themselves as an enlightened vanguard of the "sexual revolution."

Women were not necessarily passive victims. Many intelligent and educated women, critical of so many facets of modern male-dominated society, willingly accepted the illusion that the Pill was safe. They did this for many reasons: they did not want to have to touch their own genitals; they wanted to be able to make love any time, anywhere, without advance preparation; they wanted to shift the burden of responsibility, which men had shifted on to them, to the Pill itself. Whatever their personal reasons, women took an enormous risk with their own lives for the most meager gains in contraceptive effectiveness and convenience.

Even "liberated women" found it hard to escape worshipping the Pill. The McGill *Birth Control Handbook,* the first of many "people's medicine" pamphlets to be published on contraception, advised women:

> Most active drugs are dangerous, but it is not the danger of all contraception that makes it the subject of such special consideration by the media and society in general. The Pill is the first 100% effective contraceptive, the first drug to weaken male society's control over women. Women with control over their own bodies are in a better position to demand and obtain control over their own lives. Male chauvinism cannot tolerate such a possibility and searches to introduce a new fear into women.[27]

The McGill Handbook provides this advice for the stated purpose of "providing men and women with the information they need to control their own bodies." For the same ostensible purpose, the Washington Women's Liberation group took an opposite stand. Having fought their way in front of the TV cameras covering the 1970 Senate hearings on contraception, this group angrily protested "unsafe contraceptives foisted on uninformed women for the profit of the drug and medical industries—and for the convenience of men."[28]

Obviously, women are as divided on this issue as men. One may recall Claire Booth Luce's comment in 1969 that, thanks to the Pill, "modern woman is at last free to dispose of her own body, to earn her living, to pursue the improvement of her mind, to try a successful career."[29] But one can also turn to Barbara Seaman, a columnist for the *Ladies Home Journal,* whose best-selling book *Doctor's Case Against the Pill* informed hundreds of thousands of women about the political conniving and medical half-truths that led to the production of the pill.

The Boston Women's Health Course Collective has attempted to strike a middle ground between these two extremes." Their 1971 publication *Women and Their Bodies* summarizes the arguments of both pro- and anti-Pill positions. They report:

> Birth control pills are dangerous for some women and in other women can cause side effects which range from nuisances to major pains and changes. Many women have taken the pill with no apparent side effects at all. Also 100 percent protection against pregnancy is a very important tool for many of us as we start to take control of our lives. Many women, therefore, will continue to use the pill. We feel that every woman deserves to make, and must make, an *informed decision* (Barbara Seaman's phrase) about using birth control pills. She must know the risks, and she must know about other birth control methods that she could use. If she chooses the pill, she must see a responsible gynecologist.[30]

Of course, an "informed decision" is impossible as long as the American government fails to distribute accurate and comprehensive information to each pill-taking woman, and as long as doctors rely on drug companies for their information and the revenue for their medical journals. An "informed decision" is also impossible for the millions of women given contraceptives under programs (both domestic and international) financed by government agencies like HEW, OEO, and AID, who often do not have the opportunity to consult a competent gynecologist regularly.*

Even were the information available, the question remains: How can "radical" women—or men—believe that women who take hormonal contraceptives are "taking control over their bodies and their lives"? Blind trust in the benevolence of technology leads women to believe they "control their own bodies" when in fact they are forfeiting control to the FDA, the drug industry, and to the chemical compounds in their bloodstream.

Uncommon Common Sense

When rational control exceeds its limits, it becomes a world view complete unto itself, subject to no one's control.

Dickenson W. Richards, Nobel laureate in medicine in 1956, wrote in *Drugs In Our Society*:

> With all the vast technologies and powers now available, it would appear that man is moving along rather complacently in the belief that he will one day conquer nature and bring all its forces under his control. Perhaps he will. On the other hand there is evidence that he is not controlling nature at all but only distorting it . . . . His powers have extended so far that nature itself, formerly largely protective, . . . seems to have become largely retaliatory. Let man make the smallest blunder in his far reaching and complex physical or physiological reconstructions, and nature, striking from some unforeseen direction, exacts a massive retribution.[31]

One could argue that, even if it were proven that the pill *was* related to enormously higher incidence of cancer, heart

---

* Some women's groups have asserted that Pill manufacturers, aware of the possibility of a massive boycott of the Pill by angry and fearful American women, have planned to protect their investment in hormonal contraceptives should such a boycott actually begin. They would simply export their pills to the Third World markets where women consumers do not know the facts.

disease, and other diseases, it would still be up to the individual woman to weigh benefits against risks and to make up her own mind. But young women in their late teens and twenties who *do* want eventually to have children should remember that someone else's well-being is involved as well. What these mothers-to-be do to their own reproductive systems and hormonal balance, they do to their own children. We do not know how extensive the impact of prolonged use of hormones affect offspring, but *we do know that we do not know*. After the medical profession had assured women for several years that hormones were not excreted into breast milk, tests were finally conducted which showed that hormones were indeed present in the milk. Moreover, mothers on the pill showed a decrease in milk supply. The experts were wrong once; they can be wrong again.[32]

Dr. Alan Gutmacher, President of Planned Parenthood, told the readers of *Good Housekeeping* that "[t]here are no statistics to indicate that the pill has any residual effects on the embryo." We must add that there are no statistics to indicate that the pills do *not* have any residual effects. One can see the harm that the pills do to women who take them; one can only *foresee* the harm they will do to children.

The engineers of the technological revolution are not diabolical culprits. The Pill was invented; it was marketed; and millions bought it. To focus only on political or economic institutions would be to fail to recognize how much the technicians' world view characterizes us all. Those millions of consumers are ourselves.

Aside from the women who use the Pill for various medical reasons, women on the Pill—and men who love them—have let their own faculties atrophy as they empower technical experts with supreme judgment. Where are the unpretentious men or women who can still speak of common sense or intuition without feeling guiltily apologetic?

The simple-minded person would assume that forcing a woman's body to suppress a normal monthly process (ovulation), to be primed up unremittingly for an event which never happens (childbirth), might be damaging. He or she would suppose that natural hormones, when artificially replaced by more powerful synthetic ones, would be thrown into imbalance. The body, stuck in an unresolved early pregnancy year after year, might forget how *not* to be pregnant. He or she might also wonder if, after a woman stops taking Pills and then really becomes pregnant, her body might not be reluctant to believe that, finally, the hormonal cry of "Wolf" was real, and might not therefore respond with less vitality to the physical demands of child-bearing. The uncluttered mind would reason that, if natural hormonal changes during pregnancy have an identifiable and strong impact on the woman's emotional life, synthetic hormones in standardized dosages would have an even greater impact: it is known that progesterone has a depressant effect on the central nervous system; and that both progesterone and estrogen affect the metabolism of chemicals which influence emotional life, particularly acute depression.[33] Finally, the untrained man or woman might well fear that, since the Pill's synthetic hormones accumulate in the body over many months or even years, the children conceived during the months right after stopping the Pill would be harmed. In fact, the chief gynecologist of the US Air Force has documented an alarming frequency of miscarriages for women who conceived in the first month after discontinuing Pills. (20 percent as against 8.6 percent for non-pill-users).[34]

But there are few simple, untrained minds among us, and their voices have no microphones. Many of us have been trained too well. We lead our lives as if we were anchored to statistics, as if we only knew what tests and experiments show now, about the present, and through the eyes of the present.

Technological man is in a rush. To where, he does not know. But he cannot wait. The vain glories of progress prod him onward ever faster. We love our technical solutions so deeply that we refuse to acknowledge the distortions they create. That we destroyed Vietnamese villages in the process of saving them is not just a tragedy of war, but a tragedy of our own psyches. Now we are about to "save" the world from overpopulation by destroying the health of many women, and perhaps the growth of their children.

The medical controversy surrounding the Pill, argues Morton Mintz, cannot be separated from other technological issues, such as the use of DDT and other pesticides, the neglect of urban rapid transit, the SST and the construction of nuclear power plants. All lead inexorably to Rene Dubos' warning:

> Since we make so little effort to investigate the effects of social and technological innovations on human life, we are practicing —not by intention but irresponsibly—a kind of biological warfare against nature, ourselves and especially against our descendants.[35]

Having sex and having children—the two are deeply intertwined. We may separate them biologically, or even intellectually, but they will remain bound together in our minds . . . like lovers' bodies. Who can blame us for trying to buy deliverance from this existential dilemma—these "facts of life"? It is offered at such a low price, as a result of scientific progress, for the good of the economy, with the blessings of the state, and in the name of a stable planetary population. Because all the noblest adult rationales are summoned to rally around this new invention, it requires of us our strongest radical will to see the truth.

The Last Resort:
Abortion

Few adults in America argue anymore that contraception is immoral; or, to put it bluntly, that all eggs which pass down the Fallopian tubes have the God-given right to be impregnated. Virtually everyone is in accord that the unfertilized egg is not a "person" and so has neither a soul sacred unto God nor a citizen's protection under law. But, at the moment of conception, the scales of justice shift. It is better to prevent conception, in other words, than to prevent the birth of what has already been conceived. Some would call abortion "murder"; others, a "woman's right"; others, "a medical question." But, whatever their political stand, very few men and women deny that the ethics of abortion are more ambiguous than the ethics of contraception.

Though all women should have access to abortion, the destruction of the fetus should never be a first resort. America today is a nation already caught in the genocide of Vietnam. Life would truly lose its sacredness if having abortions became as common as catching colds. *As surely as women should have access to safe abortions, they should rarely need them.* If access to, and education about, birth control were universal, very few abortions would be required. Contraception could make abortions, though legal, nearly absolete.

It is nevertheless true that the Pill, which should be avoided if at all possible, is *more* effective (and *more* dangerous) than other forms of contraception. Assured by the blanket guarantee, some women will therefore "logically" select the Pill despite its alarming dangers unless they have a legal and reliable access to that *post*-conception "contraceptive"—abortion. Just as the availability of contraceptives should make abortions a legal but largely unnecessary right, the availability of abortions as a last resort should encourage women to avoid foolproof—but foolish—hormonal contraception.

We encountered in preceding chapters many examples of children who, though fortunate enough to have parents who anticipated their birth with joy, were nonetheless exposed to the severest threats to their physical and mental health and abandoned to inventions and institutions which can crush a child's spirit. What, then, may the "unwanted" child expect in such a world? The fortunate ones may be adopted and find permanent, loving homes, but the vast majority are destined for multiple foster families, care-taking agencies, and other institutions for abandoned children. They will most likely not be nursed tenderly, nor consistently cared for. They will be deprived of many of the experiences of infancy that are so directly involved in full development. Already on this planet there are too many children and too little food and care. We cannot, in good conscience, increase the imbalance to ever more tragic proportions. It makes no sense to so reverently abstract "life" and so coldly devalue the quality of life we call "growth."

Children,
or Not

Perhaps as a generation we know more about logarithms and syntax than our predecessors did, but we probably know less about babies or families. Traditional social life has been violently uprooted by technology; old relationships of family and generations no longer serve as useful guides; our schooling has been virtually devoid of any emphasis on the human. We were never encouraged to think about sex roles, about child-rearing, pregnancy, or old age. It was assumed that this need not be taught in school because it was learned in "life."

But attitudes toward life and the reproduction of life have become extraordinarily dislocated. *Technology has altered every one of the traditional justifications for having children.* Contraceptive technology virtually assures sex without conception, and surgical technology attends to any unfortunate oversights. Babies will soon not only arrive when the parents want, but in the desired sex[36] and, in perhaps only a few decades, with the desired genetic makeup as well. Meanwhile, even "made-to-order" children are no longer economic assets but incredible liabilities. Industrial technology has made child labor inefficient, while at the same time raising the cash cost of child-rearing. Moreover, when parents become old, they will not be supported by their children but by pension funds and social security benefits derived from years of hard-earned paychecks. Medical technology has lowered the childhood death rate of the well-to-do so that fewer births will produce proportionately more adults. The automation of industry and warfare no longer makes expansion of national wealth or power contingent on the expansion of population. Industry needs relatively fewer, but more highly trained workers. The same in war: "with automated war the combatants are *technicians*" whose power preferably rests in gadgetry rather than manpower.[37] Finally, urban congestion, combined with high per capita energy consumption and waste production, has made zero population growth in the advanced countries seem highly desirable.

Even the nonmaterial rationales for having children have been undermined. Except for the most protected enclaves of Catholicism, the religious exhortation to "replenish the earth" has lost its authority. And the psychological satisfaction of having children who will keep the family's name alive is being eroded by the rapidity of change which makes the transmission of values between generations more problematical.

"Why should we have any children at all?" we ask. To have children no longer serves a heart-felt need, nor accelerates economic growth, nor contributes to national grandeur. It costs a lot, limits our movement, compromises our freedom, and guarantees no cultural immortality.

And so among many of the postwar generation having children is mentioned more often with foreboding than with joy. It is an inconvenience to be avoided, put off; a painful duty to be gotten over, drugged away; a commitment which interferes with personal freedom and ties one down. It requires such stability and commitment of us, and such hope. A man and woman must be sure of themselves, sure of each other, and sure, too, of the biological and political world in which they live. Is this still possible in our technological age? Faced with such uncertainties, why should one leave youth behind at all?

Stopping the use of contraceptives is apparently even harder than starting. With the rewards of child-rearing so ephemeral, the sacrifices loom larger. It is hard to find time for the weekly newsmagazine, not to mention children.

How can a young woman on her way to an alluring career, conscious of herself as young, informed, shapely, and free—

how can she stop it all in order to become pregnant? Why would she choose to become heavy and protruding, tie herself to one man and to one child, attend to her nursing infant several times a day for weeks or months on end, and become ultimately responsible for another human being—however small—at a time when no one seems to be responsible for anything but themselves?

Pregnancy, a life-stage of extraordinary potential growth, has become drained of much of its meaning. Never having witnessed a birth, probably distant from her own mother, separated from her husband by hospital rules, untrained and uninformed about labor and delivery, thrust into an unfamiliar white-walled environment, and often drugged as well— the fate of the prospective mother is one which holds little joy for the young woman today. The pregnant woman is like the old model car whose market value plummets after she loses her showroom virginity.

A man's anxiety is different, but frightening just the same. No tradition propels him toward parenthood: to be a single man, successful in his career, is not a negative future. He can easily have sex with many women; change cities at a moment's notice; work hard, travel wherever necessary, or entertain often; all without giving a thought to cumbersome family obligations. He can act out that seductive Playboy fantasy: the single, carefree bachelor who lives life to the fullest, surrounded by every pleasure-giving apparatus on the market— including the contracepted woman.

It is hard enough to care for one's husband or one's wife, whom one has chosen willingly. What of a child, thrust upon one sight unseen? Though society has sanctioned divorcing one's spouse, it is still unacceptable to "divorce" one's small child. One cannot plead mental cruelty and simply leave one's sons and daughters to fend for themselves.

Beneath the suave single sex roles type-cast in Hollywood and Madison Avenue are many young men and women who remain childless simply because they are afraid. They do not know what a family means. As children, the young adults of the present generation have spent less time with their parents than did those of preceding generations. During youth, this age segregation was yet more stringent. College youth are actually herded away from kids and away from adults; it is on this isolation that the "freedom" of youth culture rests. Some students diligently study the work of scholars who deal with "stages of growth," or "psychological development," or "the life cycle." But after years in the desert of impersonal, technical "knowledge," a drink at these intellectual oases only serves to remind these students of how estranged they have become from the life cycle as a whole.

During youth, estrangement reaches its peak. Neither children nor parents, and only sometimes lovers, keep time with the rhythm of our growth. Unable to recall, unwilling to envision, we have only the moment. So we do not simply glorify the here-and-now; we idolize it, trying to squeeze from it every drop of meaning. Who can wait and plan for the birth of another being when we can be magically, effortlessly, instantaneously "reborn" ourselves at the drop of a pill?

Drugs:
In Protest

Users of "psychedelic" drugs claim unique stature for their compounds because they "expand consciousness."* But what "confined" consciousness in the first place?

It was college youth, unmarried and childless, who first proselytized for psychedelics among middle-class white society. Their non-college peers, to a large extent, were founding families. They had no time, and too many responsibilities, to go tripping on acid or whizzing on speed. College kids on the other hand, raised in a technological world in which drugs were very much at home, were quick to find in this different

---

* This will not be a thorough or impartial discussion of drugs. I have done this elsewhere (cf. *The Whole World Is Watching*, Viking, 1969, pp. 173-214). Interested readers are encouraged to turn to other books on psychedelic drugs as well. Let me specify here that my criticisms are directed more at laboratory drugs like LSD than at organic substances like marijuana and peyote.

sort of drug an escape from the alienation they felt all around.

It is actually amazing that psychoactive drugs—LSD, peyote, mescaline, DMT, methedrine, uppers, and downers —have been considered part of the counter culture. The technological society has introduced various kinds of chemical compounds at virtually every stage of life. They are peddled by highly profitable corporations, plugged by the media, stuffed into livestock, sanctioned by the government, and endorsed by Lawrence Welk. The proposition that "psychedelic" drugs are a cultural protest warrants skepticism from the outset.

Each claim for the psychedelics begs a question. "When I'm high I feel so much more in tune with my body, all my senses are alive." (How did you get alienated from your body and senses to begin with?) "My mind makes connections so much better. I get out of the straightjacket of words and rationality and think in images and broad patterns." (What put you in the straightjacket?) "I discover a deeper creativity within myself. My poems are more original." (Why were you cut off from this creativity before?) "I can contact my feelings and other people's so much easier, and so I get closer to people." (How did you get alienated from your feelings, and made distant from others?) "So vividly I saw my whole life in metamorphosis. My face passed before my eyes, nursing at my mother's breast, up to the present, and into old age. It was incredible, really mystical!" (Why can't you experience this mystical awareness of the unity of your life without drugs?)

Drug experience is a repository for all those human qualities which the user has failed to develop but wants to develop. It embodies the backlog of traits which a young man or woman has chosen to—or been compelled to—neglect. It represents an attempt to reclaim stolen or forfeited self-awareness.

The purpose of the preceding questions is not to be hostile or moralistic, but to set the question of drugs into a more human, a more "radical" frame of reference. If quietly asked to respond these counterarguments, the drug-user might well recall certain episodes or tensions in his childhood and adolescence which led to his "inadequately"-expanded consciousness (which we have called "technical creativity"). He might well refer to familial, educational, cultural, and interpersonal pressures similar to those discussed in this book. Though he accurately attributes his unrealized potentials to human and social influences, he seeks to rectify or to counteract these influences, not by searching for other human and social settings which will stimulate his growth, but by taking drugs.

Though drugs may provide pleasure, and even occasional flashes of artistic inspiration or personal insight, they cannot give back to the young what technological life has taken away: *the sense that from birth to death life can hold together, perhaps even beautifully*. Erikson writes:

> . . . somewhere between the exploitation of nature and the self-exploitation of mercantile and mechanized man, a gigantic transformation has taken place . . . the creation of middle-men between man and nature. And it dawns on us that the *technological* world of today is about to create kinds of alienation too strange to be imagined.[38]

This alienation goes far deeper than any of the fragmented movements our generation has fostered—deeper than our social institutions (and beyond the solutions proposed by vying groups of political reformers and revolutionaries); deeper than our violation of nature (the ecology movement and "going back to the land"); deeper than our inability to communicate with each other (encounter groups, rock festivals, communes, etc.), and deeper than our alienation from our own bodies (yoga, meditation, body sensitivity, diets, etc.).

We are alienated from the human life cycle itself. We have become cut off from others and from ourselves, cut off from our past and from our future. We are left with a "now," stark and unconnected. The technological change in which we grew up has made our lives appear so "strung out" that we no longer feel personally connected to the chapters of our life history that we have lived or have yet to live. Transfixed in a drug-like trance to our own point in the life cycle, we have lost the rhythm of human growth and the cadence of generations.

Drugs offer a soothing security because they let us accept how adrift we are, huddled about our stereos and staring at the latest flicks. They camouflage our real needs: to center on our own childhood and to free ourselves from the alienations it produced in us; to form communities with our friends; and to create a fertile, human environment for our children. As long as childhood is a memory to escape, and adulthood a future to avoid, the young will always bring too much of their hope to the timeless world of psychedelics and too little of themselves to this fragile, temporal world which needs their hope and work so much.

The Cycle Broken

This "alienation too strange to be imagined" lies behind our fear that marriages cannot last and that having children might as well be left to someone else. "Future shock," "the biological time-bomb," "ecocide" and "terracide," "limits of growth," and "forecasting the future"—all are fragments of a shattered faith in the regeneration of life. Our generation cannot confidently promise our children, as many of our parents promised us, a better start in life than their parents had. We may have dreams for our kids, a determination to protect their development, a desire to let them touch the earth, to feel with inner strength the bright joys and dark fears that color every moment from birth to death. But a gnawing apprehension remains: that the life to which we gave birth in a climax of pleasure may not have the biological support and the social freedom to unfold.

Without traditional confidence or instinctive courage, we could easily *contra*ceive forever. For child-rearing, in a sense, is antithetical to the technical spirit. Accustomed to assuming limited responsibility, the technical parent seeks to construe his relations to his children as a specialized role. He is held only marginally accountable for his child's growth. Like a prime contractor with many subcontracts, he delegates authority—and blame—to the other specialists involved.

Obstetricians take charge at birth; pediatricians are responsible for a child's ailments and cures; the teacher for his intelligence; the coach for his physique; the supermarket and food industry for his food; television for his myths; the minister for his soul; and the psychiatrist, if necessary, for the feelings wedged in between. Technical parenthood is narrowed to housing and clothing these various component parts so that they hang together in a legally coherent form which can be identified as John or Mary.

Perhaps a technician needs no "center," no ethical goal or spiritual values for his work. But a parent does. A father or mother cannot view life as a mass of disconnected technical questions which must be left up to the expert in charge. For parents, the facts alone are not enough. Parents must decide what the facts *mean,* and on that basis what they should *do.* They cannot shift responsibility to another department, or to the officer who gave the order, or to another worker down the line. Any struggle that influences the children's growth must become the parents' struggle as well.

The machine cannot regenerate human life. This is the fatal flaw in the technological future. Parental responsibility may be shifted from families to women, then from women to institutional staffs, and finally from staffs to their various gadgets and techniques. Adults may be "freed" from the tasks of parental care. Freed, in other words, from adulthood itself. They may be induced to remain in a post-adolescent limbo of puerile, Playboy sexuality and mindless, competitive self-advancement while their children are programmed to repeat their dead-end development. They may become, in the end, so loyal to what were technically their self-interests that they sacrifice their selves. Though life may go on, it ceases to be human.

Getting Together:
Love

Responsible parenthood, both in the biological and the ethical senses, has never been easy. The future is never guaranteed. For parents who care about their children's growth, having children has always been an act of faith. So even if the odds we face are unprecedented; even if we feel the world is coming apart at the seams; let us not conclude that having and caring for children is now meaningless. In no way do we improve the future of mankind if we succumb to our fears about leaving the freedom of youth for the ethical responsibilities of collective parenthood.

It is, in fact, not a choice between freedom and responsibility but between humanity and inhumanity. As R. D. Laing recalls Franz Kafka:

> You can hold yourself back from the suffering of the world, this is something you are free to do and is in accord with your nature, but perhaps this holding back is the only suffering that you might be able to avoid.[39]

A society built for machines will simply not survive. Babies need not only mothers but also "families to protect the mothers, societies to support the structure of families, and traditions to give a cultural continuity to systems of tending and training. All of this," writes Erikson, "is necessary for the human infant to evolve humanly . . . ."

> For man's psychosocial survival is safeguarded only by the vital virtues which develop in the interplay of successive and overlapping generations, living together in organized settings. Here, living together means more than incidental proximity. It means that the individual's life stages are "inter-living", cogwheeling with the stages of others *which move him along as he moves them.*[40]

With this insight, the concept of "self-interest" is made human. Parenthood must be rooted in the realization that one's *self-interest* will feed upon itself and stagnate unless one becomes *interested* in the growth of others.

The vital human interplay between parent and child, the birthplace of all love, is inaccessible to economists' charts, politicians' voting patterns, and businessmen's consumer reports. Human growth is unlike the other kinds of "growth" with which the technological society is so obsessed. Like male and female, childhood and adulthood are meaningful only relative to each other. Even if a man or woman chooses not to have his or her own children, it is difficult to imagine a fulfilling adulthood which does not express the parental impulse to guide and help the next generation. And, even if a child is not raised by his or her biological parents, there can be no full childhood development without the care of at least one sustaining adult. Each generation must be responsive to, and ultimately responsible for, the growth of the next.

As we have seen in the preceding chapters, virtually every major American industry and the government agencies which "police" them must be transformed so that children can grow. This children's revolution requires tens of thousands of radical, ethical parents. In Jonothan Kozol's words, they must be "radical, strong, subversive, steadfast, skeptical, rage-minded and power-wielding." They must penetrate the energy conglomerates, the military-industrial complex, the medical-drug-hospital establishment, the auto-petroleum-highway interests, the food-advertising-agribusiness industry. They must become building code examiners, defense attorneys, city planners, economists, advertisers, government officials, disarmament experts, news reporters, TV producers, professors, nutritionists, and on and on. Today, this is as much a parent's business as changing diapers.

III.

... And the disciples rebuked them. But Jesus said, suffer little children, and forbid them not to come unto Me ...

Matthew 19:14

12.
Adulthood

if you give to your children

What man is there of you, whom if his son ask bread, will he give him a stone?

Or if he ask a fish, will he give him a serpent?

If ye then know how to give good gifts unto your children, how much more shall your Father which is in Heaven give good things to them that ask him?

Matthew 7: 9-11

Concerned by the threats of the postwar technological society, the first generation of postwar Americans has begun to meet the challenges of adulthood with basically three different reactions. Each of these reactions stresses some aspect of adulthood at the expense of others.

1. Once the most vocal and visible members of the postwar generation, one group emphasizes the *political* responsibilities of adulthood. These young men and women feel that the peril to human life is so great that their energies should be directed almost exclusively toward politics itself. Long hours, mobility, financial hardship, legal risks, and all-consuming commitment are required of them. None of these conditions are conducive to raising children. Besides, they feel having children is not as important as making the world a better place for them to enter. Enough children are already alive who are starving and homeless; better to adopt them as their own, if they have time for children in their life style, than to add more to the chaos.

These political activists also tend to de-emphasize education, arguing that it is not what you *know* but what you *do* that will make a difference.

2. A second group of young people have reacted to the crisis of adulthood by stressing its occupational or *profes-*

sional aspects. They feel that it will be impossible for them to influence the technological state unless they have the technical training and the professional stature which today are the preconditions for power. To achieve this, they must undergo prolonged and intensive education followed by unstinting devotion to the requirements of their particular career. They would argue that they cannot hope to influence decisions on any of the multitude of technical matters which now face America unless they have an ever renewed knowledge of their field. Consequently, devotion to knowledge must take precedence over all else, including active politicking and any major sacrifices for parenthood.

3. In contrast to the groups concerned with the political and professional responsibilities of adulthood, a third group of young people have underscored their commitment to the strictly *parental*. In their own and their friends' lives, they have witnessed adults of all political persuasions and professional background who thoughtlessly sacrificed their marriages, their children's welfare, their home life, or even their own health, in order to survive in the technological state. After much searching, this group has minimized the importance of any social activism in order to create a protective, private life style which could welcome children into a pure, if confined and isolated, world of intimate relationships. Throughout America today, set along dirt roads in the woods or the farm country, they have built new homesteads. By farming, doing odd jobs, living simply, and sharing what they own, they have created islands of peace into which children can be brought with great enthusiasm. Since a farm can feed many mouths, and since children's voices are like music in the awesome silence of country evenings, these new pioneers want children and, more often than not, they choose to have many.

Although these three reactions to the common tasks of adulthood often overlap, their emergence as three separate cultural phenomena during the 1960s attests to the growing tension involved in *integrating the political, professional, and parental responsibilities of adulthood into a coherent, meaningful way of life.*

These three anticipatory reactions to adulthood symbolize fundamentally different conceptions of the future: the first, a diligent organizing to prepare for imminent political upheaval; the second, earnest self-education toward gaining control of an essentially technocratic state; and third, a greening-of-America vision of megalopolises spontaneously diffusing into idyllic homesteads. So divergent are these orientations toward the future that they point out their common failing: each tends to exclude the others.

As beautiful and authentic as the rural commune is, it alone is fatally inadequate. To what schools will the children of these communes be sent? Who will raise taxes—and fine or jail taxpayers if they are delinquent? What if a nuclear power plant is built next door, or a shopping plaza? Nowhere within the borders of the United States can one live incognito, pretending that seclusion is possible. It simply will not work. To protect one's children, the adult must concern himself with the political and professional as well as the narrowly parental.

To say that all three are part of the "counter culture"—the political activist in Washington; the young doctor in the neighborhood clinic; and the meditating farmer with his organic vegetables and geodesic barn—is simply to say that they have all exercised some creativity. To be *radically* creative, however, those of us involved on each level of opposition must regain a sense of brotherhood in our shared search for a more human future. It is important to stress the interdependence of politics, work, and parenthood, because only at the core of these spheres does a whole adulthood become possible. Only by respecting and sharing our varying concerns will we keep each other honest, and our children safe.

Politics:
Parenthood Writ Large

Technology undeniably poses formidable problems for a parent who wants to be politically responsible. For adults today it often seems nearly impossible to be a citizen anymore. In addition to family responsibilities and keeping up at work, an adult today must have an extraordinary breadth of knowledge if he is to exercise his rights of citizenship.

First, one must discern the truth about political events. (Did American bombers strike North Vietnamese hospitals? Did the GOP support the Watergate Five who burglarized Democratic headquarters?) Then there are the social dynamics which underlie politics. (Does economic growth require military spending? What are the tax loopholes and who profits from them? Are the Russians friendly now or must we remain on military alert?) Most difficult of all, are the complex scientific questions which now intrude on virtually every public debated. (Is MSG dangerous? Is the ABM effective? Will the Alaska pipeline, or underground bomb tests cause environmental damage? How nutritious are breakfast cereals? And so on.)

Earning a living and raising children require energy enough. But even if the average citizen could delegate those tasks to someone else, he or she would still not have enough time to understand many political issues. Democracy and technocracy, in this sense, are opposed—on the one hand, the need for universal citizen participation and, on the other hand, the intensely specialized knowledge required. This tension between democracy and technocracy leaves many adults intellectually besieged and politically impotent. "Here are these great issues," writes Theodore Roszak, "coming at them daily like bullets fired point blank. They *must* decide . . . and yet how *can* they decide? The world is just no longer their size."[1]

In this super-technological world, certain features of democracy seem to be nearing obsolescence. In a letter written shortly after the American Revolution, Thomas Jefferson asked his friend James Madison "whether one generation has a right to bind another." In answering his own question strongly in the negative, Jefferson did not speak figuratively of posterity, but quite literally of the next generation:

> . . . [L]et us provide in our constitution for its revision at stated periods. What these periods should be, *nature* herself indicates.

> By the European tables of mortality, of the adults living at any moment of time, a majority will be dead in about nineteen years. At the end of that period, a new majority is come into place; or, in other words, a new *generation*. Each generation is as independent of the preceding one, as that was of all which had gone before. It has then, like them, a right to choose for itself the form of government it believes most promotive of its own happiness. . . . [I]t is for the peace and good of mankind that a solemn opportunity for doing this every nineteen or twenty years should be provided by the constitution; so that it may be handed on, with periodical repairs, from generation to generation, to the end of time . . . .[2]

Jefferson was adamantly in favor of the next generation re-designing the revolution he had helped make. To prevent one generation's liberation movement from becoming the tyranny of the next, Jefferson realized that *children and youth must develop freely so that they may reorder the previous generation's priorities.*

Two hundred years later, Jefferson's vision of generational freedom has been declared an anachronism by technicians eager to swarm into the childhood years. The vanguard of this movement, represented by B. F. Skinner, is already describing a "technology of behavior" by which America may efficiently mold the kinds of citizens it needs.[3] Victor Ferkiss writes:

> It is now theoretically possible, given a certain investment of resources and access to the persons involved, to control human personal and social development in a systematic way . . . . No longer does ignorance or impotence offer us an escape from the possibility of control by means of social technology. The power exists . . . . To rail at Skinner as a monster is irrelevant, since the choice he places before us is a real one, and insofar as it exists technological man exists.[4]

And so we approach the antithesis of Jefferson's image of man: instead of each generation being "as independent of the preceding one as that was of all which had gone before," the next generation will become the creatures of the previous generation's planners.

This book has chronicled the biological, psychological, and

social intervention in child development. Neither the Left nor the Right has actively defended children against the threat of dangerous radiation, childbirth drugs, food processing and additives, etc. Neither Democrats or Republicans seem sensitive to the fate of the child in the nuclear family, the levels of DDT in milk, or the magnified effects of polluted air and water on infant health. And neither liberals nor conservatives have appeared concerned about the implications of Skinnerian psychology, computerized instruction, or television programming for the personalities of growing children. Of what relevance, then, is adult politics to children's growth?

Political scientists have found that the most salient factor differentiating "liberal" from "conservative" policies is the set of interest groups to which they respond. "Congressmen are guided in their votes, Presidents in their programs, and administrators in their discretion, by whatever *organized* interests they have taken for themselves as most legitimate."[5] This of course is pluralism: the faith that government will serve as a just arbitrator between the *competing* claims of various groups. The words "organized" and "competing" have been emphasized because children are the largest and most helpless of the groups who can do neither. By this definition, politics excludes children—if not by legal statute, then by biological and psychological fact.

Responsible parents, therefore, cannot rely on party affiliation. Our generation cannot use hand-me-down political labels for defining our allegiances. We must instead grapple with every program, every expenditure, and every law, to test whether it is in our children's best interest or only in the interest of one or another group of competing adults. If this leads us to a "capitalist" approach, or if this leads to "socialism," so be it. If the defense of our children makes us "radical" one day and "conservative" the next, then too: so be it. What counts is that we escape from the rigid political self-definitions which have for so long been the anchors for adult identities in times of crisis. Only then may we let ourselves perceive the world anew.

In sum, we must evolve a life-style of *politically responsible parenthood,* independent of present ideologies and political parties. We cannot reduce to platforms, policies, and parties what is in fact a human, ethical dilemma. As Ignazio Silone wrote:

> To oppose fascism, we need neither heavy armaments nor bureaucratic apparatuses. What we need above all is a different way of looking at life and human beings. My dear friends, without this different way of looking at life and human beings, we shall ourselves become fascists.

As regional, educational, ethnic, and economic indicators of political affiliation become less salient, the adult's attitude toward children and technology—to the quality of human creativity—becomes more crucial. The question now must be answered: which is the true measure of progress, and to which do we entrust the future—our inventions or our children?

To reply that it is not a question of either/or is to evade the ethical choice. If not in politics, then certainly in life, man can have only one "ultimate concern."

Work:
Voting with Our Lives

So much worthless and wasteful work was required of the first postwar generation that they naturally tended to rebel against the very idea of work. Pressured during high school into a post-Sputnik acquisition of technical skills, many of these young people embraced new values but rejected skills altogether. Some of them were so enthralled with their new-found "radical consciousness" that virtues like competence, workmanship, or "doing a good job" seemed old-fashioned. As a result, the first rituals endorsed by the counter culture—anti-war marches, drugs, and rock festivals—required of their participants no individual skills whatsoever.

Most of this generation has realized that simply rebelling

against technology and the skills it requires is not enough. This is, and will be, a technological era in which *values lose their political impact unless they are grounded in skills.* We submerge ourselves in pretechnological dreams only by forfeiting our power to control the potentially catastrophic technology that now exists. This is why a politically responsible adult is one who has placed his skills in the service of radical values, not one who has ceased to use his skills at all.

Despite the idyllic panoramas of Woodstock, the ascendancy of technology has made *work* far more crucial today than ever before. Our alternative life-styles or social organizations will fail unless we begin to express our "political" values every day in the way we earn our living and raise our children. A successful *post*-technological revolution depends as much on our work as our political activity, and maybe more.

For some young people work may mean politics itself, but certainly not for most. The vast majority of any generation must work in the so-called "nonpolitical" activities of child-care, education, transportation, health and sanitation, communication, finance, industry, regulatory agencies, science, and the professions. In these areas, radicals are needed as desperately as in formal politics. We can change these institutions only by working in them. Unless we begin what the German student activist Rudi Dutschke called "the long march through the institutions,"[6] the levers of control will be left in the hands of others. Voting and campaigning are important, but the way we invest our daily, life-long labor is ever more important.

Economic and political philosophy have, until quite recently, underestimated the political impact of technical work. "The steady invasion of technology is the commanding reality that shapes the economic relations of man to nature in our day," notes Robert Heilbroner. "How extraordinary, then, that the two most important economists of full-blown capitalism, Alfred Marshall and Lord Keynes, have virtually nothing to say about the impact of technology on the economic system."[7]

Sharing Heilbroner's conviction that social theory has not kept pace with technological practice, Robert Lane foresees technicians superseding politicians as technology becomes increasingly autonomous.[8] "The higher the state of technological development," writes another political scientist, Franz Neumann, "the greater the concentration of political power".[9] The leadership emerging in the technological state, argues Daniel Bell, will be comprised of "the Scientists, the mathematicians, the economists, and the engineers of the new complex technology. The leadership of the new society will rest . . . with the research corporation, the industrial laboratories, the experimental stations, and the university."[10] This has been called "the new priesthood,"[11] an oligarchy of technicians which will result in "the tyranny of experts."[12] The father of the criticism of technology, Jacques Ellul, concludes in *The Political Illusion*:

> . . . [T]he decisions fundamentally affecting the future of a nation are in the domains of technology . . . . [T]hese innumerable decisions are the fruits of the technician's labor . . . [and] will no longer be taken on the basis of philosophic or political principle or on the basis of doctrine or ideology, but on the basis of technicians' reports outlining what is useful, possible, and efficient . . . . The politician finds himself inside a framework designed by technicians, and his choice, if it is serious, will be made on a technological grounds . . . .[13]

What such scholars have in common—regardless of whether they consider technology a godsend (Bell), a curse (Ellul), or something in between (Lane and Neumann)—is their underestimation of the first post-technological generation which has presently come of age.

Until our generation challenged the image of technological man and his way of thinking, its critics were few. We must remember that as late as the mid-1960s sociologists still were certain that "each age produces its own type of hero: soldier, diplomat, theologian, scholar, statesman, businessman. Today, who can deny that the technologist occupies the hero's niche?"[14] Others observed bluntly: "Technology is the new metaphysics."[15] Surrounded by the nearly unanimous revolutionary fervor of the technicians, it is not surprising that their few, lonely critics adopted an anguished and embittered tone. Like Ellul, they railed against the inhumanity of technique as if it were a daemonic force beyond human control.

Though understandable, self-righteous wailing at the gates of technology's palace is not solution. In fact, "out-radicalizing" each other by ever intensified hostility toward the "system" or toward "technology" ultimately represents the most reactionary position of all. Once one believes that the technological state is so dehumanizing that nothing can save it, one's belief becomes self-confirming. The only options then available are guerilla warfare or apathy, both of which the technological state can easily deal with.

The problem has been that technocracy has not been perceived as a political phenomenon—neither by those who work in it nor by those affected by it. To use Theodore Roszak's metaphor: the public was so busy watching the competing political teams that it forgot about the umpire, technology, which "sets the limits and goals of the competition and judges the contenders."[16] By questioning the rules of the game as well as the merits of the opposing teams, a generation has at last become conscious of technology's power and methods.

With this consciousness in hand we cannot limit ourselves to a life-style of cultural freedom on the one hand and political protest on the other. Some attitude researchers argue that two revolutions are occurring, one "cultural" and the other "political," and that from 1970 to 1972 the former gained strength at the expense of the latter.[17] Such deceptive dichotomies avoid dealing with a third revolution: the new breed of knowledge workers who will force their way into every setting where technical decisions are made. Among technicians who pride themselves on using new methods, inventing new products, and exploiting new markets, this group will bring new ethical judgment to the decision of when *not* to use, *not* to invent, and *not* to exploit.

Adult who have adopted counter cultural life-styles and

"leftist" political attitudes, must now decide *to what ends we will devote our labor.* How long could an opposition survive, if, after returing from the barricades, it had to rely on its ad-versaries for child-care, nourishment, news, education, enter-tainment, literature, and even finances? Conversely, how long could a counter culture survive if no one worked to dis-mantle and redesign the war-and-waste machine which saps the vitality of *all* culture, counter or not. Unless both the "cultural" and "political" revolutions are translated into work, they will die before our children are old enough to give them new life.

Getting Together:
Work

Without a corps of radical professionals, the only opponents of technology would be bleak and categorical neo-Luddites. These uninformed critics of technology would simplistically call for a complete renunciation of the inventions of tech-nology: from drugs to computers, and from combustion engines to mass production. They would call for an end to further scientific research and development. The technicians rightfully dismiss this minority of strident critics, since the problems of the technological society cannot be solved by leaving our technical knowledge unused. Rather it must be used within a human frame of reference.

Economic planning, educational control, ecological exploi-tation, dehumanized national priorities—all exact a price from the next generation's freedom. To counteract this basic "conservatism" of technology, we must now deal not only with *current* conflicts of interest—between a corporation's right to dump wastes in a river and the downstream people's right to pure drinking water, for example—but with *future* conflicts as well.

This is, perhaps, the most complicated task we face. Each fundamentally radical alternative to the technicians' brave new world that is proposed will be met with the epithet "reactionary." There are clearly reactionary overtones in the mistrust of nuclear reactors, in the renewed desire for organic and natural foods, in the search for drug-free methods of controlling childbirth pain. But what makes these proposals radical, and not reactionary, is that they do not constitute a blind and regressive denial of technology, but a selective adoption of technology within a human frame of values. No greater task lies before the present generation of young adults than the task of developing the combination of technical skills and man-centered values which will enable them to avoid both primitivist escapism and technological brinkmanship.

One guide between these two extremes is the concept of childhood. *Every institution must become in its own way a children's lobby.* This change in orientation is perhaps nowhere more crucial than in the university. For the university is desperately needed in order that ethical *values* may be translated into creative *skills*.

Educated young people must learn to use their knowledge on behalf of society and their own children. A university empty of values and commitment is an easy target for powerful economic or state institutions. The German university system inherited by Hitler was a strictly supervised and hierarchically ordered system which left students no voice whatsoever in what they were taught. Students were expected to appreciate, not to question. Thus it is no surprise that, once the Nazis came to power, university students in Germany quietly listened and learn the Nazi "body of material."[18]

The German educational system was effective in forming intellectuals like Hitler's obedient architect Albert Speer, men who became "immured in isolated, closed-off areas of life." These men efficiently performed their specific technical tasks while remaining mindless of the direction of society as a whole. Like Speer, they rarely reflected on the purpose or value of their work; they were more concerned with career advancement.[19] It is no wonder that they sold their skills to the highest bidder, Adolf Hitler.

We cannot afford to spend twenty years in prison, as did Speer, to recognize that the danger of specialized irresponsibility is not accidental to, but integrally part of, the technological society. Modern man must develop ethical responsibility as well as technical proficiency. Unless he is to destroy the very basis of life, he must realize that, as Alvin Toffler puts it, "so far as technology is concerned, *no one* is in control."[20]

If the university is so tied to a deification of knowledge which serves technology that it fails to be the intellectual birthplace of our children's welfare, then it is no longer a university but simply a personnel office. When an ambitious student long ago asked Buddha about the nature of the universe, he replied: "I do not know and it is of no concern to me because whatever the answer is it does not contribute to the one problem which is of concern: how to reduce human suffering." We must learn this truth—that the ultimate *veritas* is *caritas*. To protect the development of children and of humanity itself, each of the interlocking parts of the technological state must be transformed.

1. The Technological Sciences.   Often considered the field most remote from "social issues," the technological sciences nevertheless have had the greatest impact on society. A new scientific ethics must question the value of expanding knowledge rapidly and "efficiently" in terms of limiting and controlling the application of that knowledge.[21] Technical scientists in the past have not sufficiently analyzed themselves and their society in order to assess their personal motivations or their social impact. The fact that a machine or a drug or a process or commodity *could* be invented inevitably meant to them that it *ought* to be invented and used on the widest possible scale.[22] Although scientific planners ostensibly pursued their work for the welfare of society, only rarely was the long-range impact of those inventions on human development seriously considered.[23]

2. The Biological Sciences.   With the destructive processing of our food, the high intake of establishment and anti-establishment drugs, the noise and density of urban living, and the industrial pollution of water and air, we have been thrust unprepared into a new biological and ecological world. The physiological integrity of man must be defended by natural as well as social scientists, who alone have the ability to forewarn us of the secondary effects of technical, economic, and political decisions on nature—and on human nature. We now require, as one biologist has put it, a "bioethics" in which to ground the more abstract ethics of politics, psychology, philosophy, and religion—none of which has prevented our ecological crisis.[24] The interlocking scientific puzzles and social complexities require the training of radical ecologists who are knowledgeable also in business, community decision-making, and even international politics.[25] If the imperiled human ecosystem is to be saved, biologists who have had the courage to move beyond their traditional intellectual habitat will play the leading role. Without their participation, the numerous social-action organizations will have understanding no deeper than their opponents.[26]

3. Medicine.   How the knowledge generated by the technical and biological sciences is translated into health care is determined by medical doctors. While the standards of medical schools have assured the American public of competent medical specialists, professional medical organizations are frequently so reactionary in their political views that this medical competence does not efficiently reach the sick. To oppose attempts to insure adequate health care for the poor produces far more illness than even the most diligent doctors could treat. For the average citizen it is political suicide to remain inactive when pollution has begun to produce genetic defects[27] and when DDT has been found in dangerous quantities in mother's milk.[28] For a doctor it is professional irresponsibility.

Fortunately some doctors have begun to mobilize against the sterile definition of medical responsibility bequeathed to them by the AMA.[29] They have recognized that the "social responsibility of the scientist" applies especially to those who are responsible for human health.[30]

4. The Social Sciences.   These technical, biological, and medical professions together may provide the scientific component of the post-technological revolution, but they cannot do so without a direct study of man and society. Because the social sciences can expose social inequality and human alienation, they have been the source of student activism throughout the world.[31] The raging debate in these fields is, to borrow Marx's phrase, whether their task is to interpret the world or to change it.[32]

Seeing themselves as value-free interpreters, social scientists have generally shared the goals of the managerial elite when studying domestic issues and of the federal policymakers when studying international affairs.[33] With aspirations to "objectivity," they have provided rationales for their class or national allegiances. Scientific rigor does exist in some parts of these disciplines. Where controversy over basic values reigns, however, scientific technique is of no avail. Although one economics professor, for example, may claim that the sole responsibility of any corporation is to produce profits, another may charge that the concept of profit is false when social and human costs are not included in the analysis. Until social scientists commit themselves on socioeconomic conflicts like these, they cannot begin to exert a positive influence on the reshaping of society.

5. Psychology.   Both the technical and the social scientists must link their research to the concrete needs of human development. Apparent technical and economic "progress" can camouflage deeper failures in social organization and human relationships. The voice of a radical psychology must be heard among scientists to ensure that the changes advocated by those scientists will indeed benefit children trying to grow up.

"Potentially one of the most revolutionary intellectual enterprises ever conceived by the mind of man,"[34] psychology today does not merit this praise. Few psychologists have committed themselves to ensuring that their hard-won knowledge will indeed improve the real condition in which children grow. What does "progress" in physiological psychology mean to malnourished children? Or "expanded knowledge" in cognitive growth to ghetto school children? Increasingly sophisticated experimental, analytical, or therapeutic methods will amount to little more than intellectual playthings as long as the values of technological capitalism remain unchallenged. Today psychology's contributions to knowledge are primarily seized upon when they promise new means of control for established authority or new products for enterprising firms.[35]

6. The Humanities. It has fallen to the humanities to be the watchdog of the sciences. By its very name, this field was meant to be concerned with the "human," to be for mankind the "antennae of the race." If those in the humanities are to fulfill this mandate even in the midst of this accelerated technological age, their vision must be powerful and their descriptions precise. Without them, values will become the exclusive domain of the technician. We will not reach a new, humanistic synthesis of the "two cultures," but simply a victory by default of the scientific over the artistic.[36]

We must, in other words, get our heads together as well as our hearts. When Freud was once asked what basic abilities a normal, healthy adult should have, he answered: *Lieben und arbeiten.* "To love and to work." Even if our political categories are considered useful in distinguishing between adults as voters, they are clearly inadequate in describing the range of alternatives available to adults as workers, and as lovers. To describe even tentatively the responsible adulthood for which we are searching, we must begin to think about how the three elements of our adult lives—political, professional, and parental—can mutually support each other. Only then will we find enough vitality, strength, and love in our own lives so that we may share them with our children.

The Divided Child

Both the culture and the political economy are increasingly determined by the technologies on which they are based. As

President Kennedy said in a 1962 commencement address at Yale University, the problems facing American society in the 1960s, unlike those of the 1930s, would require "technical answers—not political answers".[37] Kennedy's statement was designed to indicate a readiness to move beyond cold-war ideological fanatacism that had dominated the 1950s. As Arthur Schlessinger put it later,

> . . . the rise in the last generation of the mixed society—of the view that it is possible to give the state sufficient power to bring about social welfare and economic growth without thereby giving it the power to abolish political and civic freedom— has revealed classical capitalism and classical socialism as nineteenth century doctrines, *left behind by the onward rush of science and technology. The world has moved beyond these obsolete ideologies toward a far more subtle and flexible social strategy.*[38]

Though this may have heralded "the end of ideology" as far as politics was concerned, it obviously marked "the beginning of ideology" as far as technology was concerned. For now the question was: these men who would provide these objective "technical" answers—what political values and social ethics did *they* have?

Instead of accepting this pseudo-utopian "end of ideology," we would be far wiser parents if together we reformulated a new and comprehensive, man-centered ideology. Given the magnified importance of technological decisions, *we must now choose our work with the same ethical passion with which we chose our politics.* Military technology decides who can control whom; economic technology, who can outproduce whom; and communications technology, who can ultimately convince whom. Men and women whose lives and livelihoods are bound up with this technology, therefore, are as involved in the overall "political" process as those who work for the government itself. As William Barrett puts it:

> Now that we have airplanes that fly faster than the sun, intercontinental missiles, space satellites, and above all atomic explosives, we are aware that technology itself has assumed a power to which politics in any traditional sense is subordinate.

> If the Russians were to outstrip us decisively in technology, then all ordinary political considerations would have to go by the boards. The classical art of politics, conceived by the Greeks as a thoroughly human act addressed to humans, becomes an outmoded and fragile thing beside the massive accumulation of technological power. The fate of the world, it now appears, turns upon sheer mastery of things.[39]

To cope with such a world, we need not end, but rather extend, ideological values. Ideology need not mean a rigid, closed, "totalistic" set of ideas. It can mean simply that as parents we must have a vision of the future that makes work meaningful and that gives knowledge and "facts" social purpose.

Envisioning a desirable future, and selecting the ways to reach it, are not tasks that can be left to hired "futurologists," elitist "planning boards," or high-powered "think tanks." On the contrary, these are tasks for which every parent must feel responsible if his work is to help ensure a reasonable welcome for his children into the world. To be "ideological," then, means that we care where we are going and where we are taking our children. It is by caring, at last, that we become parents, and by working like parents that we extend our care to all.

The political, professional, and parental aspects of adult responsibility are separate in name only. Yet we feel between these groups a sense of divisiveness, even hostility, despite the fact that *all* these groups' concerns must be present to ensure our children's growth. They should overlap to form a strong, personal center. Such adults whom we quite naturally call "together," engage in work and politics with the care and dedication of a parent; they do their politicking and parenting with a long-term committedness that others reserve for work; and they recognize that being a parent, like being a worker, has political impacts. These adults' lives "hang together" because they are centered in care.

Our generation has thought these mature adults were less common in our society than they actually are. After all, our childhoods were spent stranded in classrooms and enveloped by the media. But the truth is that such adults are rare simply because the basic model of parenthood these adults had—their own parents—could not be applied to the technological world they had created.

As the technicians delegated intrinsically social issues to private policy-making groups of "experts," they subjected traditionally private matters (food, child-rearing, family life, education, etc.) to external social control. With the public having become private and the private public, the technicians mistakenly subdivided adulthood as if it were but another problem of management. Political responsibility came to be limited to biennial ballots; professional responsibility to be based on fulfilling standardized requirements for advancement; and parental responsibility reserved for what were called "family matters." The resulting tragedy was that even "good mothers and fathers" would support a war which required their sons to kill or be killed meaninglessly; would vote for politicians willing to spend extravagantly on bombs and lunar modules but so very stingily on children; and would betray their children to repressive school systems or accept fake foods.

The Cycle Joined

But the dehumanization does not affect only children. If the new fate of the very young is to be seated in rows at mechanical consoles monitored by computers, then the equally tragic fate of the very old is to be deserted in a wicker rocking chair, segregated with other aged and ailing castaways in dismal nursing homes. The very old have also become the victims of the tangle of conflicting hopes and fears of those younger than themselves who are grasping at life like losing gamblers at a roulette wheel.

The young are the responsibility of the old—this much is clear. But what about the very old? Are they not also the victims of a technological ethic which values productivity and despises dependency? If an isolated child seated at a computer console troubles the parental conscience, should not a stooped, lonely resident of a nursing home trouble us too.

Instead of veneration and care, the old have received political solicitation. Aside from overtures for the "senior citizen" vote and promises from retirement profiteers, they have been shunted aside with a callousness unknown to earlier generations. Just as the quality of childhood in a society reveals that society's real goals, so Simone de Beauvoir argues that "by the way in which a society behaves towards its old people, it uncovers the naked, and often carefully hidden, truths about its real principles and aims . . . *their unhappy fate proclaims the failure of our civilization as a whole.*"[40]

Given our alienation from nature, how logical that technological man should be alienated from the human gateways to nature, birth and death, and the stages of life that follow and lead to them, childhood and old age. Thus technology threatens those who go out from, as well as those who come in to, adulthood. The wisdom of the venerable village elder has been replaced by the updated know-how of the middle-aged executive and the quick expertise of the fresh trainee. This technically defined obsolescence, combined with the stripped-down family unit, has left the old in a "no-man's land" walled off from the rest of society by a manufactured youthfulness. Consequently, we tolerate an "American way of death"[41] as distorted by technique as the rites of birth. When the deodorized, cosmeticized anesthesia wears off and we finally realize that even technological man grows old and dies, it is too late.

Although power to decide the common fate of all ages rests most heavily with those equidistant from birth and death, perhaps a certain wise innocence belongs to those who have yet to enter, and those who have already passed, adulthood. How else can we explain the strange and healing bond which seems to be developing between the forgotten old and the alienated young?

Radical political groups at the Democratic Convention in Miami in 1972 purposefully planned joint events with elderly citizens with whose fate they identified. High school and college students on Ralph Nader's staff spent months researching the plight of nursing home residents. Young singers have dedicated albums to the elderly; conscientious objectors have often sought service in old-age homes; students in high schools have initiated programs to develop contacts with the old.

This link between the "over-aged" and the "under-aged" is the human equivalent of the link between "reactionary" and "radical." To connect their two disparate histories, the "grandchildren" seek assurance that they do indeed come from somewhere and that some durable human continuity still survives. The "grandparents" seek the peace that comes from knowing that, despite the publicized revolutions which their children and their children's children claim to have made, the conception of life which gave them strength to survive the century still holds meaning and may live on.

In such gentle ways does humanity reassert itself. Unless generations experience "progress" and "growth" in their own life cycles, these goals inevitably become abstract and counterfeit. This is why, no matter how rigorous the demands or how seductive the diversions with which technological civilization may present us, each generation must go back "to the root"—to the interweaving of daily lives where truly human progress and growth are achieved. When our lives come to the end of a revolution around the wheel of time, we will gain the courage to pass peacefully from life with the knowledge that we have replenished it—not just with new lives, but with fuller ones.

We will not build Utopia. Probably Marx's vision of a society in which "the full and free development of all is the ruling principle" will still be unrealized. But at least we will have secured for the next generation, our children, the freedom and dignity to reach again for this goal.

This is the human essence of the Creation in which we are all joined. It will never be timed by ticking clocks or measured calendars; never determined by projected curves or computed plans; never captured in a test tube or recorded on microfilm; and never destroyed, we hope, by the hidden war-

heads of hate. This Creation is neither mechanically controlled, nor divinely preordained, but so fragile, so human.
It unfolds to its fullest only as each generation offers to the
next their deepest creativity.

Notes

Introduction

1. Joseph Lelyveld, "The Status of 'the Movement'," *New York Times Magazine,* November 7, 1971.
2. Christopher Lasch, *The Agony of the American Left* (Random House, New York; 1969).
3. Ibid.
4. Daniel Yankelovich, *The Changing Values on Campus* (Pocket Books, New York; 1972).
5. Quoted by Alvin Toffler, *Future Shock,* p. 419 (Bantam, New York; 1970).
6. Howard Zinn, "Marxism and the New Left," in Alfred E. Young, *Dissent,* p. 359 (N. Illinois Univ. Press, DeKalb, Ill.).
7. Andrew M. Greeley, "The End of the Movement," *Change,* 4:13, April 1972.
8. Staughton Lynd, "The Movement: A New Beginning," in *Liberation.*
9. Michael Lerner, "Respectable Bigotry," *The American Scholar* (Fall, 1969); originally published in the *New Journal,* a student publication at Yale.
10. Jonothon Kozol, *Free Schools* (Houghton Mifflin, Boston; 1972).
11. Speech commemorating the 100th Anniversary of Lenin's birth, celebrated in 1970.
12. Dirk J. Struik, ed., *The 1844 Manuscripts of Karl Marx* (International Publishers, 1968).
13. Erik Erikson, Godkin Lectures, delivered at Harvard University, Spring 1972.
14. Herb Gintis, "Towards a Political Economy of Education," in *This Magazine is About Schools,* April 1972.
15. Rubem Alves, *Tomorrow's Child:* Imagination, Creativity, and the Rebirth of Culture.

Radicalism

1. *Webster's New World Dictionary of the English Language,* College Edition (World Publishing Company, New York; 1962). Cf. Crane Brinton, *The Anatomy of Revolution,* p. 276.
2. For differing interpretations of Marx's celebrated statement, cf: Erich Fromm, *Sane Society,* 221 ff; (Holt, Rinehart & Winston, New York); Dwight MacDonald, *The Root is Man,* 273 ff; (Gordon Press); and Veljke Karac, "In Search of Human Society," in Fromm's *Socialist Humanism* (Doubleday, New York).

3. Erich Fromm, *Marx's Concept of Man*, p. 58 (Ungar, New York).

4. Marx's statement from *Das Kapital* is quoted in Fromm, *Sane Society*, p. 223.

5. R.A. Spitz. "Hospitalism," *Psychoanalytic Study of the Child*, Vol. 1. (1945). S. Provence and R. C. Lipton, *Infants In Institutions* (International Univ. Press, New York; 1962). J. Bowlby, *Maternal Care and Mental Health* (Schocken, New York; 1951).

6. John Flavell, *The Developmental Psychology of Jean Piaget*, p. 203 (Van Nostrand-Reinhold, New York; 1963).

7. Ibid., pp. 204–5; also Barbell Inhelder and Jean Piaget, *The Growth of Logical Thinking from Childhood to Adolescence*, pp. 341–2 (Basic Books, New York; 1958).

8. Erikson, *Insight and Responsibility*, p. 245 (Norton, New York; 1964).

9. These concepts have been developed by William G. Perry in "Forms of Intellectual and Ethical Development in the College Years," Bureau of Study Counsel, Harvard University.

10. Lawrence Kohlberg's work explains these concepts of the development of moral reasoning during childhood and adolescence.

11. Erikson, op. cit., p. 125.

12. Erikson, "A Memorandum on Identity and Negro Youth," *Journal of Social Issues*, 20:41, October 1964.

13. Inhelder and Piaget, op. cit., p. 337.

14. cf. Sigmund Freud, *New Introductory Lectures in Psychoanalysis*, p. 177f (Norton, New York); and Paul Roazen, *Freud: Political and Social Thought*, p. 320 (Knopf, New York).

15. Roazen, op. cit., p. 259.

16. Erik H. Erikson, *Identity: Youth and Crisis*, p. 23 (Norton, New York; 1968).

17. John Lukacs, *Historical Consciousness*, pp. 233–4 (Harper and Row, New York; 1968).

The Technological Revolution

1. Karl Popper, *The Open Society and Its Enemies*, p. 83 (Princeton Univ. Press, N.J.; 1966).

2. V. I. Lenin, "Left-Wing Childishness and the Petty Bourgeois Mentality", in *Collected Works*, Volume 27, p. 349 (Progress Publishers, Moscow, 1964).

3. Edvard Kardelj, *Socialist Thought and Practice,* No. 21, pp. 7–8; Belgrade 1966.

4. Quoted in Erich Fromm, *Revolution of Hope* (Harper and Row, New York; 1970).

5. Kardelj, op. cit., p. 8.

6. Herbert Marcuse, *Revolution and Counterrevolution,* p. 50 (Beacon Press, Boston; 1972).

7. Roger Garaudy, *Crisis in Communism,* p. 24 (New York; 1970).

8. Emmanuel G. Mesthene, *Technological Change* (New American Library; 1970).

9. For various interpretations see the work of Peter Drucker, Michael Harrington, J. K. Galbraith, Erich Fromm, Roger Garaudy, Zbigniew Brzezinski, Herbert Marcuse, and others cited.

10. John K. Galbraith, *The New Industrial State,* p. 267 (Houghton Mifflin, New York; 1969).

11. Fletcher Byrom, Address at the Krannert Graduate School of Industrial Administration, Purdue University, June 23, 1970.

12. The best job has been done by Fritz Machlup in *The Production and Distribution of Knowledge in the United States* (Princeton Univ. Press, New Jersey).

13. Clark Kerr's estimate, quoted by Michael Harrington in *Toward A Democratic Left,* p. 65 (MacMillan; 1968).

14. Peter Drucker, *The Age of Discontinuity,* p. 263 (Harper and Row, New York).

15. Michael Harrington, *Socialism,* p. 359 (Saturday Review Press, New York; 1972).

16. Philip Slater, *The Pursuit of Loneliness* (Beacon, Boston; 1970).

17. Herbert Marcuse, *Five Lectures,* p. 96 (Beacon, Boston; 1970).

18. *Youth's Agenda for the Seventies:* A Report on the White House Conference on Youth with a Summary of the Recommendations, (ed. Wade Green; the John D. Rockefeller Fund, New York, 1971).

19. For a more scholarly approach to the dynamics of science-bred change, cf. Thomas S. Kuhn, *The Structure of Scientific Revolutions* (Univ. of Chicago Press; 1962).

20. Barry Commoner, *The Closing Circle,* p. 129 (Knopf, New York; 1971).

21. Galbraith, op. cit., chapters 1 and 2.

22. Garaudy, op. cit., pp. 49–55.

23. Galbraith, op. cit., chapter 1.

24. Erich Fromm, *Revolution of Hope,* p. 84 (Harper and Row, New York; 1970).
25. Donella Meadows et. al., *The Limits to Growth,* p. 143 (Universe, New York; 1972).
26. Dennis L. Meadows, in testimony before Senate Subcommittee On Air and Water Pollution in Support of Senate Bill 1113, May 3, 1971.
27. Ronald S. Glasser, M.D., *365 Days* (Braziller, New York; 1971).

The Children's Revolution

1. Robert Coles, *Children of Crisis,* p. 319 (Dell, New York; 1968).
2. For a more thorough discussion of personal (as distinct from legal) freedom, cf. Christian Bay, *The Structure of Freedom* (Stanford Univ. Press).
3. Herbert Marcuse, *Eros and Civilization,* Preface (Beacon Press, Boston; 1955).
4. Kenneth Keniston, *The Uncommitted,* p. 254 (Dell, New York; 1970).
5. Cf. Robert K. Merton's introduction to Jacques Ellul, *The Technological Society* (Knopf, New York; 1964).
6. Robert Boguslaw, *The New Utopians: A Study of Systems Design and Social Change* (Prentice-Hall, Englewood Cliffs, N. J.; 1968). This is one of the best critiques of systems analysis available.
7. Keniston, op. cit. p. 254ff.
8. Garrett, Hardin, quoted in Barry Commoner, *The Closing Circle* (Knopf, New York; 1971).
9. Commoner, op. cit. p. 188.
10. Brewster Chiselin, *The Creative Process,* p. 14 (New American Library, New York).
11. James Simon Kunen, *Strawberry Statement* (Random House, New York).
12. *Report to the President,* pp. 262, 241 (White House Conference on Children, 1971).
13. Cf. for example Marvin Leiner and Robert Udell, "Day Care in Cuba: Children are the Revolution," *Saturday Review,* April 1972. This is an illustration of a proper *emphasis* on childcare, not necessarily the proper *method.*
14. Maria Montessori, *The Secret of Childhood,* pp. 362–3 (Fides, Notre Dame, Indiana).

15. Charles Hampden-Turner, *Radical Man,* p. 309 (Schenkman, Cambridge, Mass.; 1970).
16. Quoted by Nan Berger, "The Child, The Law, and the State," in *Children's Rights: Toward the Liberation of the Child,* p. 179 (New York; 1971).
17. Montessori, *The Secret of Childhood,* pp. 257 and 263–4.
18. Erikson, *Childhood and Society,* Revised Edition (Norton, New York; 1963).
19. Erich Fromm, *The Crisis of Psychoanalysis* pp. 55–6 (Harcourt Brace and World, New York; 1970).

The Embryo

1. Commoner, p. 50.
2. Ibid, p. 53.
3. Cited in Commoner, p. 195.
4. *The Federalist Papers* (Pocket Books, New York; 1964).
5. Commoner, p. 197.
6. Cf. John M. Fowler, *Fallout* (Basic Books, New York; 1960).
7. Commoner, p. 60.
8. Neil Fabricant and Robert M. Hallman, *Toward A Rational Power Policy: Energy, Politics, and Pollution,* pp. 122–3 (Braziller, New York; 1971).
9. Ibid., pp. 132ff.
10. Glenn T. Seaborg and Duston L. Bloom, "Fast Breeder Reactors," *Scientific American,* November 1970.
11. Ernest J. Sternglass, *Low-Level Radiation,* p. 14 (Ballantine, New York; 1972)
12. Ibid.
13. Ibid., p. 147.
14. Fabricant et al., op. cit., pp. 112–3.
15. "Nuclear Reactor Safety: At the AEC the Way of the Dissenter is Hard," *Science,* May 5, 1972.
16. Fabricant, p. 124.
17. *Science,* loc. cit.
18. Fabricant, p. 135.
19. Fabricant et al.
20. Richard S. Lewis, *The Nuclear Power Rebellion* (Viking, New York; 1972); H. Peter Metzger, *The Atomic Establishment* (Simon and Schuster, New York; 1972).
21. Quoted by Michael Harrington in *Socialism,* p. 349.
22. "Energy Crisis: Are We Running Out?," *Time,* June 12, 1972.

Childbirth

1. Irwin Chabon, *Awake and Aware,* p. 70 (Dell, New York; 1966).
2. T. Berry Brazelton, "What Childbirth Drugs Do To Your Baby," *Redbook,* February 1971.
3. Watson A. Bowes et al., "The Effects of Obstetrical Medication on Fetus and Infant," *Monographs for the Society for Research in Child Development,* 35 (4) :24 (1970).
4. Ibid., p. 9.
5. Ibid., p. 15.
6. Margaret Mead and Niles Newton, "Cultural Patterning of Perinatal Behavior," in Richardson and Guttmacher, *Childbearing: Its Social and Psychological Aspects* (William and Wilkins, New York; 1967).
7. Bowes, op. cit., p. 6.
8. J. R. Fouts, "The metabolism of drugs by the fetus," in J. M. Robson et al., *Embryopathic Activity of Drugs,* pp. 43–55 (Little, Boston; 1965).
9. Bowes, op. cit., p. 5.
10. H. B. Atlee, *Natural Childbirth* (Springfield, Ill.; 1956).
11. Niles Newton, *Maternal Emotions* (New York; 1955).
12. Brazelton, "Psychophysiologic reactions in the neonate," *Journal of Pediatrics* 58: 512–8 (1961).
13. Brazelton, op. cit.
14. Such inquiry has been rare because it straddles one of the innumerable barriers between medical specialties: in this case, between pediatrics and obstetrics. Because pediatricians frequently are uniformed (or unconcerned) about a specific child's birth experience, they are unlikely to relate pediatric pathology to it. The converse is true for the obstetrician.
15. In Bowes et al., op. cit., p. 33.
16. Bowes, op. cit., p. 7; and Benaron "Subsequent effects of anoxia," *American Journal of Obstetrics and Gynecology,* 80: 1129 (1960).
17. Ashley Montagu, *The Humanization of Man* (Grove Press, New York).
18. *Medical World News,* p. 17, May 22, 1970.
19. Ibid.
20. Erik H. Erikson, *Childhood and Society,* p. 420.
21. MacDonald, Robert L., "The Role of Emotional Factors in Obstetric Complications: A Review," *Psychosomatic Medicine,* 30: 222 (1968).

22. Frederick T. Melges, "Postpartum Psychiatric Syndromes," *Psychosomatic Medicine*, 3: 95 (1968).
23. Niles Newton, op. cit., p. 115f.
24. Ashley Montagu, op. cit., p. 115f.
25. Quoted in *Prevention* Magazine, p. 26, December, 1970.
26. Niles Newton, op. cit., p. 38.
27. Jonothan Kozol, op. cit.
28. Macy Conference Report, *The Midwife in the United States*, Address by Dr. George A. Silver, "Mother and Child Care: One View of the Problem."
29. Ibid.
30. Irwin Chabon, op. cit., pp. 26–7.
31. Niles Newton, op. cit., p. 40.
32. Dr. Norma Morris, Introduction to Leon Chertok, *Motherhood and Personality: Psychosomatic Aspects of Childbirth* (Lippincott, Boston; 1969).
33. Leon Chertok, op. cit., p. 200.
34. Niles Newton, op. cit., pp. 36–7.
35. Arthur J. Mandy, et al., "Is Natural Childbirth Natural?" *Psychosomatic Medicine*, 14: 431 (1952).
36. Irwin Chabon, op. cit., p. 66.
37. Barbara and John Ehrenreich, *The American Health Empire*, p. 17 (Random House, New York; 1970).
38. *Prevention*, p. 422, December, 1970.
39. Erik H. Erikson, *Childhood and Society*, 422.
40. Erik H. Erikson, *Identity and the Life Cycle*, p. 100, (New York; 1959).

Feeding

1. Phillippe Aries, *Centuries of Childhood*, pp. 374f (Knopf, New York; 1962).
2. Alice Gerard, *Please Breast-feed Your Baby*, p. 28 (Avon, New York).
3. Ibid.
4. Gustav Eckstein, *The Body Has A Head*, p. 201 (Harper and Row, New York; 1970).
5. Gerard, op. cit., pp. 29–31. Cf. "The Uniqueness of Human Milk," *American Journal of Clinical Nutrition*, August, 1971.
6. Bruno Bettelheim, lecture at the University of Chicago, 1970.
7. Erik H. Erikson, *Identity, Youth, and Crisis*, p. 219.
8. Ibid., pp. 97–8; also Melges, op. cit.
9. Gerard, op. cit., Chapter 2.

10. Ashley Montagu, op. cit.
11. Brazelton (1961), op. cit.
12. Studies by Kron et al., quoted in Niles Newton and Michael Newton, "Psychologic Aspects of Lactation," *New England Journal of Medicine,* 277: 1179–1188 (November 1967).
13. Cf. Newton and Newton, loc. cit.
14. Ibid.
15. Gerard, op. cit., p. 56.
16. Ibid., p. iv.
17. Newton and Newton, op. cit.
18. *Forbes* Magazine, December 15, 1970.
19. In a letter to Congressman Henry S. Reuss, reported by UPI in the *Indianapolis Star,* December 7, 1970.
20. Leon Walther, quoted by Jacques Ellul, op. cit., pp. 20 and 352.
21. Newton and Newton, op. cit.
22. Gerard, op. cit., Chapter 2.
23. Charles F. Wuster, "DDT in Mother's Milk," *Saturday Review,* May 1, 1970.
24. Ibid.
25. Gerard, op. cit., p. 118.

Eating and Infancy

1. *Hunger USA.* Report of the Citizen's Board of Inquiry into Hunger and Malnutrition in the United States (Beacon, Boston; 1968).
2. Hearings before the Senate Subcommittee on Nutrition and Human Needs, Part I. Review of the Results of the White House Conference on Food, Nutrition, and Health.
3. *Hunger USA,* pp. 18f. Cf. H.G. Birch and J.D. Gussow, *Disadvantaged Children: Health, Nutrition, and School Failure* Grune, New York; 1970).
4. Ibid.
5. Ibid., p. 41.
6. Ibid.
7. Ibid., p. 50.
8. Dept. of HEW, "Health Services to the Poor," December, 1967.
9. *Congressional Record,* June 28, 1967, H8243.
10. George McGovern, "The Child and the American Future," *American Psychologist,* February, 1970.
11. *Time,* May 8, 1972.
12. Julian Chisolm, Jr., "Lead Poisoning," *Scientific American,* February 1971.

13. Gordon Rattray Taylor, *The Doomsday Book,* pp. 134–5, 146–7, 160, 181, 228 (World Publishers, New York; 1970); and Commoner, op. cit., pp. 82 and 93.

14. Citizen's Board Report, op. cit., p. 46.

15. Roper Research Study, published by Sugar Information, Inc. For a more complete analysis read John Yudkin, M.D., *Sweet and Dangerous,* Chapter 17: "The Sugar Industry's Defense Strategy: Attack."

16. James S. Turner, *The Chemical Feast* (Grossman, New York; 1970); See also *Making Your Own Baby Food,* by Mary and James S. Turner.

17. Ibid., p. 88.

18. Ibid., p. 88ff.

19. Cf. Sidney Margolius, *The Great American Food Hoax* (Walker, New York; 1971); and Beatrice Trum Hunter, *Consumer Beware* (Simon and Schuster, New York; 1971).

20. *Prevention,* loc. cit., pp. 78ff.

21. Jacques Ellul, op. cit., p. 327.

22. Gene Marine and Judith van Allen, *Food Pollution.*

23. James S. Turner, op. cit., pp. 60 and v.

24. U.S. Dept. of Agriculture, Agriculture Research Service, 62–17, June 1968.

25. New York *Times,* November 9, 1969.

26. Boston *Record-American,* August 28, 1969.

27. Gene Marine et al., op. cit.

28. Cf. *Ramparts* Magazine, May 1972.

29. Frances Moore Lappé, *Diet for a Small Planet* (Ballantine, New York; 1971).

30. Ibid., p. 11. See also the Berkeley Women's Health Collective, *Feeding Ourselves,* c/o 2214 Grove Street, Berkeley, Cal. 94704.

The Family

1. An article by Marya Mannes, World News Service, reported in the Indianapolis *Star.* Cf. "Bibliography on the Battered Child," Dept. of HEW, July 1969 (revised); and D.G. Gil, *Violence Against Children: Physical Abuse in the United States* (Harvard Univ. Press, Cambridge, Mass.; 1970).

2. *U.S. News and World Report,* p. 38, April 24, 1972.

3. White House Conference on Children, 1970, p. 253.

4. CBS News, May 9, 1972.

5. White House Conference Report, op. cit.

6. James Miller, "The War Against Children," *Life,* May 19, 1972.

7. Ibid.
8. *U.S. News and World Report,* loc. cit.
9. *Newsweek,* "Never too Young to Learn," May 22, 1972.
10. Erik Erikson, *Identity: Youth and Crisis,* p. 116 (Norton, New York; 1968).
11. Michael Wallach, "Creativity and the Expression of Possibilities," in Jerome Kagan, *Creativity and Learning* (Houghton Mifflin, Boston; 1968).
12. Piaget, quoted by Charles Silberman, op. cit., pp. 218–9.
13. Ibid.
14. Arnold Gessell and Frances L. Ilg, *Child Development,* p. 260 (Harper and Row, New York; 1949).
15. Alvin Toffler, op. cit., p. 242.
16. See *Autokind vs. Mankind,* Kenneth R. Schneider (Norton, New York; 1971), also *The Accessible City,* Wilfried Owen Brookings Institute, Washington D.C.; 1972).
17. Gessell and Ilg, op. cit., pp. 34 and 157.
18. John K. Galbraith, *The New Industrial State,* p. 363 (Houghton Mifflin, Boston; 1968).
19. Patricia Kay Sexton, *The Feminized Male,* pp. 29 and 137, (Random House, New York; 1967).
20. Ibid., p. 20.
21. Cf. Urie Bronfenbrenner, *Two Worlds of Childhood: US and USSR* (Russell Sage, Beverly Hills, Cal.; 1970).
22. Lecture at the University of Chicago, Fall 1970. For a similar discussion cf. Bettelheim, *Children of the Dream,* p. 63 (Macmillan, New York).
23. Edna J. LeShan, *The Conspiracy Against Childhood,* p. 26 (Atheneum, New York; 1967).
24. *Newsweek,* May 22, 1972.
25. Quoted by Erich Fromm, *Marx's Concept of Man,* p. 31 (Ungar, New York).
26. Cf. Toffler, op. cit., "The Fractured Family."
27. Robin Morgan, *Sisterhood is Powerful,* p. 250 (Random House, New York; 1970).
28. Maria Montessori, *Spontaneous Activity in Education,* p. 16 (Schocken, New York; 1965).
29. Sexton, op. cit., p. 116.
30. Ibid.
31. Quoted in Theodore Roszak, "The Hard and the Soft," in Betty and Theodore Roszak, *Masculine/Feminine,* pp. 86–106 (Harper and Row, New York; 1969).
32. For example, Gayle Rubin, in Roszak and Roszak, op. cit.
33. Ibid., p. 235.

34. Michael Rossman, *Wedding Within the War* (Vintage, New New York).

35. *Newsweek,* May 25, 1972.

36. Benjamin Spock, *Baby and Child Care,* p. 571 (Pocket Books, New York; 1968).

37. William V. Shannon, "A Radical, Direct, Simple, Utopian Alternative to Day-Care Centers," *New York Times Magazine,* May 14, 1972.

38. Herbert Marcuse, *Eros and Civilization,* op. cit., p. iv (Vintage, New York; 1962).

39. Erikson, *Childhood and Society,* pp. 291 and 285–6.

40. Ibid., p. 292f.

41. One of the most eloquent articles written by a woman activist on this subject is Alice Embree's "Media Images 1: Madison Avenue: Brainwashing—the Facts," in Robin Morgan, *Sisterhood is Powerful,* op. cit., pp. 175–191.

Television

1. Fritz Machlup, *The Production and Distribution of Knowledge in the United States* (Princeton Univ. Press; 1962).

2. Erik H. Erikson, lecture at Harvard University, Fall, 1969.

3. William Kessen, op. cit., pp. 43–44.

4. Earl of Shaftsbury, "A Speech on moving for leave to bring in a bill to make regulations respecting the age and sex of children and young persons employed in the mines and collieries of the United Kingdom." House of Commons, June 7, 1842; In Kessen, pp. 45–56.

5. Harvey Swados, *Year of Conscience: The Muckrakers,* p. 168 (World Press, New York, 1962).

6. Ibid., p. 165–66.

7. Vance Packard, *The Hidden Persuaders,* pp. 135–143 (McKay, New York, 1957).

8. Erik H. Erikson, *Identity: Youth and Crisis,* p. 122.

9. Packard, op. cit., pp. 137–8.

10. White House Conference on Children and Youth, 1950.

11. Ibid.

12. Bronfenbrenner, op. cit., p. 102.

13. Newton N. Minow, Chairman, Federal Communications Commission. Address to the 39th Annual Convention of Broadcasters, May 9, 1969.

14. Studies quoted in Bronfenbrenner, pp. 109ff.

15. Schramm, Wilbur, et al., *Television in the Lives of Our Children,* p. 162 (Stanford Univ. Press, 1961).
16. Study by Eleanor Maccoby cited in Schramm, op. cit., p. 69.
17. Cited in Schramm, p. 134.
18. Bernard Berelson et al., *Human Behavior: An Inventory of Scientific Findings,* p. 535 (Harcourt, Brace and Jovanovich, New York, 1967).
19. Schramm, op. cit., p. 190.
20. Schramm, p. 180.
21. Quoted without reference in *Reader's Digest,* March 1972.
22. New York *Times,* p. 65, January 11, 1971.
23. Ibid.
24. Anna Freud, *Normality and Pathology in Childhood: Assessment of Development,* p. 126 (International Univ. Press, New York, 1966).
25. Erikson (1968), p. 219.
26. In William Y. Elliott, *Television's Impact on American Culture,* (Michigan State Univ. Press, East Lansing, 1958).
27. Schramm, op. cit., p. 160.
28. Chlee and Aaron, "The Alternate-Media Guerillas," *New York Magazine,* October 17, 1970.
29. *Law and Social Action,* Spring 1972.
30. *Time,* p. 75, April 17, 1971.
31. John Holt, "Big Bird, Meet Dick and Jane," *The Atlantic,* May 1971.
32. Bronfenbrenner, op. cit.

School

1. Charles Silberman, op. cit., 146f and 339.
2. Toffler, op. cit., p. 355.
3. Raymond E. Callahan, *Education and the Cult of Efficiency: A Study of the Social Forces that Have Shaped the Administration of the Public Schools* (Univ. Chicago Press, 1962).
4. Reprinted in Haimowitz and Haimowitz, *Human Development,* p. 528 (T.Y. Crowell, New York, 1966).
5. This sales pitch comes from both university-based program designers and industry promoters.
6. William A. Shanner, "A System of Individual Instruction Utilizing Currently Available Instructional Materials," American Institute of Research, Westinghouse Learning Corp.
7. Ibid.
8. Ibid.
9. Montessori, *Spontaneous Activity in Education,* p. 194.

10. Mumford, op. cit.; p. 286.

11. "A Growth Industry Grows Up," *Time,* March 1, 1972.

12. Cf. D. Alpert and D.L. Bitzer, "Advances in Computer-Based Education," *Science,* March 20, 1970; and D. Bitzer and D. Skaperdas, "The Design of an Economically Viable Large-Scale Computer-Based Educational System," CERL Report X-5, February 1969.

13. Robert Borguslaw, *The New Utopians: A Study of Systems Designs and Social Change* (Prentice-Hall, Englewood Cliffs, N.J., 1968).

14. CERL Report X-2, May 1968. This report includes the two examples cited, as well as a full listing of the available programs as of its publication. Additional examples may be found in Anthony Oettinger, *Run, Computer, Run,* pp. 135ff. (Harvard Univ. Press, 1969).

15. Richard C. Anderson, et al., CERL Report X-11, February 1970.

16. Roger's essay is reprinted in Harold H. Anderson, *Creativity and its Cultivation,* pp. 69–83 (Harper and Row, New York, 1959).

17. Maria Montessori, *Spontaneous Activity in Education,* 175ff.

18. Robert Glaser, Director of Pittsburgh's Learning Research and Development Center; quoted in Oettinger, op.cit., p. 141.

19. The following information of performance contracts, unless otherwise noted, has been taken from two issues of *The Knowledge Industry Report,* a trade magazine subscribed to by firms in communications and education. The two issues I have used are Volume 4, Nos. 2 and 5, June-July 1970.

20. Boston *Globe,* February 28, 1971.

21. Robert W. Locke, "Has the Education Industry Lost Its Nerve?" *Saturday Review,* January 16, 1971.

22. Charles Silberman, *Crisis in the Classroom* (pp. 186ff), provides one of the most thorough analyses of the cost and technique claims of the computer sellers. (Random House, New York, 1970).

23. Silberman, op.cit.

24. Jerome Kagan, op.cit., 55.

25. Betty J. Sawyers, "You and the Machine," *Teacher* 89:5 (January 1972).

26. In many mass magazines during 1970.

27. Bruno Bettelheim, "Redundant Youth," *Realités,* December 1970.

28. Cf. Wallach's article, in Kagan, op.cit.

29. Edward T. Ladd, "Pills for Classroom Peace?" *Saturday Review,* November 21, 1970.
30. "Pep Pills to Quiet the Over-Peppy Child," New York *Times,* March 14, 1971. Cf. "Report of the Conference on the Use of Stimulant Drugs in the Treatment of Behaviorally Disturbed Young School Children," Dept. of HEW (Washington), January 11–12, 1971.
31. Ladd, op.cit.
32. Careth Ellingson, in Ladd, op.cit.
33. Cf. Barbara Fish's "The 'One Child, One Drug' Myth of Stimulants in Hyperkenesis" (*Archives of General Psychiatry* 25:193–203 (1971), for a most sensitive medical analysis of the complex question of treating hyperkenesis.
34. The irrationality of this fear of movement is documented by Silberman, op.cit., pp. 128ff.
35. Ladd, op.cit.
36. New York *Times,* March 14, 1971.
37. Ibid.
38. Dr. Selig Greenberg, *The Quality of Mercy,* Atheneum, 1971; Cf. also Dr. Harry F. Dowling, *Medicines for Man,* Knopf, 1970.
39. In his introduction to the book based on the CBS documentary by Daniel Schorr, entitled *Don't Get Sick in America,* Aurora Publishers, Nashville, Tenn., 1970.
40. *New York Times Magazine,* March 14, 1971. Cf. Claire Townsend, et al., *Old Age: The Last Segregation* (Bantam, 1971).
41. Quoted by Silberman, 141.
42. George A. Miller, "Some Psychological Perspectives on the Year 2000," *Daedalus,* p. 883, Summer 1967.
43. This process once again has its obvious industrial parallel, as Charles Hampden-Turner demonstrates in his discussion of various forms of management-worker control in corporate structures. Cf. "Corporate Radicalism," in *Radical Man* (Schenkman, Cambridge, Mass., 1970).
44. Holt, op.cit., p. 119.
45. Karl Marx, *Das Kapital,* Vol. I, pp. 461–2, 680–1 (Kerr and Co., 1906).
46. Silberman, op.cit., 200.
47. Fromm, *Marx's Concept of Man,* op.cit., p. 76.
48. Diane Divoky (ed.), *How Old Will You Be in 1984? Expressions of Outrage from the High School Free Press* (Avon, 1971), and Marc Libarle and Tom Seligson (eds.), *The High School Revolutionaries* (Random House, New York, 1970).
49. Banesh Hoffman, *The Tyranny of Testing* (Macmillan, New York, 1964).

50. Walter and Miriam Schneir, "The Joy of Learning—In the Open Corridor," in *New York Times Magazine,* April 4, 1971; cf. Silberman, loc.cit., on the British School for further background. It might be noted here that some performance contract schools have indeed paralleled this human innovation, and brought in mothers at a minimal salary rather than more teachers. Assuming that the mothers do not need more money, this seems like a welcome alternative to more characteristically technical solutions.

51. Silberman, quoting from NEA's Journal *Discipline in the Classroom.*

52. The best book I know of on this subject is *Children Teach Children: Learning by Teaching,* Alan Gartner et al. (eds.) (New York, 1971).

Youth

1. Kenneth Keniston, "Youth: A 'New' Stage of Life," *American Scholar* (Fall 1970), Vol. 39 No. 4, pp. 631–654.

2. Erik Erikson, "Memorandum on Identity and Negro Youth," *Journal of Social Issues,* 20:41, October 1964.

3. Quoted by James Ridgeway, *The Closed Corporation,* p. 47 (Ballantine Books, New York).

4. Irving Louis Horowitz et al., *The Knowledge Factory,* p. 137.

5. Harrington, op.cit., p. 154.

6. Drucker, *The Age of Discontinuity,* p. 246.

7. Normal Birnbaum, "Is there a Post-Industrial Revolution?" *Social Policy,* p. 10, July–August 1970.

8. Daniel Bell, in *The Public Interest,* p. 30, Winter 1967.

9. Kenneth Keniston and Mark Gerzon, "Human and Social Benefits of Higher Education," a paper presented at the 54th Annual Meeting of the American Council on Education, Washington, D.C., October 6–8, 1971; published in 1972 by the A.C.E. In this paper we discuss at greater length the differences between creative and technical education.

10. Monique Segre, Lucie Tanguy, and Marie-France Lortic, "A New Ideology of Education," *Social Forces,* Vol. 50, March 1972.

11. For a more personal account, see my *The Whole World is Watching* (Viking, New York, 1969; Paperback Library, New York, 1970), especially chapters on high school and college.

12. Written by Dr. Robert A. Wilson, a New York gynecologist, *Forever Feminine* sold over 100,000 copies and was reprinted

in many women's magazines. He argued essentially that the Pill made women sexier, regardless of age. Published in 1966, Wilson's book nowhere mentioned that he had been heavily funded by the Searle Foundation, created by G.D. Searle & Company, manufacturers of the first Pill.

13. Morton Mintz, *The Pill: An Alarming Report,* pp. 14–15 (Boston, 1969).
14. Dr. Robert Kistner, *The Pill* (Dell, New York, 1968); quoted by the Boston Women's Health Collective, *Women and Their Bodies.* Copies available c/o New England Free Press, 791 Tremont Street, Boston, Mass.
15. "Biochemistry of the Pill Largely Unknown," *Chemical and Engineering News,* pp. 44–49, March 27, 1967.
16. Ibid.
17. Paul Vaughan, *The Pill on Trial,* p. 225 (New York, 1970).
18. Barbara Seaman, *The Doctors' Case Against the Pill,* p. 28 (Avon, New York, 1970).
19. *Second Report on the Oral Contraceptives,* Advisory Commission on Obstetrics and Gynecology, FDA, August 1, 1969.
20. Quoted by Mintz, op.cit., p. 117.
21. Mintz, p. 115.
22. Quoted by Seaman, op.cit. p. 198.
23. *A Prescription for Family Planning: The Story of Enovid,* A Reference for Professional Use from G.D. Searle & Company, 1964.
24. Quoted by Seaman, p. 190.
25. Mintz, p. 24f.
26. Seaman, pp. 195–7.
27. Birth Control Handbook, P.O. Box 1000, Station 6, Montreal 130, P.Q., Canada. 8th edition revised, October 1971.
28. Vaughan, p. 226
29. Seaman, p. 157.
30. Boston Women's Health Collective, pp. 45–6.
31. Mintz, p. 116.
32. Cf. "Mother and Child," pp. 100–107, in Mintz, *The Pill.*
33. Arthur and Libby Colman, Pregnancy: *The Psychological Experience,* pp. 10–11 (New York, 1971).
34. Cited by Seaman, pp. 154–5.
35. Mintz, p. 17.
36. David M. Rorvik and Landrum B. Shettles, *Your Baby's Sex: Select, Don't Settle* (Dodd, Mead, & Co., New York, 1970).
37. Air War Study Group Cornell University, *The Air War in Indochina* (Beacon, Boston, 1972).
38. Erik Erikson, *Insight and Responsibility* (Norton, New York, 1964).

39. R.D. Laing, *The Divided Self,* Penguin.
40. Erikson, *Insight and Responsibility,* p. 114.

Adulthood

1. Theodore Roszak, *Where the Wasteland Ends,* p. 53 (Doubleday, New York, 1972).
2. Saul Padover, *The Complete Jefferson,* pp. 124–5 and 291–3.
3. B. F. Skinner, *Beyond Freedom and Dignity* (Knopf, New York, 1971).
4. Victor C. Ferkiss, *Technological Man: The Myth and the Reality,* p. 84 (Mentor, New York, 1969).
5. Theodore J. Lowi, *The End of Liberalism,* p. 58ff (Norton, New York, 1969).
6. Quoted by Herbert Marcuse, *Revolution and Counterrevolution,* p. 55 (Beacon Press, Boston, 1972).
7. Douglas, op.cit., p. 175.
8. Robert E. Lane, "The Decline of Politics and Ideology in a Knowledgeable Society," *American Sociological Review,* 31: 649–662 (1966).
9. Franz L. Neumann, "Approaches to the Study of Political Power," *Political Science Quarterly,* 65:161–180 (1950).
10. Quoted in Victor C. Ferkiss, op.cit., p. 111.
11. Ralph E. Lapp, *The New Priesthood: The Scientific Elite and the Uses of Power* (New York, 1965).
12. J. Lieberman, *The Tyranny of Experts* (Walker & Company, New York, 1970).
13. Jacques Ellul, *The Political Illusion* (Knopf, New York, 1967).
14. Robert Nisbet, "The Impact of Technology on Ethical Decision-Making," in Douglas, op.cit., p. 40.
15. William Kuhns, *The Post-Industrial Prophets: Interpretations of Technology.*
16. Theodore Roszak, op.cit., p. 9.
17. Cf. Daniel Yankelovich, "The New Naturalism," in *The Changing Values on Campus* (Pocket Books, New York, 1972).
18. Amos Elon, *Journey Through a Haunted Land,* p. 217ff.
19. Albert Speer, *Inside the Third Reich* (Macmillan, New York).
20. Alvin Toffler, op.cit.
21. Erikson *Identity: Youth in Crisis* p. 259; Mumford, op.cit., p. 187.
22. Hasan Ozbekhan, *The Triumph of Technology: "Can" Implies "Ought"* (Santa Monica, Cal., 1967).
23. Fromm, *Revolution of Hope,* op.cit., p. 97.

24. Van Rensselaer Potter, "Bioethics, The Science of Survival," *Perspectives in Biology and Medicine,* Autumn 1970; from his book *Bioethics: Bridge to the Future* (Prentice-Hall, Englewood Cliffs, N.J., 1970).
25. Graham C.J. Smith, "The Ecologist at Bay," *Saturday Review,* January 2, 1971.
26. A full list of environmental agencies and organizations is available from Common Cause: *Report from Washington,* Vol. 5, No. 1 (1971).
27. New York *Times,* p. 14, January 31, 1971.
28. Charles F. Wuster, "DDT in Mother's Milk," *Saturday Review,* May 2, 1970.
29. Barbara and John Ehrenreich, *The American Health Empire: Power, Profits and Politics* (Random House, New York, 1970). Especially Chapter XVII, "The Student Health Organization."
30. Ed. Martin Brown, *The Social Responsibility of the Scientist* (MacMillan, New York, 19).
31. Daniel and Gabriel Cohn-Bendit, *Obsolete Communism,* pp. 34–40, provides a case history of a sociology department which contributed many radicals to the French student movement.
32. Cf. Alvin Gouldner, *The Coming Crisis in Western Sociology* (Basic Books, New York, 1970).
33. Cf. Loren Baritz, *The Servants of Power* (Wesleyan Univ. Press), and Noam Chomsky, *American Power and the New Mandarins* (New York, 1967), especially "Objectivity and Liberal Scholarship" and "The Responsibility of Intellectuals."
34. George W. Miller, "Psychology as a Means for Promoting Human Welfare," Presidential Address, American Psychological Association, September 1969.
35. The central conflict in the field of psychology was personified in a dialogue between Carl Rogers and B.F. Skinner, "Some Issues Concerning the Control of Human Behavior," *Science,* November 30, 1956.
36. A reading of C.P. Snow's *The Two Cultures* (Cambridge Univ. Press, 1969) is particularly interesting in this context if followed by Lionel Trilling's essay, "The Leavis-Snow Controversy," in *Beyond Culture: Essays in Literature and Learning* (New York, 1959).
37. Roszak, op.cit., pp. 8–9.
38. Quoted in Yankelovich, op.cit., pp. 183–4.
39. William Barrett, *Irrational Man* (Anchor Books, 1962).
40. Simone de Beauvoir, *Coming of Age,* English translation (G.P. Putnam's Sons, New York, 1972).
41. Jessica Mitford, *The American Way of Death* (Simon and Schuster, New York, 1963).